OXFORD MEDIEVAL TEXTS

General Editors
V. H. GALBRAITH   R. A. B. MYNORS
C. N. L. BROOKE

THE
EPISTOLAE VAGANTES
OF
POPE GREGORY VII

THE
EPISTOLAE VAGANTES
OF
POPE GREGORY VII

EDITED AND TRANSLATED

BY

H. E. J. COWDREY

OXFORD
AT THE CLARENDON PRESS
1972

Oxford University Press, Ely House, London W. 1

GLASGOW NEW YORK TORONTO MELBOURNE WELLINGTON
CAPE TOWN IBADAN NAIROBI DAR ES SALAAM LUSAKA ADDIS ABABA
DELHI BOMBAY CALCUTTA MADRAS KARACHI LAHORE DACCA
KUALA LUMPUR SINGAPORE HONG KONG TOKYO

72- 195673

(ʹ) ℓ-51-b · ℓ ℓℓℓ-ℓ/ℊ

PRINTED IN GREAT BRITAIN
AT THE UNIVERSITY PRESS, OXFORD
BY VIVIAN RIDLER
PRINTER TO THE UNIVERSITY

PREFACE

I AM most grateful to the custodians of the manuscripts detailed in the List of Manuscripts Used, who have made them available for the preparation of this edition, as well as to the photographic departments or agents of the several libraries and archives for their expert services. Various scholars have helped and encouraged me with advice and information. Professor C. N. L. Brooke, a general editor of this series, has not only shown generous interest at every stage of the work, but has read, criticized, and greatly improved my typescript. Dr. S. Mähl and Dr. G. Tangl, of Munich, supplied me with some particularly valuable information. Professor J. G. Plante, curator of the Monastic Manuscript Microfilm Library, St. John's University, Collegeville, Minnesota, also advised me about manuscripts in certain Austrian archives and sent me invaluable photographs of otherwise inaccessible items. Two further scholars kindly allowed me to use the papers of eminent medievalists of the last generation: Professor S. Kuttner, of the Institute of Medieval Canon Law at Berkeley, supplied me with references and notes from the papers of the late Professor W. Holtzmann; and Professor A. M. Stickler (now Prefect of the Vatican Library) allowed me to examine the papers of the late Don G. B. Borino at the Pontificio Ateneo Salesiano in Rome. In Oxford it is a pleasure to acknowledge my continued indebtedness to the staffs of the Bodleian Library and of the Clarendon Press. I am also most grateful to the Research Committee of the British Academy and to the Board of the Faculty of Modern History at Oxford University for assistance towards the expenses of preparing this book.

I must also make an acknowledgement of a different kind. Carl Erdmann died in 1945 while still a fairly young man. Had he survived the Second World War the *Epistolae uagantes* of Pope Gregory VII would long since have been edited as he alone could have performed the task. The following pages will make abundantly clear how largely I have drawn upon his published work. Yet such a measurable debt is but a small part of what a medievalist working within the vast area of Erdmann's interests must

quickly become aware of owing to his fine intelligence and immaculate scholarship. Their stimulus and inspiration have in no way diminished with the years.

H. E. J. C.

St. Edmund Hall, Oxford
January 1972

CONTENTS

LIST OF PRINTED BOOKS AND ARTICLES,
   AND ABBREVIATIONS   ix

INTRODUCTION   xvii

TEXT AND TRANSLATION   I

APPENDIX A   150

APPENDIX B   154

ADDITIONAL NOTE
   The Date of Nos. 6–11   160

LIST OF MANUSCRIPTS USED   162

INDEX OF LETTERS   165

INDEX OF REFERENCES TO GREGORY VII'S *REGISTER*
   AND PRIVILEGES   167

INDEX OF QUOTATIONS AND ALLUSIONS   169

GENERAL INDEX   171

LIST OF PRINTED BOOKS AND ARTICLES, AND ABBREVIATIONS

Abh. Gött.: *Abhandlungen der Akademie der Wissenschaften zu Göttingen, phil.-hist. Klasse.*

Analecta iuris pontificii, x (Rome, 1869).

Annalista Saxo, ed. G. Waitz, *M.G.H. Scr.* vi. 542–777.

Baluze, É., *Miscellanea*, 7 vols. (Paris, 1678–1715).

Baronius, C., *Annales ecclesiastici*, 19 vols. (Antwerp and Cologne, 1597–1630).

B.É.C.: *Bibliothèque de l'École des chartes.*

Becker, A., *Studien zum Investiturproblem in Frankreich* (Saarbrücken, 1955).

Beno, *Gesta Romanae ecclesiae contra Hildebrandum*, i, ed. K. Francke, *M.G.H. L. de L.* ii. 369–73.

Bernard of Constance, *Apologeticus*, ed. F. Thaner, *M.G.H. L. de L.* ii. 58–88.

Bernold, *Chronicon*, *M.G.H. Scr.* v. 385–467.

Berthold, *Annales*, *M.G.H. Scr.* v. 264–326.

Bibliotheca Cluniacensis, ed. M. Marrier (Paris, 1614).

Blaul, O., 'Studien zum Register Gregors VII.', *Archiv für Urkundenforschung*, iv (1912), 113–228.

Bock, F., 'Annotationes zum Register Gregors VII.', *S.G.* i (1947), 281–306.

Bonizo of Sutri, *Liber ad amicum*, ed. E. Dümmler, *M.G.H. L. de L.* i. 568–620.

Borino, G. B., 'Può il Reg. Vat. 2 (Registro di Gregorio VII) essere il registro della cancellaria?', *S.G.* v (1956), 391–402; vi (1959–61), 363–90.

——'Le lettere di Gregorio VII e di Sigfrido arcivescovo di Magonza', *S.G.* vi (1959–61), 265–75.

——'I decreti di Gregorio VII contro i simoniaci e i nicolaiti sono del sinodo quaresimale del 1074', *S.G.* vi (1959–61), 277–95.

Briefsammlungen der Zeit Heinrichs IV., edd. C. Erdmann and N. Fickermann, *M.G.H. B.D.K.* v (1950).

Bruno, *Saxonicum bellum*, edd. E. Lohmann and F.-J. Schmale, *Q.G. HIV.*, pp. 192–405.

Bullarium Cluniacense, ed. P. Simon (Lyons, 1680).

Cartulaire de l'abbaye de Lérins, edd. H. Moris and E. Blanc, i (Paris, 1883).

Cartulaire de l'abbaye de Sainte-Croix de Quimperlé, edd. L. Maître and P. de Berthou (2nd edn., Rennes and Paris, 1904).

Cartulaire de Saint-Vincent de Mâcon, ed. M.-C. Ragut (Mâcon, 1864).

Caspar, E., 'Studien zum Register Gregors VII.', *N.A.* xxxviii (1913), 144–226.

Catel, G. de, *Mémoires de l'histoire du Languedoc* (Toulouse, 1633).

Conrad, *Vita Wolfhelmi abbatis Brunwilarensis*, ed. Surius, *De probatis sanctorum historiis*, ii. 781–98; ed. R. Wilmans, *M.G.H. Scr.* xii. 180–95.

Corpus iuris canonici, ed. A. Friedberg, 2 vols. (Leipzig, 1879).

Cowdrey, H. E. J., *The Cluniacs and the Gregorian Reform* (Oxford, 1970).

C.S.E.L.: *Corpus scriptorum ecclesiasticorum Latinorum.*

D.A.: *Deutsches Archiv für Erforschung des Mittelalters.*

D'Achéry, L., *Spicilegium*, iii (Paris, 1723).

Delisle, L., 'Trois Lettres de Grégoire VII et la *Bibliotheca rerum Germanicarum* de Philippe Jaffé', *B.É.C.*, 6th ser., i (1865), 556–61.

De unitate ecclesiae conseruanda, ed. W. Schwenkenbecher, *M.G.H. L. de L.* ii. 173–284.

Douglas, D. C., *William the Conqueror* (London, 1964).

Duchet, T., *Additions et corrections au recueil des manuscrits de Saint-Omer* (n.d.).

Duckett, G. F., *Charters and Records from among the Archives of the Ancient Abbey of Cluni from 1077 to 1534*, ii (Lewes, 1888).

Eccard, J. G., *Corpus historicum medii aeui*, ii (Leipzig, 1723).

Ekkehardi chronicon uniuersale ad a. 1106, ed. G. Waitz, *M.G.H. Scr.* vi. 33–231.

Ep. coll.: Gregorii VII, *Epistolae collectae*, in *Monumenta Gregoriana*, ed. P. Jaffé, *Bibliotheca rerum Germanicarum*, ii (Berlin, 1865), 520–76.

Erdmann, C., *Die Entstehung des Kreuzzugsgedankens* (Stuttgart, 1935).

—— 'Die Bamberger Domschule im Investiturstreit', *Zeitschrift für bayerische Landesgeschichte*, ix (1936), 1–46.

—— 'Die Anfänge der staatlichen Propaganda im Investiturstreit', *Historische Zeitschrift*, cliv (1936), 491–512.

—— 'Tribur und Rom. Zur Vorgeschichte der Canossafahrt', *D.A.* i (1937), 361–88.

—— 'Gregor VII. und Berengar von Tours', *Q.F.I.A.B.* xxviii (1937-8), 48–74.

—— *Studien zur Briefliteratur im elften Jahrhundert* (Schriften der *M.G.H.* i, Stuttgart, 1938).

Fabre, P., *Étude sur le Liber censuum* (Paris, 1892).

Fliche, A., *Le Règne de Philippe Ier, roi de France (1060–1108)* (Paris, 1912).

—— *La Réforme grégorienne*, ii (Louvain and Paris, 1926).

Franchi, D. de, *Historia del Patriarcha S. Giovan Gualberto* (Florence, 1640).

Frutolf of Michaelsberg, see *Ekkehardi chronicon*.

Fuhrmann, H., 'Zur Benutzung des Registers Gregors VII. durch Paul von Bernried', *S.G.* v (1956), 299–312.

Gams, P. B., *Series episcoporum ecclesiae catholicae* (Regensburg, 1873).

Gattula, E., *Historia abbatiae Cassinensis*, i (Venice, 1733).

G.C.: *Gallia Christiana*, 16 vols. (Aix, Trier, Tours, Vienne, 1715–1865); new edn. of i–v (Paris, 1870–7).

Gerhoh of Reichersberg, *Commentarius in Psalmum X*, ed. E. Sackur, *M.G.H. L. de L.* iii. 414–18.

—— *Epistola ad Innocentium papam*, ed. E. Sackur, *M.G.H. L. de L.* iii. 202–39.

Giesebrecht, W. von, *De Gregorii VII registro emendando* (Brunswick, 1858).

—— *Geschichte der deutschen Kaiserzeit*, iii (3rd edn., Brunswick, 1869).

Giry, A., 'Grégoire VII et les évêques de Thérouanne', *Revue historique*, i (1876), 387–409.

G.P.: *Germania Pontificia*, ed. A. Brackmann, 3 vols. (Berlin, 1911–35).

Gwynn. A., 'Gregory VII and the Irish Church', *S.G.* iii. 105–28.

Hahn, S. F., *Collectio monumentorum*, i (Brunswick, 1724).

Haller, J., *Das Papsttum. Idee und Wirklichkeit*, iii (2nd edn., Darmstadt, 1962).

Halphen, L., *Le Comté d'Anjou au xie siècle* (Paris, 1906).

Hauck, A., *Kirchengeschichte Deutschlands*, iii (3rd and 4th edn., Leipzig, 1920).

Hauthaler, W., 'Die grosse Briefhandschrift zu Hannover', *N.A.* xx (1894–5), 209–20.

Heidrich, K., 'Die Datierung der Briefe in Brunos Sachsenkrieg', *N.A.* xxx (1904–5), 115–40.

Holder-Egger, O., 'Fragment eines Manifestes aus der Zeit Heinrichs IV.', *N.A.* xxxi (1906), 183–93.

Holtzmann, W., 'Kanonistische Ergänzungen zur *Italia Pontificia*' *Q.F.I.A.B.* xxxvii (1957), 55–102.

Hugh of Flavigny, *Chronicon*, *M.G.H. Scr.* viii. 280–503.

I.P.: *Italia Pontificia* , ed. P. F. Kehr, 9 vols. (Berlin, 1906–62).

Jakobs, H., *Der Adel in der Klosterreform von St. Blasien* (Cologne, 1968).

J.L.: *see Regesta pontificum Romanorum.*

Klewitz, H.-W., *Reformpapsttum und Kardinalkolleg* (Darmstadt, 1957).

Kost, O.-H., *Das östliche Niedersächsen im Investiturstreit. Studien zur Brunos Buch von Sachsenkrieg* (Göttingen, 1962).

Krause, V., 'Die Acten der Triburer Synode, 895', *N.A.* xvii (1891–2), 283–326.

Labbe P., and Cossart, G., *Sacrosancta concilia ad regiam editionem exacta*, x (Paris, 1671).

Ladner, G. B., 'Two Gregorian letters on the sources and nature of Gregory VII's reform ideology', *S.G.* v (1956), 221–42.

Lampert of Hersfeld, *Annales*, edd. O. Holder-Egger and W. D. Fritz (Ausgewählte Quellen zur deutschen Geschichte des Mittelalters, ed. R. Buchner, xiii, Berlin, n.d.).

Lanfranci opera quae supersunt omnia, ed. J. A. Giles, 2 vols. (Oxford, 1844).

Leonis Mariscani et Petri Diaconi Chronica Monasterii Casinensis, ed. W. Wattenbach, *M.G.H. Scr.* vii. 551–844.

Loewenfeld, S., 'Papsturkunden in Paris', *N.A.* vii (1882), 145–67.

—— Die Canonsammlung des Cardinals Deusdedit und das Register Gregors VII.', *N.A.* x (1884–5), 311–29.

—— *Epistolae pontificorum Romanorum ineditae* (Leipzig, 1885).

Lühe, W., *Hugo von Die und Lyon* (Leipzig, 1898).

Mabillon, J., *Annales ordinis sancti Benedicti*, v (Paris, 1713).

Manegold of Lautenbach, *Ad Gebehardum liber*, ed. K. Franke, *M.G.H. L. de L.* i. 300–430.

Mansi: *Sacrorum conciliorum noua et amplissima collectio*, ed. J. D. Mansi, 31 vols. (Florence and Venice, 1759–93).

Marca, P. de, *Dissertationes de concordia sacerdotii et imperii*, ed. É. Baluze, ii (Paris, 1663).

Marianus Scottus, *Chronicon*, ed. G. Waitz, *M.G.H. Scr.* v. 481–568.

Martène, E., *Veterum scriptorum et monumentorum collectio noua*, i (Rouen, 1700).

—— and Durand, U., *Thesaurus nouus anecdotorum*, 5 vols. (Paris, 1717).

Martin, F., 'Zwei Salzburger Briefsammlungen des 12. Jahrhunderts', *M.Ö.I.G.* xlii (1927), 313–42.

Mas Latrie, L. de, *Trésor de chronologie d'histoire et de géographie* (Paris, 1889).

Meltzer, O., *Papst Gregors VII. Gesetzgebung und Bestrebungen in Betreff der Bischofswahlen* (Leipzig, 1869).

Meyer von Knonau, G., *Jahrbücher des deutschen Reichs unter Heinrich IV. und Heinrich V.*, 7 vols. (Leipzig, 1898–1909).

M.G.H.: *Monumenta Germaniae Historica.*

—— *B.D.K.*: *Die Briefe der deutschen Kaiserzeit.*

—— *Dipl.*: *Diplomata.*

—— *Ep. sel.*: *Epistolae selectae.*

—— *L. de L.*: *Libelli de lite imperatorum et pontificum.*

—— *Scr.*: *Scriptores.*

Miccoli, G., *Pietro Igneo. Studi sull'età gregoriana* (Rome, 1960).

M.I.Ö.G.: *Mitteilungen des Instituts für Österreichische Geschichtsforschung* (1923–42: *M.Ö.I.G.*).

Monumenta Bambergensia, ed. P. Jaffé, *Bibliotheca rerum Germanicarum*, v (Berlin, 1869).

Morghen, R., 'Richerche sulla formazione del registro di Gregorio VII', *Annali di storia del diritto*, iii–iv (1959–60), 35–75.

Morice, H., *Mémoires pour servir de preuves à l'histoire ecclésiastique et civile de Bretagne*, i (Paris, 1742).

Morin, G., 'Lettres inédites des papes Alexandre II et saint Grégoire VII', *R.B.* xlvii (1936), 117–28.

Murray, A., 'Pope Gregory VII and his letters', *Traditio*, xxii (1966), 149–201.

Nachr. Gött.: *Nachrichten von der Gesellschaft der Wissenschaften zu Göttingen, phil.-hist. Klasse.*

N.A.: *Neues Archiv der Gesellschaft für ältere deutsche Geschichtskunde.*

Neuss, W., and Oediger, F. W., *Das Bistum Köln von den Anfängen bis zum Ende des 12. Jahrhunderts* (*Geschichte des Erzbistums Köln*, i, Cologne, 1964).

Paul of Bernried, *Gregorii VII uita*, in *Pontificum Romanorum uitae*, ed. Watterich, i. 474–546.

Peitz, W. M., 'Das Originalregister Gregors VII. im vatikanischen Archiv', *SB. Wien*, clxv (1911), Abh. 5.

Pflugk-Harttung, J. von, *Acta pontificorum Romanorum inedita*, 3 vols. (Tübingen, 1880–8).

Pivec, K., 'Studien und Forschungen zur Ausgabe des *Codex Udalrici*', i, *M.Ö.I.G.* xlv (1931), 409–85; ii, *M.Ö.I.G.* xlvi (1932), 257–342; iii, *M.Ö.I.G.* xlvii (1933), 322–413.

P.L.: *Patrologia Latina*, ed. J. P. Migne, 221 vols. (Paris, 1844–64).

Pontificia Hibernica. Medieval papal chancery documents concerning Ireland, 640–1261, ed. M. P. Sheehy, i (Dublin, 1962).

Pontificum Romanorum uitae, ed. J. B. M. Watterich, 2 vols. (Leipzig, 1862).

Poole, R. L., *Lectures on the history of the papal chancery* (Cambridge, 1915).

Q.F.I.A.B.: *Quellen und Forschungen aus italienischen Archiven und Bibliotheken.*

Q.G. HIV.: *Quellen zur Geschichte Kaiser Heinrichs IV.* (Ausgewählte Quellen zur deutsche Geschichte des Mittelalters, ed. R. Buchner, xii, Berlin, 1963).

Quinque compilationes antiquae, ed. A. Friedberg (Leipzig, 1882).

Ramackers, J., 'Analekten zur Geschichte des Reformpapsttums und der Cluniazenser', *Q.F.I.A.B.* xxiii (1931–2), 22–52.

Ramackers, *P.U.F.*: J. Ramackers, 'Papsturkunden in Frankreich, N.F. v, Touraine, Anjou, Maine und Bretagne', *Abh. Gött.* 3rd ser., xxxv (1956).

R.B.: *Revue bénédictine.*

Reg.: *Gregorii VII Registrum*, ed. E. Caspar, 2 vols. *M.G.H. Ep. sel.* ii (Berlin, 1920–3).

R.H.F.: *Recueil des historiens des Gaules et de la France*, 24 vols. (Paris, 1738–1904).

Regesta pontificum Romanorum, ed. P. Jaffé, 2 vols. (2nd edn., Leipzig, 1885–8).

Roye, F. de, *Vita, heresis et poenitentia Berengarii Andegauensis archidiaconi* (Angers, 1657).

Sancti Anselmi Cantuariensis archiepiscopi opera, ed. G. Gerberon (2nd edn., Paris, 1721); ed. F. S. Schmitt, iii (Edinburgh, 1946).

Santifaller, L., 'Beiträge zur Geschichte der Beschreibstoffe im Mittelalter, i, Untersuchungen', *M.I.Ö.G.*, Ergänzungsband xvi, Heft i (Graz, 1963).

Santifaller, *Q.F.*: L. Santifaller, *Quellen und Forschungen zum Urkunden- und Kanzleiwesen Papst Gregors VII., Teil i, Quellen: Urkunden, Regesten, Facsimilia* (Studi e testi, cxc, Vatican City, 1957).

SB. Wien: *Sitzungsberichte der Wiener Akademie der Wissenschaften, phil.- hist. Klasse.*

Schieffer, T., *Die päpstlichen Legaten in Frankreich vom Vertrage von Meersen (870) bis zum Schisma von 1130* (Historische Studien, cclxiii, Berlin, 1935).

Sdralek, M., *Wolfenbüttler Fragmente* (Kirchengeschichtliche Studien, i. 2, Münster, 1891).

Severt, J., *Chronologia historica successionis hierarchicae archiantistitum Lugdunensis archiepiscopatus*, ii (2nd edn., Lyons, 1628).

S.G.: *Studi Gregoriani*, 8 vols. (Rome, 1947–70).

Sigebert of Gembloux, *Chronica*, ed. L. C. Bethmann, *M.G.H. Scr.* vi. 300–74.

Stenton, F. M., *Anglo-Saxon England* (2nd edn., Oxford, 1947).

Sudendorf, H., *Registrum oder merkwürdige Urkunden für die deutsche Geschichte*, 3 vols. (Jena and Berlin, 1849–54).

Surius, L., *De probatis sanctorum historiis*, ii (Cologne, 1571).

Thaner, F., 'Papstbriefe', *N.A.* iv (1878), 401–6.

Tosti, L., *Storia della badia di Monte Cassino*, i (Naples, 1842).

Ughelli, F., *Italia sacra*, 10 vols. (2nd edn., Venice, 1717–22).

Ussani, V., 'Gregorio VII scrittore nella sua corrispondenza nei suoi dettati', *S.G.* ii (1947), 341–59.

Ussher, J., *Veterum epistolarum Hibernicarum sylloge* (Dublin, 1632).

Vita Altmanni episcopi Patauiensis, ed. W. Wattenbach, *M.G.H. Scr.* xii. 226–43.

Wattenbach, W., and Holtzmann, R., *Deutschlands Geschichtsquellen im Mittelalter. Die Zeit der Sachsen und Salier*, ii, pts. 3 and 4 (new edn. by F.-J. Schmale, Darmstadt, 1967).

Wiederhold, *P.U.F.*: W. Wiederhold, 'Papsturkunden in Frankreich, vii: Gascogne, Guienne und Languedoc', *Nachr. Gött.* (1913).

Zema, D. B., 'Economic Reorganization of the Roman See during the Gregorian Reform', *S.G.* i (1947), 137–68.

INTRODUCTION

THE pontificate of Gregory VII (1073–85) ushered in the long period of effective papal predominance in western Europe which continued without decisive setback until the last years of Boniface VIII (1294–1303). Gregory's work was itself in part prepared for by the events of the thirty years before his accession. In 1046 the Emperor Henry III (1039–56) delivered the papacy from the hands of the local Roman families and instituted a succession of German popes who between 1046 and 1057 began to exercise its authority more firmly. Leo IX (1048–54), in particular, took a strong lead in seeking to extirpate the moral abuses which contemporary reformers so vociferously condemned. Chief amongst these abuses were the two 'heresies' of simony—the buying and selling of orders and offices in the church—and 'nicolaitism'—clerical marriage and unchastity. With Henry III's death and the succession of his son Henry IV (1056–1106), a child not yet six years old, the pace of reform tended to quicken. The years from 1057 to 1073 saw a succession of four popes from Lorraine and Tuscany who were not restrained, as even Leo IX had been, by the existence in the background of a strong German protector. The Election Decree of 1059 gave the cardinals of the Roman church the decisive part in papal elections and reduced the emperor's role to a shadow; while the treaty of Melfi in the same year was intended to provide the papacy with Norman allies in south Italy who would enable it to dispense with German support. From 1059 Hildebrand, the future Gregory VII, stood near to the centre of affairs as archdeacon of the Roman church.

When he became pope he sought with an altogether new resolution and zeal to bring to fruition the work which his predecessors had initiated. Simony and clerical marriage quickly became and always remained the objects of his energetic action. But from the very beginning of his reign he also sought wider ends which had been foreshadowed but not clearly articulated and pursued by the Lotharingian and Tuscan popes: as well as aspiring to secure the reform of the church he also set himself with demonic zeal to

achieve what he and his supporters called its 'liberty'. By this cardinal concept of the Gregorian reform they meant, negatively, the
freeing of the church, so far as it might be possible, from every
kind of subordination to lay control or lordship; and, positively,
its consequent subjection to the exclusive lordship of St. Peter as
prince of the apostles and as recipient of Christ's commission to
feed his sheep.

In this, Gregory's motive was overwhelmingly a religious one.
As he himself expressed it towards the end of his life in letter 54
below: 'my greatest concern has been that holy church, the bride
of Christ, our lady and mother, should return to her true glory and
stand free, chaste, and catholic'. To this end the church must have
liberty in exclusive subjection to St. Peter and his vicar; and to
this end Gregory felt himself constrained to proclaim to the whole
world, clerical and lay alike, the inexorable demands of what he
called 'iustitia' (righteousness). By this he meant far more than
moral virtue or conformity with Christian law: he meant an active
and total collaboration of all men of whatever rank or class to
achieve the right order of a single human society having Christ as
its head and displaying the holiness which fitted it to stand as his
bride the church. The fullness of this righteousness it was for the
pope to announce to the church, just as the prophets of old, upon
whose office Gregory so largely modelled his papal commission,
had announced a foreshadowing of it to Israel; and papal sanctions
were not less formidable than the prophets'. By obedience to it the
rulers of a radically fallen world might learn to obey the demands
of the grace of God; if they defied it they declared their adherence
to the Antichrist who for Gregory was so mightily at work in the
world. Gregory's conception of righteousness had its roots in his
reading of the Vulgate and especially of St. Paul, and in the Latin
dogmatic tradition which had been formed by St. Augustine of
Hippo and which came to him through Pope Gregory I and the
augustinisme politique of Carolingian times.

Gregory's unrelenting insistence upon liberty as his demand for
the church and upon righteousness as a universal duty brought him
into dispute and conflict with lay rulers. Most of all it led to the
'Investiture Contest' with Henry IV of Germany, who came of age
in 1065; the development of their conflict is the principal theme
which underlies the texts which follow. It also impelled him to
show an unprecedented activity in the exercise of papal authority

at the nerve-centre of the church's government. Gregory felt bound
to be the vicar of St. Peter not only in name, but to make St. Peter's
authority everywhere effective. To this end he exploited all the
means at his disposal. At his Lent and November councils in
Rome, a legacy from his immediate predecessors which he developed greatly, he conducted all manner of ecclesiastical business,
took decisions about disobedient lay rulers, and held to account
both greater and lesser clergy from all over Europe. If the world
was made to come to Rome, Roman authority was also to be made
locally effective in all kingdoms and dioceses with which communi-
cation was possible. Gregory repeatedly sent legates to whom,
within the terms of their commissions, he delegated full Petrine
authority to act on his behalf. In this, again, he imitated his predecessors; but as the burden of business grew and as his conflict with
Henry IV developed, Gregory made the innovation of appointing
standing legates to represent him permanently in wider localities—
Hugh of Die and Lyons in northern and central France, Amatus
of Oléron in the south and west, Altmann of Passau in south
Germany, and Anselm II of Lucca in Lombardy. Finally, in his
attempts to further his purposes Gregory sent letters wherever it
was possible for them to reach. The purpose of the present volume
is to make more widely and conveniently available for study certain
of these letters.

THE LETTERS OF POPE GREGORY VII

The principal source for Gregory's letters is his *Register*, which is
preserved in the Vatican Archives as Registrum Vaticanum 2.[1]
Leaving aside a score or so of records of Lent and November
councils at the Lateran, privileges, oaths, and other miscellaneous
items, it contains some 360 letters. For a pontificate of more than
twelve years which was one of the most active, propagandist, and
momentous in the whole of papal history, this is a surprisingly
small total; particularly as for some of Gregory's busiest years,
1075–6, 1077–8, and 1080–1, fewer than 25 letters from each find
a place in the *Register*, and for 1076–7 and 1079–80 only between
25 and 30. For each of Gregory's first two years as pope the number
is well over 70, and whether or not Reg. Vat. 2 is Gregory's original
register—a question which it is at present best to regard as an open

---

[1] Ed. E. Caspar, *M.G.H. Ep. sel.* ii (Berlin, 1920–3).

one[1]—it would be difficult to believe that it contained by any means all of Gregory's letters. In fact nearly 70 other letters have for long been known, which it is convenient to describe as his *Epistolae uagantes*, or as his *extrauagantes*. They are the chance survivals of a larger number of letters which escaped registration in Reg. Vat. 2 if it is an original register, or which may have been included in another register if such there was. Following the most plausible estimate which has hitherto been attempted, it appears reasonable to suppose that there were perhaps some 600–700 letters over and above those in Reg. Vat. 2,[2] though there may have been considerably more. The number of *extrauagantes* to survive is thus not more than about a tenth, at most, of the probable total. But it includes some of the most important and characteristic of Gregory's letters, and many which bear the marks of his own dictation. The *Epistolae uagantes* must be studied together with the *Register* as a source for the history of Gregory's pontificate.

THE MANUSCRIPTS OF THE *EPISTOLAE VAGANTES*

None of the letters in this edition has survived as an original product of the papal chancery;[3] this is not surprising, for in the eleventh century the keeping of letters in the archives of their recipients was virtually unknown. The principal means by which copies of the most important of the *extrauagantes* have been handed down has been their incorporation in literary works, which fall into three groups:

I. *The* Gregorii VII uita *by Paul of Bernried*

This biography was written *c.* 1128. Its author, a regular canon of Bernried (dioc. Augsburg), was a staunch Gregorian. Copies of

---

[1] The case that Reg. Vat. 2 is Gregory's original register was powerfully stated by W. M. Peitz, 'Das Originalregister Gregors VII. im vatikanischen Archiv', *SB. Wien*, clxv (1911), Abh. 5, and confirmed by Caspar in his printed edition and elsewhere. Although their conclusions have since been widely accepted, a number of scholars have called them in question, notably Santifaller and Borino in studies which are cited in the Bibliography of this book. A fresh examination of Reg. Vat. 2 itself is highly desirable in the light of Santifaller's work.

[2] A. Murray, 'Pope Gregory VII in his Letters', *Traditio*, xxii (1966), 149–202. His conclusions about the probable number of Gregory's letters are, in general, acceptable whether or not Reg. Vat. 2 is regarded as Gregory's original register. Mr. Murray himself regards 600–700 as the highest reasonable estimate.

[3] There are only three surviving originals of letters in the *Register*: *Reg.* p. x.

it are found in the four manuscripts of the *Magnum Legendarium Austriacum*, all of which are of twelfth-century date: Vienna, Österreichische Nationalbibl. 336, fos. 248ʳ–269ʳ; Heiligenkreuz, Stiftsbibl. 12, fos. 181ᵛ–199ʳ; Admont, Stiftsbibl. 24, fos. 129ᵛ–143ᵛ; and Melk, Stiftsbibl. 492, fos. 87ᵛ–115ʳ.[1] In most cases—nos. 18 and 25 being something of an exception—Paul of Bernried provides the best available text of those of Gregory's *extrauagantes* which he included.

II. *Chronicles*

(a) *Hugh of Flavigny*, Chronicon. Hugh first emerges as a monk of the Lotharingian monastery of Saint-Vanne, Verdun. In 1085, at the age of twenty-one, he fled to France with his Gregorian abbot, Rudolf. He eventually associated himself with the high Gregorian circle of Archbishop Hugh of Lyons and Abbot Jarento of Saint-Bénigne, Dijon. In 1096 he became abbot of Flavigny, near Semur, in the duchy of Burgundy. However, after bitter conflicts with his diocesan, the bishop of Autun, and with local monks and clergy, he finally left Flavigny in 1101. He turned in despair to the imperialist party in Lorraine, becoming for a short time the imperialist abbot of his former monastery of Saint-Vanne until he disappears from sight. His *Chronicon* was composed in stages beginning *c.* 1090 when he was at Dijon, and he discontinued it in 1102. His autograph manuscript survives as Berlin, Deutsche Staatsbibl. Phillipps 1870. His years in France gave him access to French sources, notably the documents of Archbishop Hugh of Lyons. He drew upon them, together with Lotharingian sources and perhaps, directly or indirectly, Gregory's *Register*, when he compiled the four groups of Gregory's letters which he included in the second book of his *Chronicon*.[2]

(b) *Bruno*, Saxonicum bellum. Bruno was initially a clerk in the household of Archbishop Werner of Magdeburg. After the archbishop's death in 1078 he attached himself to Bishop Werner of Merseburg, to whom he dedicated the *Saxonicum bellum*. He wrote his work, an ardently partisan defence of the Saxon cause against

---

[1] So far as Gregory's *extrauagantes* are concerned these four MSS. provide remarkably consistent texts with no significant variant readings. While noting folio references to all the MSS. I have referred only to the Vienna text in the textual apparatus of the present edition.

[2] Cf. Caspar's analysis: *Reg.* pp. xii–xiv.

Henry IV, *c.* 1082. The earliest complete manuscript of it which is still extant, Leipzig, Universitätsbibl. 1323, was written *c.* 1500 and came from the monastery of Altzelle bei Nossen; while offering a text which includes all four of Gregory's *extrauagantes* which Bruno incorporated, it is somewhat marred by textual errors. Another text of them in Bruno's tradition survives in the *Annalista Saxo*, a vast compilation of *c.* 1150 which included much of Bruno. The autograph manuscript of its author, Abbot Arnold of Berge, near Magdeburg, is now Paris, Bibl. nat. lat. 11851.

III. *Letter collections*

During the eleventh and twelfth centuries letter collections came rapidly to the fore in western Europe as a literary form.[1] As Erdmann remarked, the development of letter writing and copying had something of the importance for the spread of the Gregorian reform in Germany that the development of printing was to have for the Reformation, and it ensured a wide hearing for Gregory's letters. However, the essentially literary character of the major letter collections must be borne in mind. They frequently included letters which are of the greatest value to the historian on account of the circumstances and purpose of their writing and of their earlier circulation for propagandist purposes. But they were themselves designed to preserve and to make available material to promote the *ars dictaminis*, the practice of cultivated poetic and epistolary composition, by demonstrating the achievements of past writers and by providing patterns for reading and imitation. Although they were compiled in circles which were more or less committed one way or the other in the struggle of pope and emperor they tended to be eclectic and to reflect little, if any, *parti pris*. Thus the inclusion of letters in letter collections often diminished their value as historical sources: because they had a literary purpose, personal names and place-names were often indicated only by an initial letter if they were not altogether omitted; later compilers not infrequently sought to improve the style of their

---

[1] The study of letter collections was an especial concern of Erdmann; what follows is a summary of his conclusions in his studies, 'Die Bamberger Domschule im Investiturstreit', *Zeitschrift für bayerische Landesgeschichte*, ix (1936), 1–46; 'Die Anfänge der staatliche Propaganda im Investiturstreit', *Historische Zeitschrift*, cliv (1936), 491–512; and 'Briefsammlungen', in W. Wattenbach and R. Holtzmann, *Deutschlands Geschichtsquellen im Mittelalter*, ii (2nd edn. by F.-J. Schmale, Darmstadt, 1967), pp. 415–42.

material according to their own taste and discretion; both from
their context in the midst of other material and on account of in-
ternal changes in their text letters lost something of their propagandist point and force. As authorities for the original text and
character of letters, then, letter collections tend to be less satisfactory than biographies, chronicles, and, above all, simple copies.
In general, the later and the greater the letter collection, the less
satisfactory is its authority for the original text of a letter.

Nevertheless, especially in Germany, letter collections played
an important part in preserving Gregory's *extrauagantes*, and for
some of them they are of first-rate significance. The following
German collections are important in this connection:

(*a*) *The Hanover Collection.* In its totality this collection, now
Hanover, Niedersächsische Landesbibl. xi. 671, is a sixteenth-
century compilation of five previously separate collections. Codex I
occupies the first 90 folios and consists of 35 items, almost all
dating from between 1073 and 1095. Imperialist in its background
it took its present form in the twelfth century from material which
seems to have been assembled at Bamberg *c.* 1095. It contains five
of Gregory's *extrauagantes*. One further letter owes its survival
to its inclusion in Codex III, where it forms part of an eleventh-
century collection associated with Hildesheim.

(*b*) *The Wolfenbüttel Collection.* The twelfth-century manuscript
of this collection is now at Wolfenbüttel, Herzog-August Bibl.
Helmstedt 1024. It contains 40 items dating from up to 1116 and
is of uncertain provenance: Erdmann suggested Mainz as a possibility. It is probably a rather later abbreviation of a collection made
c. 1116–25, and is characterized by a tendency to make crude errors
and considerable omissions in the transmission of the text.

(*c*) *The* Codex Udalrici. This is by far the largest and most important of the twelfth-century German letter collections in which
Gregory's *extrauagantes* occur. Its compiler, Ulrich, was a member
and perhaps for a time the provost of the cathedral chapter at Bamberg; he also served as *scholasticus* of the cathedral school. The
Codex Udalrici was dedicated in 1125 to Bishop Gebhard of Würzburg (1122–5). It comprises three books: a brief Book I consisting
of the dedication and of mainly poetic material; Book II, of 121
charters; and Book III, of some 250 letters. Of these letters about
110 are of the time of the Emperor Henry IV (1056–1106); about
90 are from that of Henry V (1106–25); while the remainder form

a later supplement of letters dating up to *c.* 1134. In the whole series there are 66 papal letters. The *Codex Udalrici* thus presents a heterogeneous and comprehensive literary collection of poetry, charters, and letters intended for purposes of reading and instruction. There are two manuscript copies of the complete work, both of twelfth-century date: Zwettl, Stiftsarch. 283, and Vienna, Österreichische Nationalbibl. 398. Two further manuscripts of the same century contain excerpts from it: Munich, Bayerische Landesbibl. lat. 4594, and Vienna, Österreichische Nationalbibl. 611.[1] So far as Gregory's letters are concerned Ulrich borrowed his material from other letter collections. In his version of the texts he made many changes of detail, and some of substance, in his endeavours to improve the style of the letters as he found them in his own sources, and especially in the somewhat unsatisfactory Wolfenbüttel Collection.

The three principal letter collections which have just been referred to stand in a close relationship to each other which Erdmann brilliantly elucidated in studies which, if necessarily hypothetical in many of their conclusions, have not met with serious challenge. He noticed that the *Codex Udalrici* (*CU*) contains all of the 40 letters in the Wolfenbüttel Collection (*W*), and also 25 of the 35 letters in Codex I of the Hanover Collection (*H*). But Ulrich did not take his material from these two letter collections in their present form. Erdmann inferred from the different order in the manuscripts of the letters common to *W* and *CU* and from a study of the textual variations between them that Ulrich drew upon an earlier and larger form of *W*, designated *w*, the whole of which he probably incorporated in *CU*. Erdmann next turned to the letters of 1075–84, 15 in number, which are common to *W* and *H*; these he regarded as evidence for the common drawing by *w* and the earlier form of *H*, designated *h*, upon a small 'papalist' collection (*p*), consisting of at least these 15 letters and going back to, or almost to, Gregory's own day. Probably of Lotharingian provenance it may also have been known to Hugh of Flavigny who himself used a number of the letters in question. Erdmann's suggested pattern of dependence is as follows:

---

[1] The *Codex Udalrici* was printed according to the order of the letters in the MSS. by Eccard, *Corp. hist.* ii. 1–374. The greater part of it was also printed, in a better text but with the order disarranged, by Jaffé, *Monumenta Bambergensia*, *Bibliotheca rerum Germanicarum*, v (Berlin, 1869), pp. 1–469.

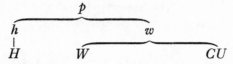

Such appear to have been the relationships of the principal German letter collections. Elsewhere than in Germany and its immediate environs letter collections were of less significance for the preservation of Gregory's *extrauagantes*. But a collection of incoming letters made by the church at Tours and originally containing some 40 items probably helped to keep from oblivion the remarkable number of letters relating to Archbishop Ralph of Tours which appear in the following pages.[1] Again, all six manuscript collections of St. Anselm's letters contain no. 34 of the present edition, which is not otherwise known.

Some of Gregory's letters seem to have circulated and to have been copied, particularly in Germany, as small propagandist compilations, e.g. no. 7 below, which formed part of a series of four items preserved in Munich, Bayerische Landesbibl. lat. 18541*a*, fos. 221ᵛ–222ᵛ; or as additional material to support the public writings of German bishops, e.g. the 'Manifesto' edited by Holder-Egger, *N.A.* xxxi (1906), 186–91. Isolated letters or fragments found a place in the works of polemists like Bernard of Constance, Berthold, Manegold of Lautenbach, or Gerhoh of Reichersberg, e.g. nos. 8, 32; and others again in saints' *Lives*, e.g. nos. 2, 20. For the rest, the *extrauagantes* mainly depended for their survival upon the chance of their being included in cartularies and similar records, or copied into convenient spaces of liturgical and other manuscripts.

PRINTED COLLECTIONS

During the eighteenth and nineteenth centuries four principal collections were made of Gregory's letters, which included a number of the *extrauagantes* as follows:

(i) Mansi, xx (1767), 370–86; which included nos. 1, 2, 13, 14, 16–18, 25, 26, 45–7, and 51 of this edition;

(ii) *R.H.F.* xiv (1806), 565–666; which included nos. 4, 12, 16, 21, 30, 38, 40, 45–7, 50–3, and 72–3;

---

[1] Cf. Erdmann, *Studien zur Briefliteratur Deutschlands im elften Jahrhundert*, p. 14.

(iii) *P.L.* cxlviii (1853), 643–734; containing a large assortment of letters and privileges from printed sources;

(iv) *Ep. coll.* (1865).

Of these four collections the last, in which Jaffé built upon the work of Giesebrecht, is the most comprehensive (for its contents see the Index of Letters, below, pp. 164–5). The present edition includes all of the material assembled by Jaffé, except for the following items already edited by Santifaller in his recent collection of Gregory's privileges:

Ep. coll.	J.L.	Addressed to	Santifaller, *Q.F.*
12	4973	Liutprand, a priest of Milan	106
19	5016	The monks of Saint-Gilles	110
45	5267	The monks of Conques and Figeac	216

In addition, *Ep. coll.* no. 34 (J.L. 5154, to Bishop Henry of Liège), is omitted from this edition because it is an artificial conflation by Deusdedit, *Collectio canonum*, i, *c.* 159, of *Reg.* vii. 13–14, 30 Jan. 1080, pp. 477–80;[1] and *Ep. coll.* no. 51 (J.L. 5309, to Bishop Altmann of Passau) is omitted because the reference in *Vita Altmanni*, *c.* 30, *M.G.H. Scr.* viii. 238, seems to be to *Reg.* ix. 3, Mar. 1081, p. 576, not to an independent letter.[2]

During the hundred years or so since Jaffé completed his *Ep. coll.* a number of other letters have come to light; all are included in the present edition.

THE SUBJECT-MATTER

The letters which are edited below comprise items which were prepared for recipients in Germany, Italy, France, Spain, England, and Ireland. By far the most important are those relating to Germany: they illustrate the successive stages of Gregory's dealings with Henry IV. A first group—nos. 6–11—arose from Gregory's attempts during Henry's preoccupation with the Saxon rising of 1073–5 to mount a campaign against simony and clerical marriage and to enforce the collaboration of the German bishops. After his first excommunication of Henry in February 1076 Gregory sought to justify his action to those who had doubts about its justice

---

[1] See Loewenfeld, 'Die Canonsammlung des Cardinals Deusdedit und das Register Gregors VII.', *N.A.* x (1884–5), 324–5, and Caspar, *Reg.* p. 478, n. 1.

[2] See Brackmann's note, *G.P.* i, p. 168, no. 28.

(nos. 13 and 14), and during the following twelve months or so further letters—nos. 15, 17–19—provide important witness to Gregory's intentions during the events which turned upon his absolution of the king at Canossa on 28 January 1077 and the election of Duke Rudolf of Swabia as anti-king by the German princes at Forchheim on 15 March. Thereafter, when he was confronted by the problem of two kings in Germany, Gregory's letters illustrate his attempts to determine which of them exhibited a righteousness (*iustitia*) which proved him as by the judgement of God to be the rightful ruler (nos. 25–7, 31), while his campaign for the moral reform of the clergy went on (no. 32). These letters shed no light upon Gregory's second excommunication of Henry in March 1080. But from the summer of 1083 onwards further letters, which circulated widely in western Europe, exhibit his personal distress and perplexity as the king's armies pressed ever more closely upon Rome, up to his final exile at Salerno as the virtual prisoner of his Norman allies (nos. 51, 54–5). Three other letters, of uncertain date, relate to Gregory's dealings with his loyal Bavarian supporter and standing legate, Bishop Altmann of Passau (nos. 58–60); while no. 20 affords the only example in this collection of Gregory's intervening to remedy a wrong done to a German monastery by its diocesan.

So far as Italy is concerned Gregory's *extrauagantes* for the most part relate to monasteries whose dealings with respect to the temporal world and its magnates he wished to influence: Vallombrosa (no. 2), Monte Cassino (nos. 28–9), and Fucecchio and Camaldoli (no. 43). He also endeavoured to involve Countess Matilda of Tuscany in his plan of 1074 for an eastern expedition (no. 5), while certain of the letters which have been noticed as illustrating his policy towards Germany also applied to the kingdom of Italy (nos. 15, 32).

The letters which concern France show a very wide diversity of content, and illustrate the practical application of the maxims of papal authority which Gregory laid down in the *Dictatus papae*. Perhaps the most important of them concern Gregory's legates, and particularly his standing legates Hugh of Die and Lyons and Amatus of Oléron; thus, Gregory may be seen commending (no. 21), upholding (no. 49), instructing (nos. 30, 44, 53), and rebuking them (nos. 42, 50). Gregory was much concerned with the episcopate: he wrote to commend to his diocese an archbishop

of his own choosing (no. 40), while he frequently sought to secure the disciplining of scandalous or disobedient bishops (nos. 16, 24, 41, 45–7). He also supported the interests of monasteries (nos. 36, 56) and desired to have the prayers of St. Anselm and his monks at Bec (no. 34). Apart from letters already mentioned the chance of survival has preserved a small group of items concerning Cluny and the diocese of Mâcon in which it was situated (nos. 4, 38, 39), and a far larger group centring upon Archbishop Ralph of Tours and the county of Anjou (nos. 3, 22, 23, 33, 35, 37, 48, 52, 61, 63, 64).

Spain, England, and Ireland are represented by one letter each: to kings in the first and last instances (nos. 65 and 57), and to the archbishop of Canterbury (no. 1).

Many of the letters—perhaps a third of the total—appear to have been personally dictated, as a whole or in substantial part, by Gregory himself. Blaul and Caspar, in the works by them which are cited above in the List of Printed Books and Articles, have suggested criteria by which such letters may be recognized: they include peculiarities of vocabulary, the use of favourite biblical and other quotations, the use of the first person singular, warm expressions of personal emotion, and appeals to the theological springs of papal action as Gregory understood them. There is inevitably a considerable subjective factor in attempting to apply such criteria. But, with particular reference to Blaul's discussion, the following letters seem especially likely to be, whether wholly or in part, of Gregory's own dictation: nos. 1, 2, 5, 9, 10, 11, 14, 15, 17–19, 23, 27, 31–3, 37–9, 47, 51, 54, 55, 59, 65. Of the remainder of the letters, most were probably drafted on Gregory's behalf by the clerks of his curia and, for the most part, seen by him before being copied in fair, sealed with a lead *bulla*, and dispatched. A small number of letters—principally those addressed to suitors who approached Gregory for settlement of the local grievances of their own monasteries and churches—may have been drafted in anticipation by the suitors and presented at the curia for sealing. It is known that Berengar of Tours prepared such drafts in anticipation of receiving a favourable verdict from Gregory at his Lent council of 1079: see nos. †72 and †73. Similar drafts may well underlie other items in this volume. It is in such cases that the separating of genuine from forged or otherwise unapproved items is most difficult. Gregory himself was concerned that *bullae* taken from his

letters might be affixed to forged documents: see no. 45. It was not difficult to add them to drafts which had not secured papal approval, or which had not been submitted for it. Again, the copying of a letter into a cartulary is no guarantee that it had ever been given a papal seal. Thus decisions about the genuineness of such letters as nos. 56 and †74 must depend upon the impression which is created by their form, style, and subject-matter, and must often remain open to question. Indeed, Gregory's *extrauagantes* in general must be approached with a certain caution: towards the end of his life he himself declared that many writings and sayings circulated in his name of which he had no knowledge.[1] Apart from letters which are probably of Gregory's own dictation the greatest confidence may be placed in items which were preserved by chroniclers and letter collectors who were in a position to know where their material came from, and rather less confidence in items which survived in isolation and by means which cannot be satisfactorily traced.

In using Gregory's letters, whether from the *Register* or not, it must be remembered that—in common with the letters of many other medieval writers—they by no means always contained the whole of the information or directions that it was intended to communicate to their recipients. Whether the fact was stated or not, their bearers were often commissioned to pass on verbally matters which considerations of brevity or security made it inexpedient to commit to writing: see, e.g., nos. 1, 17, 19. On the other hand it seems clear that, unless an eleventh-century messenger was personally well known to the recipient of his message, he was normally expected to have letters under seal to establish his credentials.[2] Thus, even when Gregory's letters were carried by legates or other men of importance they were usually themselves substantial documents; when, as must often have happened, their bearers were humbler men who chanced to be available—pilgrims or inferior clergy[3]—they are likely to have contained the whole of the message that Gregory wished to transmit. This must also have normally

[1] *Reg.* ix. 32, 1082–3, pp. 618–19; cf. iii. 18, May 1076, p. 284.
[2] Cf. *Die Hannoversche Briefsammlung* (*i, Hildesheimer Briefe*), no. 13, *M.G.H. B.D.K.* v. 32; *Reg.* i. 42, 24 Jan. 1074, pp. 64–5; *Reg.* i. 81, 6 May 1074, pp. 115–16.
[3] Cf. Bruno, *Sax. bell. cap.* 110, edd. Lohmann and Schmale, p. 364; *Die Hannoversche Briefsammlung* (*i, Hildesheimer Briefe*), no. 15, *M.G.H. B.D.K.* v. 33.

been the case with letters which the papal chancery produced *multi-pliciter*, that is in several virtually, if not entirely, identical copies addressed to different persons; see, e.g., nos. 6, 7, 51, 54; and where letters were sent to distant destinations, like Bamberg, to be copied there and circulated in accordance with the pope's directions.[1]

METHOD OF EDITING

This edition is intended to include all of Gregory's letters which survive in Latin,[2] and which appear neither in Caspar's edition of the *Register* nor in Santifaller's of the *Privileges*. Like the *Register* it includes a few items which are not letters in form but which constitute important records of Gregory's pontificate. In all cases save no. 65 it has been possible to prepare the text from the manuscripts which are known to have survived, or, where there is no manu-script authority, from the earliest printed sources. The notes re-garding manuscript and printed sources indicate the sources which have been used, save in the case of no. 65; all the manuscript sources except those in English libraries were consulted by means of photographs or microfilms of the relevant folios.

Except where indicated the text which is printed is that of the first manuscript or printed source to be listed. Punctuation and the use of capital letters have been modernized, and e cedilla has been printed as ae. The late eleventh and twelfth centuries, from which most of the manuscripts date, was a time of transition from the Latin of the Carolingian period to the phonetic Latin of the later Middle Ages, and some letters are from copies of from thirteenth-century to eighteenth-century date. Thus there are considerable differences in spelling between different letters, and indeed within many of them individually.

The text of this edition is an attempt to represent as nearly as possible the form in which the letters were issued by the papal

[1] *Die Hannoversche Briefsammlung* (i, *Hildesheimer Briefe*), no. 58, *M.G.H. B.D.K.* v. 104. It is also not impossible that, as half a century later, papal legates were sometimes furnished with pieces of parchment, sealed with the papal seal, as alleged in Rahewin, *Gesta Frederici imperatoris*, iii. 13, *a.* 1157, ed. F.-J. Schmale (Ausgewählte Quellen zur deutschen Geschichte des Mittelalters, xviii, Berlin, 1965), p. 420.

[2] A substantial fragment of an otherwise unknown letter survives in Old French translation: Amato di Montecassino, *Storia de'Normanni*, vii. 8, ed. V. de Bartholomaeis (Fonti per la storia d'Italia, lxxvi, Rome, 1935), p. 298. It was addressed to Sichelgaita, wife of Robert Guiscard, duke of Apulia and Calabria, and written in 1073.

chancery. Because in the process of tradition which has been described the letters underwent much modification, often with an essentially literary purpose in mind, an apparatus which comprehended all transpositions of words and phrases and all minor textual differences would be intolerably cumbersome. Such transpositions have, therefore, almost always been ignored. Variant readings have been recorded wherever they are of possible significance for the historian, and also in sufficient numbers to illustrate the characteristics, limitations, and interrelations of the various sources. They are intended to show so far as is possible what happened to the text of the letters as they circulated and were copied in the regions to which they were sent.

A dagger † before the number of an item indicates that it is spurious, or falsely ascribed to Gregory VII.

THE TRANSLATION

The translation is a fairly literal one which is intended as a help for students who find the Latin difficult. They are begged to remember that a translation is at best no more than a guide to what the Latin may mean and certainly not a final and conclusive statement of what it does mean. It is inevitably an interpretation, which demands careful and critical comparison with the Latin.

THE
EPISTOLAE VAGANTES
OF
POPE GREGORY VII

C

1

To Archbishop Lanfranc of Canterbury: Gregory commends his messenger to him and desires his help and prayers amidst the tribulations of the papal office; Lanfranc is to take steps against those 'Scots' who abandon or sell their wives

(1073, after 30 June)*

Gregorius episcopus seruus seruorum Dei carissimo fratri in Christo Lanfranco uenerabili Cantuariorum archiepiscopo salutem et apostolicam benedictionem.

Qualiter nobis apostolici regiminis honor et onus impositum sit, et quantis undique stringamur angustiis, praesentium tibi portitor indicabit, cui respectu tuae dilectionis etiam nonnulla nostris adhuc familiaribus occulta aperuimus. De caetero in primis fraternitatem tuam rogamus ut Deum pro nobis iugiter exorare non pigeat, et subditos sibi uel coniunctos fratres*ᵃ* suis nos orationibus apud Deum iuuare commoneat. Quanto enim in maiore periculo positi sumus, tanto amplius tuis et bonorum omnium suffragiis indigemus. Nos etenim, si diuinae uindictae iudicium effugere uolumus, contra multos insurgere et eos in animam nostram prouocare compellimur. Nam dum omnes fere, sicut ait apostolus, quae sua sunt non quae Ihesu Christi quaerunt,[1] regnorum principes et huius mundi potentes ut cupiditates suas expleant legem Dei et iusticiam non iam neglegenter deserunt sed summis conatibus impugnant, ut illud prophetae nunc sub oculis uideamus impletum: 'Astiterunt reges terrae, et principes conuenerunt in unum, aduersus Dominum et aduersus christum eius.'[2] Episcopi uero et qui pastores animarum esse deberent, mundi gloriam et delicias carnis insatiabili desiderio prosequentes,

---

ᵃ Text uncertain in E; fratris R but second syllable scored through

---

* This letter illustrates the countenance which Gregory gave to the church of Canterbury's claims to a primacy over the whole British Isles, which Archbishop Lanfranc (1070–89) energetically pursued. Apart from his dispute with the church of York Lanfranc's later endeavours were largely directed towards Ireland: in 1074 he consecrated a monk of Worcester to be bishop of Dublin, and perhaps hoped to set up a dependent archbishopric.

To Archbishop Lanfranc of Canterbury
(*1073, after 30 June*)

Gregory, bishop, servant of the servants of God, to his most be-loved brother in Christ, Lanfranc, the venerable archbishop of Canterbury, greeting and apostolic blessing.

In what way the office and burden of apostolic rule were laid upon us, and by how many tribulations we are hemmed in on every side, the bearer of this letter will make known to you; and by reason of your love we have also disclosed to him certain matters which are as yet hidden even from our own familiar counsellors. In addition to these things, we first beseech you not to be slack in continually interceding with God on our behalf, and to urge the brethren who are your subjects or companions to help us before God by their prayers. For as the danger in which we are placed becomes greater, the more pressing is our need of your support and that of all good men. As for ourself, if we would escape the judgement of divine vengeance we must needs rise up against many and provoke them against our own life. For while almost all men, as the Apostle says, seek their own and not the things of Jesus Christ,[1] the rulers of earthly kingdoms and the powers of this world, to fulfil their own desires, no longer only carelessly desert God's law and righteousness but attack them with all their might; thus we now see the prophetic word being fulfilled before our very eyes: 'The kings of the earth stand up and the rulers take counsel together, against the Lord and against his anointed.'[2] Yet bishops and those who should be shepherds of souls follow with insatiable

J.L. 4801. MSS.: London, Brit. Mus. Cotton Claudius E.V, fo. 244[r-v], twelfth cent. (*E*). Rome, Vatican Library, Reginensis lat. 285, fos. 5[v]–6[r], twelfth cent. (*R*). Cambridge, University Library, Dd. i. 11, fos. 204[v]–205[r], fifteenth cent.[3] Printed: Baronius, *Annales eccles.* xi. 446–7. *Lanfranci opera*, ed. Giles, i, no. 40, pp. 58–9. *Ep. coll.* no. 1, pp. 520–1.

[1] Cf. Phil. 2: 21.
[2] Ps. 2: 2.
[3] I am grateful to Professor C. N. L. Brooke for drawing my attention to this MS.

non solum in semetipsis quae sancta quaeque sunt religiosa confundunt, sed subditos suos ad omne nefas operum suorum exemplo pertrahunt. Quibus non contraire quam nobis periculosum resistere autem et eorum nequiciam refrenare quam difficile sit, tua prudentia nouit. Sed quoniam quos dolores inter has patiamur angustias, ut supradiximus, huic communi filio nostro tibi referendum exeruimus, plura de his dicere supersedemus.

Tuam uero fraternitatem etsi monitore non egeat, impellente tamen nos sollicitudine admonemus quatinus grauiora usquequaque resecare uitia studeat, et inter omnia et prae omnibus nefas quod de Scottis audiuimus,[1] uidelicet quod plerique proprias uxores non solum deserunt sed etiam uendunt, modis omnibus prohibere contendat. Ad haec enim apostolica te auctoritate fultum esse uolumus, ut non solum in Scottis hoc scelus sed etiam in aliis, si quos in Anglorum insula tales esse cognoueris, dura animaduersione punias et radicem tanti mali prudenti sarculo correctionis penitus extirpare non differas.

2

To the clerks, monks, and laymen of Vallombrosa: Gregory praises the memory of Abbot John Gualbertus, exhorting his followers to imitate his zeal for reform and promising them all support (*1073, after 12 July*)*

Gregorius episcopus seruus seruorum Dei clericis monachis ac religiosis laycis disciplinam sancte recordationis Iohannis Gualberti abbatis imitantibus salutem et apostolicam benedictionem.

Licet uenerande memorie eundem Iohannem patrem uestrum corporeis oculis non uiderimus, quia tamen fidei eius puritas in

---

* Vallombrosa, in Tuscany, was founded in 1036 by John Gualbertus of Florence (died 12 July 1073). His monks followed the Rule of St. Benedict but were dedicated to strict enclosure and perpetual silence. Associated with them was a convent of *conversi* or lay brothers. Vallombrosa was a centre of anti-simoniacal propaganda in north Italy. It became especially famous as such through the ordeal by fire in which its monk Peter Igneus (later Cardinal Peter of Albano) in 1068 secured the expulsion from Florence of its simoniacal bishop, Peter Mezzabarba.

J.L. 4814. *I.P.* iii, p. 88, no. 3. MS.: Andrew of Genoa, *Vita sancti Iohannis*

lust after worldly glory and fleshly delights. They not only confound holy and religious things in their own persons, but by the example of their works they lead their subjects astray into all manner of wickedness. You well know how dangerous it is for us not to proceed against them, yet how difficult to resist and bridle their iniquity. But since, as we have already said, we have made known to this messenger, who is the son of us both, for him to relate to you, the griefs which we suffer in the midst of these tribulations, we refrain from writing more about such matters.

Although you need no one to prompt you, yet because our pastoral duty impels us we urge you to be ever zealous for the extirpation of more serious evils, and first and foremost to strive by all means to end the abomination of which we have heard concerning the 'Scots',[1] namely that many of them not only abandon but even sell their own wives. We therefore desire that you should be strengthened by apostolic authority to visit this crime with severe punishment, not only amongst the 'Scots' but also amongst others in the British Isles if you know of any who are similarly guilty, and that you should brook no delay in utterly eradicating so great an evil by the hoe of your correction.

To the clerks, monks, and laymen of Vallombrosa
(1073, after 12 July)

Gregory, bishop, servant of the servants of God, to the clerks, monks, and religious laymen who follow the discipline of Abbot John Gualbertus of holy memory, greeting and apostolic blessing.

Although we never saw with our bodily eyes John, your father of honoured remembrance, we loved him with great affection

Gualberti, cap. 82: Florence, Archivio di stato, A.S.F., Corporazioni religiosi soppresse, archivio 260, no. 223, fos. 57ᵛ–58ʳ, twelfth cent. (G). Printed: Baronius, Annales eccles. xi. 451. Franchi, Historia del Patriarcha S. Giovan Gualberto, pp. 430–1. Ep. coll. no. 2, pp. 522–3.

---

[1] It is not clear from this letter whether the 'Scotti' in question were inhabitants of Scotland or Ireland. That they may well have been the latter is suggested by Lanfranc's letter of 1074 to Toirdhealbhach, king of Ireland, in which he complained 'quod in regno uestro quisque pro arbitrio suo legitime sibi copulatam uxorem nulla canonica causa interueniente relinquit, et aliam quamlibet . . . punienda sibi temeritate coniungit' (Lanfranci opera, ed. Giles, i, no. 44, p. 63).

Tuscie partibus mirabiliter resplenduit multo cum amore dileximus. Cuius sancte conuersationis*a* quamuis uos imitatores
esse non ambigamus, ut uigor rectitudinis uestre ad extirpandam
de agro dominico zizaniam sollicitius inuigilet[1] attentiusque ferueat
paterne uobis exhortationis uerba impendimus. Vos itaque dilectissimi in quantum humana possibilitas permittit uitam illius
sequentes et uere filios eius et heredes simili uos conuersatione
probantes, uiriliter agite et confortamini in Domino et in potentia
uirtutis eius.[2] Documenta sanctarum scripturarum, quibus
hereticorum argumenta destruuntur et fides sancte ecclesie
defenditur contra membra diaboli que diuersis machinationibus
christianam religionem conantur euertere, mens uestra cotidie
meditetur et ea qua solet libertate in malorum confusione erigatur.
Eos uero qui in uobis confidunt et consilium religionis uestre
sequi disponunt more predicti patris uestri suscipite, et de his
que ad salutem eorum pertinere uidentur sanctis exhortationibus
instruite, ut non solum uestra sed et uos sequentium circumpositi
populi considerantes sancta opera glorificent patrem uestrum qui
in celis est.[3] Nos autem ipsum amorem quem patri uestro et uobis
olim impendimus donec nostros spiritus rexit artus[4] exhibere
desideramus, et tanto quidem deinceps maiori uos caritate foue-
bimus quanto uos in diuinis negotiis feruentiores esse probabimus,
quibus non solum spirituale sed et seculare,*b* si necesse fuerit,
auxilium Deo adiuuante ministrabimus. Vos igitur omnipotentem
Dominum exorate, ut ipse uires et facultates nobis tribuat,
quatinus suscepti regiminis importabile pondus possimus tollerare
et sanctam ecclesiam in statum antique religionis reducere.
Valete.

---

a add studium G   *b* et scailare, *deleted and corrected to* seculare *in the
margin G*

---

[1] Cf. Matt. 13: 24–30.
[2] Cf. 1 Cor. 16: 13, Eph. 6: 10.
[3] Cf. Matt. 5: 16. Gregory refers to such groups as the Patarenes of Milan
who had looked to John Gualbertus for help: cf. Andrew of Strumi, *Vita sancti
Ioannis Gualberti, cap.* 78, ed. F. Baethgen, *M.G.H. Scr.* xxx. 1100.
[4] Cf. Virgil, *Aeneid,* 4. 336.

because his spotless faith shone wonderfully abroad throughout all Tuscany. Although we have no doubt that you are followers of his holy life, we send you words of fatherly exhortation that the zeal of your righteousness may watch the more diligently and burn the more keenly to root out the tares from the Lord's field.[1] Wherefore, dearly beloved, so far as human strength allows, follow his ways and prove yourselves by a similar manner of life to be in truth his sons and heirs: be courageous, be strong in the Lord and in the strength of his might.[2] Let your mind meditate daily upon the lessons of the holy scriptures by which the assertions of the heretics are confuted and the faith of holy church is defended against the members of the devil who are trying to overthrow the Christian religion by their manifold devices; let your mind stand upright to the confusion of evil men in the liberty wherein it is wont to stand. As for those who trust in you and desire to follow your holy counsel, do you, after your father John's example, receive them and by your holy exhortations guide them concerning whatever matters seem to belong to their salvation, so that the peoples round about, seeing not only your own good works but also your followers', may give glory to your Father who is in heaven.[3]

We, for our part, desire so long as life still moves our limbs[4] to show you the same love as we formerly extended to your father and to yourselves. We shall continue to support you with ever greater charity according as we find you more zealous in the things of God, and with God's help we shall bring you not only spiritual but also, if need arises, temporal aid. Do you therefore beseech Almighty God to give us the strength and the means to support the intolerable burden of the office which is laid upon us, and to restore holy church to the standard of her former devotion. Farewell.

3

To Archbishop Ralph of Tours: Gregory reproves him for associating with the excommunicated Count Fulk of Anjou and summons him to answer at Rome for his conduct

(1074, after 9 Mar.) *

G. episcopus seruus seruorum Dei R. Turonensi archiepiscopo.

Apostolicae sedis benedictionem tibi libenter mandaremus, nisi excommunicato Fulconi Andegauensi comiti te communicasse grauiter doleremus. Et quia in Romana synodo haec sunt relata et probabiliter enarrata, ab uniuerso sacri concilii coetu est laudatum ut, quoniam ab apostolica sede anathematizato adherere non timuisti, uerum etiam diuina illi misteria celebrare praesumpsisti, canonicae ultionis gladius in te deberet uibrari et depositionis sententia rite posset*a* depromi. Sed interuenientibus carissimi fidelis nostri Astonis marchionis precibus hoc ad praesens distulimus et inducias tibi satisfaciendi usque ad proximam Omnium Sanctorum futuram festiuitatem[1] concessimus. Quapropter fraternitatem tuam monemus ut ad hunc terminum uenire non dimittat ne, quod absit, nos in se quod non optamus depromere cogat.

4

To the clergy and people of the church of Mâcon: Gregory commends to them their new bishop, Landeric

(1074, late Apr.)†

Gregorius episcopus seruus seruorum Dei clero et populo Matisconensis ecclesiae salutem et apostolicam benedictionem.*a*

Quanta sit erga uos et locum uestrum apostolicae sedis beneuolentia ex amore quem in episcopum uestrum[2] habemus cognoscere

---

a posse *BD*   4   *a* *om.* et apostolicam benedictionem *S*

---

* Archbishop Ralph of Tours (1073–86) took office after a vacancy of five years during which Count Fulk IV, *le Réchin*, for long opposed his nomination. The circumstances of the count's excommunication, and the archbishop's actions which caused Gregory to deal with their association at his Lent council of 9–15 Mar. 1074, are obscure. But the presence at the council of Marquis Azzo II of Este (1029–97) is referred to in *Reg.* i. 57, 17 Mar. 1074, pp. 84–5, and ii. 9, 16 Oct. 1074, p. 139.

Not in J.L. MSS.: Budapest, Bibl. nat. Széch. lat. med. aeui 5, fo. 8ʳ, *c.* 1100,

To Archbishop Ralph of Tours (*1074, after 9 Mar.*)

Gregory, bishop, servant of the servants of God, to Archbishop Ralph of Tours.

We would gladly send you the blessing of the apostolic see, if we were not deeply aggrieved that you have associated with the excommunicated Count Fulk of Anjou. Because the matter was reported and reliably set forth in our Roman synod, it was agreed by the whole assembly of the holy council that, since you have not feared to keep company with a man excommunicated by the apostolic see and indeed have even ventured to celebrate the holy mysteries for him, the sword of canonical punishment should rightly be drawn against you and that sentence of deposition might properly be passed. But because of the pleas of our very dear and trusted Marquis Azzo we have deferred this for the present and given you stay to make satisfaction until next All Saints' Day.[1] We therefore warn you not to fail to come to us at this time, lest, which heaven forbid, you compel us to pass a sentence against you which we do not desire to pass.

To the clergy and people of the church of Mâcon
(*1074, late Apr.*)

Gregory, bishop, servant of the servants of God, to the clergy and people of the church of Mâcon, greeting and apostolic blessing.

The great good will of the apostolic see towards you and your church may be seen from the love which we have towards your bishop,[2] who, as is well known, has received the blessing and

(*B*). Paris, Bibl. nat. Duchesne 4, fo. 109ʳ, seventeenth cent. (*D*). Printed: Ramackers, *Q.F.I.A.B.* xxiii (1931–2), no. 4, pp. 37–8. Morin, *R.B.* xlviii (1936), no. 2, pp. 120–1. Ramackers, *P.U.F.* v, no. 8, pp. 70–1.

† The see of Mâcon, in the duchy of Burgundy, had been vacant since 5 Mar. 1072. King Philip I of France refused his consent to the canonical election of Landeric, archdeacon of Autun, unless a simoniacal payment was made; the metropolitan, Archbishop Humbert of Lyons, therefore failed to act upon Gregory's instructions that he should perform Landeric's consecration: *Reg.* i. 35–6, 4 and 7 Dec. 1073, pp. 56–8. Gregory summoned Landeric to Rome where he consecrated him in Apr. 1074: *Reg.* i. 76, 15 Apr. 1074, pp. 107–8, cf. i. 85*a*, 28 June 1074, p. 123. Landeric thereafter took possession of his see without difficulty or resistance on the king's part.

J.L. 4857. MS.: none. Printed: Severt, *Chronologia historica*, ii. 113 (*S*). *G.C.* iv, instr. no. 27, col. 282. *Ep. coll.* no. 7, p. 527. The text is that of *G.C.*

---

[1] 1 Nov. 1074. For a similar summons to Rome by this date, see *Reg.* i. 51, 14 Mar. 1074, pp. 77–8.   [2] Landeric of Berzé (1074–96).

datur, qui episcopalis officii benedictionem et dignitatem per impositionem manuum nostrarum, auctore Deo, suscepisse dignoscitur.[b] Caeterum ut ordinationis suae certa demonstrare possit indicia, sicut oportere cognouimus cum litteris nostris[1] et apostolico sigillo eum ad uos remisimus, ammonentes uos et apostolica auctoritate praecipientes[c] ut eum omni dilectione et gaudio recipientes unanimiter honoretis, et reuerentiam quae patri debetur et episcopo fideli obedientia ac deuota subiectione sibi exhibeatis, attendentes dominica uerba: 'Qui uos audit me audit, et qui uos spernit me spernit.'[2] Tanto enim laetioribus animis hunc suscipere, uenerari, timere,[d] debetis ac diligere, quanto eum ab omni simoniaca ambitione purum et incontaminatum, nec aliunde quam per ostium[3] ad custodiam animarum uestrarum in ecclesiam introisse et episcopalis uigilantiae speculam constat ascendisse. Proinde nos multum uobis congaudentes rogamus et ammonemus dilectionem uestram quatenus ad regendam sibi commissam ecclesiam eiusque iura conseruanda, et ubi opus fuerit recuperanda, quantum ualetis consilium sibi et adiutorium praebeatis, et in omnibus quae ad christianam religionem pertinent eius ammonitionibus acquiescatis, scientes sibi ac uobis et ecclesiae cuius in Christo spiritales[e] filii estis apostolica suffragia, quantum Deo praestante possumus, ad libertatem fidei uestrae et nostram[f] profectumque salutis ubique prompta atque parata fore.

5

(To Countess Matilda of Tuscany): Gregory confides to her his desire personally to cross the sea and help the Eastern Christians under persecution, and asks whether she will join the Empress Agnes and himself

(*1074, after 16 Dec.*)*

Quanta sit mihi meditatio quantumque desiderium mare

---

[b] *add* Et hic apertius constat Landricum Romae inauguratum antistitem S, *perhaps as a comment by the editor*   [c] *add* mandamus S   [d] tuerique S   [e] speciales S   [f] *Thus in G.C.,* ? nostrae; animarum curam *for* nostram S

---

* Gregory's plans for an expedition to defend Byzantium from Turkish attacks began to take shape early in 1074. He broached them to Count William of

office of the episcopate by the laying on of our own hands. However, in order that he may be able to display sure proofs of his
ordination, as we know it to be necessary we have sent him back
to you with our letters under apostolic seal,[1] warning and com-
manding you by apostolic authority to receive him with all love
and joy, to honour him with one mind, and to show him by faithful
obedience and devoted service the reverence which is due to a
father and bishop, paying heed to the Lord's words: 'He who hears
you hears me, and he who rejects you rejects me.'[2] You should
receive, honour, fear, and love him with the more joyful minds in
that he is well known to be spotlessly clean from all simoniacal
ambition, neither did he enter the church to assume custody of your
souls nor climb the watch-tower of episcopal vigilance some other
way than by the door.[3] So, rejoicing greatly with you, we beg and
beseech you, so far as in you lies, to give him help and counsel
in ruling the church committed to him and in preserving and
where necessary recovering its rights. In all things belonging to the
Christian religion you should obey his admonitions. And you may
be sure that, so far as with God's assistance we are able, we are
ready and prepared, for the bishop's sake, for your own, and for
the church's whose spiritual sons in Christ you are, everywhere to
promote the liberty of your faith and our own and the furtherance
of salvation.

(To Countess Matilda of Tuscany)   *(1074, after 16 Dec.)*

There are some whom I blush to tell, lest I should seem to be led

Burgundy in *Reg*. i. 46, 2 Feb. 1074, pp. 69–71, and issued a general summons to
all Christians in *Reg*. i. 49, 1 Mar. 1074, pp. 75–6. Gregory met with a favourable response from Duke William of Aquitaine: cf. *Reg*. ii. 3, 10 Sept. 1074,
pp. 126–8; a letter which refers to news of a relief from pagan pressure which
had caused Gregory to delay his plans. He revived them vigorously in Dec. 1074.
He then intended himself to lead an expedition as its *dux et pontifex*; it was not
only to relieve Byzantium but also to seek to free the Holy Sepulchre and to recon-
cile the Byzantine and Armenian churches to the apostolic see: *Reg*. ii. 31, 7 Dec.
1074, pp. 165–8; ii. 37, 16 Dec. 1074, pp. 172–3. The plan was totally abortive.

J.L. 4911. *I.P.* v, p. 389, no. 14. MS.: Hanover Collection: Hanover, Niedersächs. Landesbibl. XI. 671, fo. 242^r-v, sixteenth cent. (*H*). Printed: Sudendorf,
Reg. ii, no. 21, pp. 24–5. *Ep. coll*. no. 11, pp. 532–3. *Die Hannoversche Briefsammlung (i. Hildesheimer Briefe)*, no. 43, ed. Erdmann, *M.G.H. B.D.K*. v. 86–7.

---

[1] Lost.   [2] Luke 10: 16.   [3] Cf. John 10: 1.

transeundi, ut christianis qui more pecudum a paganis^a occiduntur[1]
Christo fauente ualeam succurrere, erubesco quibusdam dicere ne
uidear aliqua duci leuitate. Sed tibi, o charissima plena dilectione
filia,[2] nil horum dubito indicare, de cuius prudentiae studio
quantum possim praesumere tu ipsa uix poteris exprimere.
Quapropter uisis super hac re nostris literis quas mitto ultra-
montanis,[3] si quid potes adhibere consilium immo creatori tuo
adiutorium summopere procura, quia si pulchrum est, ut quidam
dicunt, pro patria mori,[4] pulcherrimum est ac ualde gloriosum
carnem morticinam[5] pro Christo dare, qui est aeterna uita. Credo
enim multos milites in tali labore nobis fauere, ipsam etiam nostram
imperatricem[6] nobiscum ad illas partes uelle uenire teque secum
ducere, matre tua[7] in partibus his relicta pro tuendis rebus
communibus; quia sic tute^b Christo iuuante possemus abire.^c
Proinde praedicta imperatrix causa orationis ueniens multos ad
hoc opus una tecum posset animare. Ego autem talibus ornatus
sororibus libentissime mare transirem ut animam meam, si
oporteret, uobiscum pro Christo ponerem, quas mihi semper
cupio in aeterna patria adherere. Quid super hac re et de tuo
aduentu Romam tibi uideatur, citissime procura rescribere. Quam
Dominus omnipotens de uirtute in uirtutem ducendo dignetur
benedicere, ut uniuersalis mater longo tempore de te^d possit
gaudere.[8]

^a paginis *H*   ^b sancte *H*   ^c adire *H*   ^d dote *H*

---

[1] Cf. Sallust, *Catilina*, 58. 21; whence Hegesippus, *Historiae*, 1. 11. 2, 5. 43. 2.
Gregory used similar phrases in *Reg.* i. 49, 1 Mar. 1074, p. 75; ii. 31, 7 Dec.
1074, p. 166; ii. 37, 16 Dec. 1074, p. 173.
[2] Matilda, separated wife of Duke Godfrey of Lower Lorraine; countess of
Tuscany (1052–1115).
[3] *Reg.* ii. 37.
[4] Horace, *Carmina*, 3. 2. 13.
[5] Cf. Seneca, *Epistolae*, 122. 4.
[6] Agnes of Poitou, widow of the Emperor Henry III and mother of Henry IV.
[7] Countess Beatrice of Tuscany.
[8] Cf. Ps. 83: 8 (84: 7), Gal. 4: 26.

by a mere fancy, how firmly my mind and heart are set upon cross-
ing the sea in order that, by Christ's favour, I may bring help
to the Christians who are being slaughtered by the heathen like
cattle.[1] But to you, my most beloved and loving daughter,[2] I do
not hesitate to disclose any of these thoughts, for even you yourself
can hardly imagine how greatly I may count upon your zeal and
discretion. When, therefore, you have read my letter about this
matter which I am sending to those beyond the Alps,[3] do all that
you can to give your counsel, and still more your help, to your
Creator; for if, as some say, it is a noble thing to die for our country,[4] it is a far nobler and a truly praiseworthy thing to give our
corruptible flesh[5] for Christ, who is life eternal.

Now, I believe that many knights support us in such a task, also
that our empress herself[6] desires to come with us to distant parts
and to bring you with her, leaving your mother[7] behind to safeguard our common interests here; for so, with Christ's help, we
might depart in safety. If, moreover, the empress came and devoted
herself to prayer, she in concert with you might encourage many
to take part in this work. As for me, furnished with such sisterly
aid I would most gladly cross the sea, if need be to lay down my
life for Christ with both of you whom I always desire should cleave
to me in the heavenly country.

See that you answer as quickly as you can what seems good to
you about this matter and about your coming to Rome. May the
Almighty Lord graciously bless you and lead you from strength to
strength, so that the mother of us all may for long be able to rejoice
upon your account.[8]

6

To Archbishop Siegfried of Mainz: Gregory urges German bishops to co-operate in eliminating simony and enforcing clerical chastity, and transmits the decrees of his Lateran council (*1075, Feb.*)*

G. seruus seruorum Dei Mogontino archiepiscopo[1] salutem et apostolicam benedictionem.

Cum apostolica auctoritate et ueridicis sanctorum patrum sententiis incitati ad eliminandam simoniacam heresim et praecipiendam clericorum castitatem pro nostri officii debito exarsimus, tibi cui est clerus et populus amplissime dilatatus, cui praeterea plures et late dispersi suffraganei sunt, hoc obedientiae munus iniungere decreuimus, ut tam per te quam per coadiutores tuos hoc Romanae ecclesiae decretum uniuerso clero studiosius inculcares et inuiolabiter tenendum proponeres. Qua de re tibi etiam speciales litteras cudere bulla nostra impressas collibuit, quarum fultus auctoritate tucius animosiusque praeceptis nostris obtemperes et de sanctuario Domini simoniacam heresim et fedam libidinosae contagionis pollutionem expellas. Vnde non ab re tibi scribendum fore arbitrati sumus, nos iuxta auctoritatem sanctorum patrum in nostra synodo sententiam dedisse, ut hi qui per symoniacam heresim, hoc est interuentu precii, ad aliquem sacrorum ordinum gradum uel officium promoti sunt, nullum in sancta ecclesia ulterius locum ministrandi habeant; illi quoque qui ecclesias datione pecuniae obtinent omnino eas perdant, ne deinceps uendere aut emere alicui liceat; sed nec illi qui in crimine fornicationis iacent missas celebrare aut secundum inferiores ordines ministrare altari debeant. Statuimus etiam ut si ipsi contemptores fuerint nostrarum immo sanctorum patrum constitutionum, populus nullo modo eorum officia recipiat, ut qui pro amore Dei et officii dignitate non corriguntur uerecundia saeculi et obiurgatione populi resipiscant. Studeat ergo fraternitas tua sic se in his rebus nobis cooperatricem exhibere, sic crimina

---

* For the date, see Additional Note, pp. 160–1. In this and the two following letters, which are probably typical of others to German bishops, Gregory sought to secure compliance with the decrees, now lost, of his Lent council of 1075 against simony—the buying and selling of ecclesiastical orders and offices —and clerical marriage and concubinage. The letters are particularly noteworthy

To Archbishop Siegfried of Mainz   (*1075, Feb.*)

Gregory, servant of the servants of God, to the archbishop of Mainz,[1] greeting and apostolic blessing.

Prompted by our apostolic authority and by the truthful decrees of the holy fathers, we were enkindled by the duty of our office to banish the simoniac heresy and to enforce the chastity of the clergy. Knowing that your clergy and people are widely dispersed and that, moreover, your suffragans are many and far flung, we determined to impose upon you this obligatory task: that both by your own endeavours and by your fellow bishops' you should impress the decree of the Roman church with due zeal upon all the clergy, and set it forth to be inviolably observed. It seemed good also to furnish you with a special letter about it bearing our seal, so that by the sanction of its authority you might the more safely and boldly obey our command and drive out from the sanctuary of the Lord the simoniac heresy and the foul defilement of polluting lust.

Thus we do not deem it superfluous to write to you that we have made a conciliar injunction, by the authority of the holy fathers, that those who have been promoted by the simoniac heresy, that is, with the intervention of money, to any rank or office of holy orders may no longer exercise any ministry in holy church. Those, too, who obtain churches by the gift of money must utterly forfeit them, so that no one for the future may be allowed to sell or buy them. Nor may those who are guilty of the crime of fornication celebrate masses or minister at the altar in lesser orders. We have further appointed that if they disregard our rulings, or rather those of the holy fathers, the people may in no wise receive their ministrations, so that those who are not corrected from the love of God and the honour of their office may be brought to their senses by the shame of the world and the reproof of the people. Be zealous, therefore, so to show yourself our fellow worker in these things, and so

for Gregory's attempt to stimulate lay resistance to the ministrations of sinful clergy.

J.L. 4931. MS.: Munich, Bayer. Staatsbibl. lat. 6236, fo. 166ᵛ, eleventh cent. Printed: *Ep. coll.* no. 3, pp. 523–4.

———

[1] Siegfried (1060–84).

ista de ecclesiis tuis radicitus euellere, quatinus boni pastoris meritum apud Deum ualeas obtinere et Romana ecclesia de te sicut de karissimo fratre et studioso cooperatore debeat gaudere.

7

To Archbishop Werner of Magdeburg: Gregory urges German bishops to co-operate in eliminating simony and enforcing clerical chastity, and transmits the decrees of his Lateran council (*1075, Feb.*)*

G. episcopus seruus seruorum Dei Magdaburgensi archiepiscopo[1] salutem et apostolicam benedictionem.

Text as no. 6

8

To Bishop Otto of Constance: Gregory informs him of the decrees of his Lateran council against simony and clerical unchastity (*1075, Feb.–Mar.*)†

Gregorius episcopus[a] seruus seruorum Dei dilecto in Christo[b] fratri Ottoni Constantiensi episcopo[2] salutem et apostolicam benedictionem.

Instantia nuntiorum tuorum festinanter redire[c] uolentium non permisit nos fraternitati tue que in Romana synodo[2] constituta sunt seriatim intimare. Hec tantum necessario tibi scribenda fore arbitrati sumus, nos iuxta auctoritatem sanctorum patrum in eadem synodo sententiam dedisse, ut hi qui per symoniacam heresim, hoc est interuentu precii, ad aliquem sacrorum ordinum gradum uel officium promoti sunt, nullum in sancta ecclesia

[a] *om.* episcopus *M*   [b] *om.* in Christo *A*   [c] abire *A*

---

* For the date, see Additional Note, pp. 160–1.
J.L. 4932. MSS.: Munich, Bayer. Staatsbibl. lat. 16054, fo. 1ʳ, twelfth cent. Munich, Bayer. Staatsbibl. lat. 18541*a*, fo. 222ᵛ, eleventh cent. Printed: *Ep. coll.* no. 4, pp. 524–5.
† For the date, see Additional Note, pp. 160–1.
J.L. 4933. *G.P.* ii, pt. 1, p. 127, no. 15. MSS.: Paul of Bernried, *Greg. VII uita*: Vienna, Österr. Nationalbibl. 336, fo. 252ᵛ, twelfth cent.; Heiligenkreuz,

to tear out these offences by the root from your churches, that you may win from God the reward of a good shepherd and that the Roman church may rejoice in you as a most dear brother and zealous fellow worker.

To Archbishop Werner of Magdeburg   (1075, Feb.)

Gregory, bishop, servant of the servants of God, to the archbishop of Magdeburg,[1] greeting and apostolic blessing.

Text as no. 6.

To Bishop Otto of Constance   (1075, Feb.–Mar.)

Gregory, bishop, servant of the servants of God, to his beloved brother in Christ, Bishop Otto of Constance,[2] greeting and apostolic blessing.

The haste of your messengers wishing to return without delay did not allow us to communicate to you in due order the decrees which were approved in the Roman council.[3] We thought it necessary that you should be sent written notice of this much at least: we made a ruling in this council, by the authority of the holy fathers, that those who have been promoted by the simoniac heresy, that is, by the intervention of money, to any rank or office of holy orders may no longer exercise any ministry in holy church.

Stiftsbibl. 12, fo. 185ʳ, twelfth cent.; Admont, Stiftsbibl. 24, fo. 132ʳ⁻ᵛ, twelfth cent.; Melk, Stiftsbibl. 492, fo. 93ʳ⁻ᵛ, twelfth cent.; Rome, Vatican Library, lat. 1363, fo. 244ʳ, twelfth cent. (*V*). Manegold of Lautenbach, *Ad Gebeh. lib.*: Karlsruhe, Badische Landesbibl. Rastatt 27, fo. 28ʳ, twelfth cent. (*M*). Bernard of Constance, *Apol.*: Einsiedeln, Stiftsbibl. 169, pp. 129–30, eleventh cent. (*A*); Stuttgart, Württ. Landesbibl. HB. VI. 107, fos. 144ᵛ–145ʳ, eleventh cent. Printed: Paul of Bernried, *Greg. VII uita*, cap. 36, *Pont. Rom. uitae*, ed. Watterich, p. 490. Manegold of Lautenbach, *Ad Gebeh. lib. cap.* 17, *M.G.H. L. de L.* i. 340–1. Bernard of Constance, *Apol. cap.* 1, *M.G.H. L. de L.* ii. 60–1. *Ep. coll.* no. 5, pp. 525–6.

---

[1] Werner (1063–78).   [2] 1071–86.   [3] 24–8 Feb. 1075.

ulterius ministrandi locum habeant; illi quoque qui ecclesias datione pecunie obtinent omnino eas perdant, nec deinceps uendere aut emere alicui liceat; sed nec illi qui in crimine fornicationis iacent missas celebrare aut secundum inferiores ordines ministrare altari debeant. Statuimus etiam ut si ipsi contemptores fuerint nostrarum immo sanctorum patrum constitutionum, populus nullomodo eorum officia recipiat ut qui pro amore Dei et officii dignitate[d] non corriguntur, uerecundia seculi et obiurgatione populi resipiscant.[e] Studeat igitur fraternitas tua sic se in his nobis cooperatricem exhibere, sic crimina ista radicitus de ecclesiis tuis euellere, quatinus boni pastoris meritum apud Deum ualeas obtinere et Romana ecclesia de te sicut de karissimo fratre et studioso cooperatore debeat gaudere.

9

To Bishop Otto of Constance: Gregory insists upon his sanctions against simony and clerical unchastity, reproves Otto for disobediently conniving at the marriage of his clergy, and summons him to Rome (*1075, late*)*

Gregorius[a] seruus seruorum Dei Ottoni Constantiensi episcopo salutem et apostolicam benedictionem.

Perlatum est ad nos de fraternitate tua quod satis inuitus et mestus audiui quodque, si uel de extremo christiane plebis membro ad audientiam nostram deferretur, seueriore[b] districtioris[c] discipline censura esset proculdubio castigandum. Cum enim, apostolica auctoritate et ueridicis sanctorum patrum sententiis incitati, ad eliminandam symoniacam heresim et precipiendam clericorum castitatem pro nostri officii debito exarsimus,[d] Mogontino uenerabili[e] archiepiscopo[1] confratri nostro, cui plures et late

---

[d] *om.* dignitate *A* [e] *The rest of the letter is lacking in* V
9 [a] *add* episcopus *ZC* [b] seuerioris *F* [c] districtionis *WHFS*;
districtionis et *ZC* [d] *om.* et precipiendam . . . debito exarsimus *WZC*
[e] *om.* uenerabili *WHSZC*

---

* For the date and circumstances, see Additional Note, pp. 160–1.

J.L. 4970. *G.P.* ii, pt. 1, p. 128, no. 17. MSS.: Paul of Bernried, *Greg. VII uita*: Vienna, Österr. Nationalbibl. 336, fos. 252[v]–253[r], twelfth cent. (*V*); Heiligenkreuz, Stiftsbibl. 12, fo. 185[r–v], twelfth cent.; Admont, Stiftsbibl. 24, fo. 132[v], twelfth cent.; Melk, Stiftsbibl. 492, fos. 94[v]–95[r], twelfth cent. Wolfen-

Those, too, who obtain churches by the gift of money must utterly forfeit them, and no one for the future may be allowed to sell or buy them. Nor may those who are guilty of the crime of fornication celebrate masses or minister at the altar in lesser orders. We have further appointed that if they disregard our rulings or rather those of the holy fathers, the people may in no wise receive their ministrations, so that those who are not corrected from the love of God and the honour of their office may be brought to their senses by the shame of the world and the reproof of the people. Be zealous, therefore, so to show yourself our fellow worker in these things, and so to tear out these offences by the root from your churches, that you may win from God the reward of a good shepherd and that the Roman church may rejoice in you as a most dear brother and zealous fellow worker.

To Bishop Otto of Constance   (*1075, late*)

Gregory, bishop, servant of the servants of God, to Bishop Otto of Constance, greeting and apostolic blessing.

Tidings have reached us about you which I have been most reluctant and sad to hear, and which if they came to our ears about even the lowliest member of the Christian people we should undoubtedly punish by a most stern judgement of stringent discipline. For, urged by our apostolic authority and the truthful judgements of the holy fathers, we were enkindled according to the duty of our office to extirpate the simoniac heresy and to enforce the chastity of the clergy. We laid it as a bounden duty upon our brother the venerable archbishop of Mainz,[1] whose suffragans are many and

büttel, Hzg.–Aug. Bibl. Helmstedt 1024, no. 18, fos. 43ᵛ–44ᵛ, twelfth cent. (*W*). Hanover Collection: Hanover, Niedersächs. Landesbibl. XI. 671, no. 17, fo. 44ʳ⁻ᵛ, sixteenth cent. (*H*). Hugh of Flavigny, *Chron.*: Berlin, Deutsche Staatsbibl. Phillipps 1870, fos. 104ᵛ–105ʳ, eleventh cent. (*F*). Sélestat, Bibl. municip. 13, fo. 41ʳ⁻ᵛ, eleventh cent. (*S*).[2] *Codex Udalrici*: Zwettl, Stiftsarch. 283, pp. 103–4, twelfth cent. (*Z*); Vienna, Österr. Nationalbibl. 398, fo. 60 ʳ⁻ᵛ, twelfth cent. (*C*). Printed: Paul of Bernried, *Greg. VII uita, cap.* 37, *Pont. Rom. uitae*, ed. Watterich, i. 490–2. Hugh of Flavigny, *Chron.* ii, *M.G.H. Scr.* viii. 426–7. *Codex Udalrici*: Eccard, *Corp. hist.* ii, no. 142, cols. 141–3. *Ep. coll.* no. 8, pp. 528–9.

[1] Siegfried.
[2] This MS., originally from Hirsau, is described by F. Thaner, under its former reference no. 99, in *M.G.H. L. de L.* ii. 3. This and the following letter, together with a fragment of *Reg.* ii. 45, occur in section II.

dispersi suffraganei sunt, hoc obedientie munus iniunximus, ut tam per se quam per coadiutores suos hoc Romane ecclesie decretum*f* uniuerso clero studiosius inconculcaret et inuiolabiliter tenendum proponeret. Tibi quoque, cui plurimus Constantiensis episcopii*g* clerus et populus amplissime*h* dilatatus, ob eandem causam speciales litteras cudere bulla nostra impressas[1] collibuit, quarum fultus auctoritate tutius animosiusque preceptis nostris obtemperares*i* et de sanctuario Domini symoniacam heresim et fedam libidinose contagionis pollutionem expelleres. Apostolica namque beati Pauli prepollet auctoritas qua, fornicatores et adulteros cum ceteris sceleratis*j* connumerans, diffinitam sue iussionis sententiam subicit: 'cum eiusmodi nec cibum capere'.*k*[2] Preterea uniuersus catholice ecclesie cetus aut uirgines sunt aut continentes aut coniuges. Quicumque ergo extra hos tres ordines reperitur, inter filios ecclesie*l* siue intra christiane religionis limites*m* non numeratur. Vnde et nos,*n* si uel extremum laicum pelicatui adherentem liquido cognouerimus, hunc uelut precisum a corpore dominico membrum donec peniteat condigne a sacramentis altaris arcemus. Quomodo ergo sanctorum sacramentorum distributor uel minister esse debet,*o* qui nulla ratione potest esse uel particeps? Sed illa beati pape Leonis nos impulit auctoritas, qui subdiaconis ineundi*p* conubii licentiam prorsus abstulit;[3] quod decretum beati*q* pape*r* Leonis posteriores sancte Romane ecclesie pontifices, maxime doctor eximius Gregorius,[4] ita pro lege*s* sanxerunt ut deinceps tribus his ordinibus ecclesiasticis, sacerdotibus leuitis et subdiaconibus, uincula coniugalia omnino sint prohibita. Cum autem hec omnia tibi obseruanda pastorali prouidentia transmitteremus, tu, non sursum cor sed deorsum in terra ponens,[5] predictis ordinibus frena libidinis, sicut accepimus, laxasti, ut qui mulierculis se iunxerant in flagitio persisterent, et qui necdum duxerant tua interdicta non timerent. O impudentiam, o audaciam singularem, uidelicet episcopum sedis apostolice decreta contempnere, precepta sanctorum patrum conuellere, immo uero preceptis contraria ac fidei christiane repugnantia de superiori loco et de cathedra pontificali subiectis ingerere. Quapropter tibi apostolica auctoritate

---

f debitum *WH*   *g* ecclesiae *F*   *h* latissime *H*   *i* obtemperantes *WH*; obtemperans *ZC*   *j* excommunicatis *F*   *k* sumere *HFS*
l om. ecclesie *WHZC*   *m* terminos *ZC*   *n* om. et nos *F*   *o* potest *F*
p om. ineundi *WZC*   *q* om. beati *W*   *r* om. pape *VS*   *s* om. pro lege *W*; lege *H*; ea lege *ZC*

far flung, that both by himself and through his coadjutors he should impress this decree of the Roman church with all zeal upon his whole clergy and insist that it should be inviolably observed. We also thought fit to write a special letter,[1] sealed with our seal, concerning this matter to you as ruler of the numerous clergy of the see of Constance and of its widely dispersed people, so that upheld by its authority you might the more safely and boldly obey our commands by driving out from the Lord's sanctuary the simoniac heresy and the foul defilement of polluting lust. For the apostolic authority of St. Paul is decisive when, including fornicators and adulterers with other vicious men, he went on to make this clear and final prohibition: 'not even to eat with such a one'.[2] Moreover the whole company of the catholic church are either virgins or chaste or married. Whoever stands outside these three orders is not numbered amongst the sons of the church or within the bounds of the Christian religion. Thus, if we know for a certainty that even the least of laymen is companying with a mistress, we rightly debar him from the sacraments of the altar until he repents, as a member severed from the Lord's body. This being so, how can a man be a dispenser or minister of the holy sacraments, when he can on no account be even a partaker of them? The ruling of the blessed Pope Leo is binding upon us, by which he absolutely withheld from subdeacons the liberty to marry;[3] and subsequent popes of the holy Roman church, especially the distinguished doctor Gregory,[4] have so established the blessed Pope Leo's decree as law that thereafter the bonds of marriage are altogether forbidden to the three ecclesiastical orders of priests, deacons, and subdeacons.

Yet when we passed on all these things for you to observe by your pastoral oversight, you, setting your heart not on things above but on the earth below,[5] relaxed the reins of lust, as we have heard, to all these orders, allowing those who had joined themselves to women to continue in their shame and those who had not taken women to have no fear of your prohibition. O the impudence! O the unparalleled insolence! that a bishop should despise the decrees of the apostolic see, should set at naught the precepts of the holy fathers, and in truth should impose upon his subjects from his lofty place and from his episcopal chair things contrary to these precepts and opposed to the Christian faith! We accordingly

---

[1] See no. 7.
[2] Cf. 1 Cor. 5: 11.
[3] Pope Leo I, *Ep.* xiv. 4, *P.L.* liv. 672–3.
[4] Pope Gregory I.
[5] Cf. Col. 3: 1–2.

precipimus,[t] ut ad proximam synodum nostram prima ebdomada[u] quadragesime[vI] te presentem exhibeas, tam de hac inobedientia et sedis apostolice contemptu quam de omnibus que tibi obiciuntur[w] canonice responsurus.

10

To the clergy and laity of the diocese of Constance: Gregory condemns Bishop Otto's disobedience and releases them from their own duty of obedience to him until he obeys the apostolic see (*1075, late*)*

Gregorius episcopus[a] seruus seruorum Dei clericis et laicis, maioribus et minoribus, in Constantiensi episcopatu consistentibus, christianam legem diligentibus,[b] salutem et apostolicam benedictionem.

Misimus fratri nostro episcopo uestro[c] Ottoni litteras exhortatorias,[2] per quas pro nostri necessitate officii apostolica auctoritate iniunximus illi ut symoniacam heresim de ecclesia sua penitus excluderet et castitatem clericorum studiose predicandam susciperet et firmiter tenendam episcopali uigilantia[d] inculcaret. Nam sic eam nobis euangelice et apostolice littere, autenticarum synodorum decreta et eximiorum doctorum precepta[e] insinuant, ut eam dissimulare et negligere sine magno anime nostre et populi christiani detrimento[f] non possimus. Sed episcopus uester neque beati Petri[g] reuerentia precepti neque[h] officii sui sollicitudine attractus, ut nobis relatum est, que paterne suaseramus perficere[i] curauit, et, ut non solum inobedientie uerum etiam rebellionis offensam contraheret, quemadmodum accepimus, palam clericis suis iussioni nostre immo beati Petri omnino[j]

---

[t] mandamus *WHZC* [u] prime ebdomade *V*; proximae *H* [v] *om.* quadragesime *V* [w] obediunt *W*; obediuntur *H*
10 [a] *om.* episcopus *WHZC* [b] defendentibus *WHZC* [c] Misimus ad uos episcopo uestro confratri nostro *WZC*; Misimus episcopo uestro fratri nostro *H* [d] diligentia *H* [e] *om.* precepta *WZC* [f] periculo *WHZC* [g] *add* apostoli *WHZC* [h] nec nostri precepti nec *ZC* [i] *add* non *V* [j] *om.* omnino *F*; omnia *H*

---

* For the date and circumstances, see Additional Note, pp. 160-1.
J.L. 4971. *G.P.* ii, pt. 1, p. 128, no. 18. MSS.: Paul of Bernried, *Greg. VII uita*: Vienna, Österr. Nationalbibl. 336, fo. 253[r-v], twelfth cent. (*V*); Heiligenkreuz, Stiftsbibl. 12, fos. 185[v]-186[r], twelfth cent.; Admont, Stiftsbibl. 24, fos.

command you by apostolic authority to present yourself at our next council in the first week of Lent,[1] to answer canonically respecting both this disobedience and contempt of the apostolic see, and all the charges that have been laid against you.

To the clergy and laity of the diocese of Constance

(*1075, late*)

Gregory, bishop, servant of the servants of God, to the clerks and laymen, greater and lesser, in the diocese of Constance, who love the law of Christ, greeting and apostolic blessing.

We sent to Otto, our brother and your bishop, an admonitory letter[2] in which as our office obliges us we charged him by apostolic authority that he should utterly exclude the simoniac heresy from his church, and that he should uphold the chastity of the clergy by zealous preaching and insist with episcopal vigilance upon its being steadfastly maintained. For the words of the gospels and of the apostles, the decrees of authoritative councils, and the precepts of distinguished doctors so commend it to us that we cannot disregard and neglect it without great harm to our own soul and to the people of Christ. But your bishop has been guided neither by reverence for St. Peter's precept nor by the duty of his own office; for as we have been told he has not been at pains to carry out our fatherly exhortations. Instead, that he might incur the guilt not only of disobedience but also of rebellion, as we have heard he has openly tolerated in his clergy things altogether repugnant to our command or rather St. Peter's—that those who had women might

132^{v}–133^{r}, twelfth cent.; Melk, Stiftsbibl. 492, fo. 95^{r-v}, twelfth cent. Wolfenbüttel, Hzg.–Aug. Bibl. Helmstedt 1024, no. 19, fos. 44^{v}–45^{v}, twelfth cent. (*W*). Hanover Collection: Hanover, Niedersächs. Landesbibl. XI. 671, no. 18, fos. 45^{r}–46^{r}, sixteenth cent. (*H*). Hugh of Flavigny, *Chron.*: Berlin, Deutsche Staatsbibl. Phillipps 1870, fo. 105^{r-v}, eleventh cent. (*F*). Sélestat, Bibl. municip. 13, fos. 41^{v}–42^{v}, eleventh cent. (*S*). *Codex Udalrici*: Zwettl, Stiftsarch. 283, pp. 104–5, twelfth cent. (*Z*); Vienna, Österr. Nationalbibl. 398, fos. 60^{v}–61^{r}, twelfth cent. (*C*). Printed: Paul of Bernried, *Greg. VII uita, cap.* 38, *Pont. Rom. uitae*, ed. Watterich, i. 492–3. Hugh of Flavigny, *Chron.* ii, *M.G.H. Scr.* viii. 427. *Codex Udalrici*: Eccard, *Corp. hist.* ii, no. 143, cols. 143–4. *Ep. coll.* no. 9, pp. 529–31.

---

[1] 14–22 Feb. 1076.   [2] No. 8.

contraria permisit ita ut qui mulierculas habuerant retinerent et
qui non habebant[k] illicita temeritate[l] subintroducerent. Quod ut
audiuimus moleste ferentes, secundam ei scripsimus epistolam,[1]
indignationis ei nostre motus ostendentes[m] et idem preceptum[n]
iterato acrius inculcantes, quin etiam ipsum ad synodum Romanam que prima proxime quadragesime ebdomada futura est ad-
uocauimus,[2] ut pro se rationem reddat et inobedientie causas, si
rationabiles habuerit, in audientia totius conuentus[o] exponat.

Hec ideo, filii[p] karissimi, uobis innotescimus ut anime uestre
saluti consulamus. Si enim beato Petro et sancte sedi apostolice
fronte aperta[q] repugnans et contumax esse uoluerit,[r] liquido manifestum est quia qui matrem uel patrem inhonorat nullam a fidelibus patris et matris filiis iure obedientiam exigere aut querere
debeat. Indignum est enim ut qui magistro detrectat subesse,
magister auditoribus postulet preesse.[s] Quapropter omnibus,[t]
sicut prediximus, maioribus atque minoribus Deo et beato Petro
adherentibus apostolica auctoritate precipimus, si in obduratione
sua persistere uoluerit, nullam ei obedientie reuerentiam exhibeatis. Neque id anime uestre perniciem esse putetis. Nam si,
ut totiens iam prediximus, preceptis apostolicis uoluerit esse
contrarius, ab omni illius subiectionis iugo beati Petri auctoritate
absoluimus ita ut, si etiam sacramenti obligatione quilibet ei
fuerit obstrictus, quam diu Deo omnipotenti et sedi apostolice
rebellis extiterit, nulla ei fidelitatis exhibitione fiat obnoxius.
Non enim cuilibet persone contra creatorem suum, qui cunctis
preponendus est, aliquis debet obedire, sed debemus contra
Deum superbienti resistere ut, saltem hac necessitate coactus,[u]
ad uiam iusticie addiscat redire. Quanti enim periculi quanteque
a christiana lege sit alienationis obedientiam maxime apostolice
sedi non exhibere, ex dictis beati Samuelis prophete potestis
cognoscere, que sanctissimus papa Gregorius in ultimo[v] libro
Moralium procurauit exponere.[w] Vt autem ea sint nobis in promptu,
scripta transmisimus, quatinus indubitanter sciatis nos uobis nouam
non dicere[x] sed antiquam sanctorum patrum doctrinam propalare:

Hinc Samuel ait: 'Melior est obedientia quam uictime, et auscultare
magis quam offerre adypem arietum; quoniam quasi peccatum ariolandi

---

[k] *om.* retinerent et qui non habebant *WHZC*   [l] *add* alias *ZC*   [m] indignationis eius nostri motus ostendentes *W*; indignationem ei nostri motus
indicantes *ZC*   [n] *om.* preceptum *F*   [o] sinodi *W*; *om.* conuentus *H*;
ecclesiae *ZC*   [p] fratres *V*   [q] *om.* fronte aperta *WZC*; *om.* aperta *H*

keep them, and that those who did not have them might commit the unlawful brazenness of taking them. When we heard of it we were deeply angered and wrote him a second letter,[1] making clear to him the depth of our indignation and insisting still more sharply upon our command. At the same time we also summoned him to the Roman council called for the first week of next Lent,[2] in order that he may give an account of himself and explain in the hearing of the whole assembly the grounds for his disobedience, if he has reasonable ones.

Dearest sons, we make these things known to you in order that we may promote the salvation of your souls. For if he is determined to be brazenly hostile and unyielding to St. Peter and to the holy and apostolic see, it is clearly evident that a man who does not honour his mother or father should rightfully neither expect nor ask their faithful sons to yield obedience to himself. For it is unfitting that a man who refuses to be under a master should himself seek to stand as a master over disciples. Accordingly, as we have already said, by apostolic authority we charge all of you, both greater and lesser, who stand by God and St. Peter, that if he is determined to continue in his obduracy you should show him neither respect nor obedience. Nor need you think this a danger to your souls. For if, as we have often said already, he is determined to resist apostolic precepts, we so absolve you by St. Peter's authority from every yoke of subjection to him that, even if any of you is bound to him by the obligation of an oath, for so long as he is a rebel against God and the apostolic see you are bound to pay him no fealty. For a man should obey no one before his Creator, who must be placed before all others; but we should resist whoever waxes proud against God so that, driven at least by this constraint, he may learn to turn back to the path of righteousness. For how very dangerous it is, and how far removed from the law of Christ, not to be obedient, especially to the apostolic see, you may learn from the words of blessed Samuel the prophet which the most holy Pope Gregory undertook to expound in the last book of his *Morals*. In order that we may have them before us we are setting them down in writing; you may thus know beyond doubt that we are addressing no new teaching to you, but are rehearsing the ancient teaching of the holy fathers:

Hence Samuel says: 'To obey is better than sacrifices and to hearken than to offer the fat of rams. For rebellion is as the sin of witchcraft,

r studuerit *WHS*   *s om.* Indignum est . . . postulet preesse *F*   *t om.* omnibus *WHZC*   *u* compulsus *F*   *v om.* ultimo *F*   *w* explanare *WHFSZC*   *x* superducere *ZC*

[1] No. 9.   [2] 14–22 Feb. 1076.

est repugnare, et quasi scelus ydolatrie nolle acquiescere'.[1] Obedientia quippe uictimis iure preponitur, quia per uictimas aliena caro, per obedientiam uero uoluntas[y] propria mactatur. Tanto igitur quisque Deum citius placat quanto ante eius oculos, repressa[z] arbitrii sua superbia, gladio precepti se immolat. Quo contra ariolandi peccatum inobedientia dicitur ut quanta sit uirtus[aa] obedientie demonstretur. Ex aduerso igitur melius ostenditur quid de eius laude sentiatur. Si enim 'quasi ariolandi peccatum est repugnare et quasi scelus[bb] ydolatrie nolle acquiescere', sola est que fidei meritum possidet, qua sine quisque conuincitur infidelis, etiam si fidelis esse uideatur.[2]

11

To all the clergy and laity of Germany: Gregory urges them to resist bishops who tolerate clerical marriage and concubinage (*1075, late*)*

Gregorius episcopus seruus seruorum Dei omnibus clericis et laicis in regno Teutonicorum constitutis salutem et apostolicam benedictionem.

Audiuimus quod quidam episcoporum apud uos commorantium ut sacerdotes et diaconi et subdiaconi mulieribus commisceantur aut consentiant aut negligant. His precipimus uos nullomodo obedire uel illorum preceptis consentire, sicut ipsi apostolice sedis preceptis non obediunt neque auctoritati sanctorum patrum consentiunt. Testante diuina[a] scriptura, facientes et consentientes par pena complectitur.[3] Omnipotens et misericors Deus, qui ultra spem, qui ultra meritum miseretur et consolatur nos in omni[b] tribulatione nostra, aperiat cor uestrum in lege sua et confirmet uos in preceptis suis ut, auctoritate beati Petri[c] a cunctis peccatis absolutos, uos ad celeste regnum perducat regnaturos. Amen.

---

[y] *om.* uoluntas *WHZC*   [z] repraehensa *H*   [aa] quanti sit uirtus *WH*; quantae sint uires *ZC*   [bb] *om.* scelus *HZC*

11   [a] sancta *F*   [b] *om.* omni *F*   [c] *add* apostoli *F*

---

* For the date and circumstances, see Additional Note, pp. 160–1. The fact that this letter survives only in two sources perhaps indicates that it did not circulate widely in Germany.

J.L. 4902. MSS.: Paul of Bernried, *Greg. VII uita*: Vienna, Österr. Nationalbibl. 336, fo. 254[r], twelfth cent.; Heiligenkreuz, Stiftsbibl. 12, fo. 186[v], twelfth cent. Admont, Stiftsbibl. 24, fo. 133[r], twelfth cent.; Melk, Stiftsbibl. 492, fo.

and stubbornness is as iniquity and idolatry.'[1] Now obedience is rightly placed before sacrifices, because by sacrifices we put to death flesh which is not our own, but by obedience our own will. A man pleases God the more readily in proportion as he curbs his own pride of will and sacrifices himself before God's eyes by the sword of his precept. Disobedience, on the other hand, is likened to the sin of witchcraft in order that it may appear how great is the virtue of obedience: by contrasting them it may the more clearly be seen how highly we should praise it. For if 'rebellion is as the sin of witchcraft, and stubbornness is as iniquity and idolatry', only obedience has the reward of faith, since without it a man is proved to be unfaithful even though he appear to be faithful.[2]

To all the clergy and laity of Germany   (*1075, late*)

Gregory, bishop, servant of the servants of God, to all the clergy and laity of the kingdom of Germany, greeting and apostolic blessing.

We have heard that certain of the bishops who dwell in your parts either condone, or fail to take due notice of, the keeping of women by priests, deacons, and subdeacons. We charge you in no way to obey these bishops or to follow their precepts, even as they themselves do not obey the commands of the apostolic see or heed the authority of the holy fathers. Divine scripture testifies that an equal punishment is due to those who commit an evil and to those who assent to it.[3] May the almighty and merciful God, who beyond our hope and our deserving pities and comforts us in all our tribulation, so open your heart in his law and confirm you in his precepts that, being absolved by the authority of St. Peter from all your sins, he may bring you to reign in his heavenly kingdom. Amen.

94^{r-v}, twelfth cent. Hugh of Flavigny, *Chron.*: Berlin, Deutsche Staatsbibl. Phillipps 1870, fo. 106^{r-v}, eleventh cent. (*F*). Printed: Paul of Bernried, *Greg. VII uita, cap.* 41, *Pont. Rom. uitae*, ed. Watterich, i. 495–6. Hugh of Flavigny, *Chron.* ii, *M.G.H. Scr.* viii. 428–9. Baluze, *Miscellanea*, vii. 125–6.[4] *Ep. coll.* no. 10, p. 532.

---

[1] 1 Reg. (1 Sam.) 15: 22–3.
[2] Pope Gregory I, *Moralium*, xxv. 28, *P.L.* lxxvi. 765.
[3] Cf. Rom. 1: 32.
[4] 'Ex codice 562. monasterii S. Germani de pratis' (Baluze). It is made up from fragments of this letter and *Reg.* ii 45, 11 Jan. 1075, pp. 182–5.

12

*To the abbots and superiors of religious houses in France:
Gregory appeals to them to renew payment of the taxes
which their houses owe to the Roman see, and nominates
Bishop Hugh of Die to be the collector*   (*1075*)*

Gregorius episcopus seruus seruorum Dei omnibus abbatibus et
praelatis tam monachorum quam et canonicorum per Gallias constitutis salutem et apostolicam benedictionem.

Fraternitatem uestram, dilectissimi fratres, latere minime
credimus quasdam aecclesiarum uestrarum beato Petro et nobis
annuos census persoluere ex praecedentium patrum institutionibus
debere. Sed quia quidam uestrum partim neglegentia partim uero
tenaci induratione haec hactenus minus plene quam oporteret
egerunt, hos ut emendari et debita soluere studeant, omnes autem
ut apostolico praecepto: 'Cui uectigal uectigal, cui tributum
tributum',[1] optemperetis commonemus. Vnusquisque enim non
quod suum est sed quod alterius querat,[2] quoniam si digne red-
arguitur qui prout oportet propria non largitur, qua sententia
dignus est qui nec aliena rapere nec debita metuit retinere, dicente
Domino: 'Quae uultis ut faciant uobis, haec facite et uos illis',[3] et:
'Quod tibi non uis, alii non feceris.'[4] Nunc igitur, quia dilectum
filium nostrum Hugonem Diensem episcopum ob ecclesiasticae
utilitatis diuersa negotia in Gallias uices nostras exequuturum
mittimus, et quia nemini potius credere debemus quem in
omnibus a nobis sibi iniunctis fideliter egisse comperimus, quae
nobis ex ecclesiis uestris specialiter debetis uos illi ad nos per-
ferenda persoluere ac de retentis satisfacere iubemus.

---

* Gregory here lays claim to the taxes (*census*) which were owed by many
religious houses to the Roman see in return for privileges granted by earlier
popes. For a similar claim by Pope Urban II, cf. his *Epp.* lxxxix, xc (1093), *P.L.*
cli. 368–70. These popes' letters indicate that, until the compilation of the
Liber censuum of 1192, the papacy had no sufficient record of the amounts of
such taxes or of those who owed them. Hugh, bishop of Die (1074–82) and
archbishop of Lyons (1082–1106), became Gregory's standing legate in France.
Gregory first mentioned him as being active 'in legatione nostra' at the Lent
council of 1076: *Reg.* iii. 10*a*, p. 269. If Gregory referred to Hugh's activities in
Reg. ii. 56, 4 Mar. 1075, pp. 209–10, and ii. 64, 25 Mar. 1075, p. 219, their results
are not likely to have been known to Gregory until fairly late in 1075; this
indicates the *terminus a quo* of the present letter.
J.L. 4849. MS.: Hugh of Flavigny, *Chron.*: Berlin, Deutsche Staatsbibl.

To the abbots and superiors of religious houses in France
(*1075*)

Gregory, bishop, servant of the servants of God, to all abbots and
superiors of monks and canons throughout France, greeting and
apostolic blessing.

We are sure, dearest brothers, that you are by no means unaware
that according to the decrees of the fathers of former times some of
your churches should pay an annual tax to St. Peter and to ourself.
But since some of you, partly from carelessness but partly from
stubborn obstinacy, have hitherto fulfilled their obligation less
completely than they should, we admonish them to see to it that
they accept correction and pay their dues, and all of you to obey
the Apostle's command: 'Pay revenue to whom revenue is due,
taxes to whom taxes are due.'[1] Let everyone seek not his own good
but his neighbour's;[2] for if a man deserves reproof for not bestowing his own goods as is right, of what condemnation is he worthy
who has not hesitated to seize what does not belong to him or to
keep back what he should pay; whereas our Lord says: 'Whatever
you wish that men would do to you, do so to them',[3] and: 'What
you do not wish for yourself, do not do to others.'[4] We have sent
our beloved son Bishop Hugh of Die to France to attend on our
behalf to various matters of importance for the church. There is
no one in whom we may more fully trust, for we have found that
he has faithfully performed all the duties that we have laid upon
him; we therefore charge you to pay to him, so that he may bring
to us, whatever each of you owes in respect of your churches, and
to make good anything that you may have been keeping back.

Phillipps 1870, fo. 96ᵛ, eleventh cent.[5] Printed: Hugh of Flavigny, *Chron.* ii,
M.G.H. Scr. viii. 412–13. *Ep. coll.* no. 6, p. 526.

---

[1] Cf. Rom. 13: 7.   [2] Cf. 1 Cor. 10: 24.   [3] Cf. Matt. 7: 12.
[4] Not in this form a saying of Christ, but cf. Tobit 4: 16 (15) and *Doctrina
apostolorum, The Apostolic Fathers,* ed. J. B. Lightfoot (London, 1891) p. 225.
[5] This letter appears in the left-hand margin of the folio, in the same hand as
the rest. Approximately 4 mm. of the left-hand side of the text have been cut
away; I have taken the missing words of the letter from the *M.G.H.* edition,
which does not sufficiently indicate the condition of the MS.

13

To Bishop Henry of Trent: Gregory reproves him for failing to reply to a message and protests the justice of his own excommunication of Henry IV. He urges the bishop to send knights for the service of St. Peter

(1076, Mar.–July)*

Gregorius episcopus seruus seruorum Dei fratri et coepiscopo Tridentino Heinrico[a1] salutem et apostolicam benedictionem.

Miramur fraternitatis tue prudentiam uerba nostra neglexisse[2] ut secundum ea nullum decreueris dare responsum, maxime cum post sinodalem sententiam in Heinricum regem prolatam dilectio tua minime differre debuerit. Ad cuius nimirum sententie promulgationem nos iusticie zelo impulsos et non aliqua com-motione[b] iniurie concitatos manum exercuisse neque sollertiam tuam ignorare neque aliquem sane mentis hominem putamus posse ambigere. Quod tamen si in dubium cuiquam deueniret, constat eius rei rationem prius ex nobis fore scrutandam quam in illum preiudicium factum temere esse credendum. Verum ut-cumque sese opinio habeat factumue interpretetur, illud procul dubio clementia diuina sperantes promittimus: festum beati Petri[3] non prius transeundum quam in cunctorum noticia certis-sime clareat illum iustissime esse excommunicatum. Et inde fraternitatem tuam uolumus atque[c] monemus ut certos nos studeat facere utrum[d] Deo an hominibus magis elegerit obedire[4] utrumue iustitie obtemperando fidem Deo et sancte Romane ecclesie

---

[a] *om.* Heinrico *ZC*   [b] promotione *W*   [c] *om.* uolumus atque *ZC*
[d] utrumque *W*

---

* This letter survives only in letter collections which give no clue to its date. It could be the sequel either to Gregory's first excommunication of Henry in Feb. 1076: *Reg.* iii. 10*a*, pp. 268–71, or to his second in Mar. 1080: *Reg.* vii. 14*a*, pp. 483–7. The later date was proposed by J. Haller, *Das Papsttum. Idee und Wirklichkeit*, ii (2nd edn., Darmstadt, 1962), 610, and accepted by F. Baethgen, 'Zur Tribur-Frage', *D.A.* iv (1940), 395, n. 4. Haller pointed to the similarity between Gregory's assertion in his letter that the justice of Henry's excom-munication would be made plain before the 'festum beati Petri', and the familiar tradition, generally associated with the year 1080, that Gregory predicted Henry's death or deposition before St. Peter's Day: Bonizo of Sutri, *Liber ad amicum*, ix, *M.G.H. L. de L.* i. 616; Beno, *Gesta Romanae ecclesiae*, i. 7, *M.G.H. L. de L.* ii. 371; cf. Sigebert of Gembloux, *Chron. a.* 1080, *M.G.H. Scr.* vi. 364. But Bonizo and Beno did not precisely date their stories, and only a similar

To Bishop Henry of Trent (1076, Mar.–July)

Gregory, bishop, servant of the servants of God, to his brother and fellow bishop Henry of Trent,[1] greeting and apostolic blessing.

We are surprised that you should have so disregarded our message[2] that you have decided to make no reply to it; for particularly after our conciliar sentence against King Henry you should certainly not have delayed to answer. We believe that neither you nor anyone of sound mind could doubt that we were brought to pass this sentence because we were driven to it by zeal for righteousness, not because we were aroused by some merely personal wrong. If anyone should still be in doubt about this, he ought to find out from us the truth of the matter before rashly believing that an injustice was done to the king. But whatever men think and however they may construe what has happened, with unwavering trust in God's mercy we make this prophecy: the feast of St. Peter[3] will not have passed before it is quite certainly made known to all men that the king was most justly excommunicated. We therefore desire and admonish you to assure us without fail whether you choose to obey God rather than men,[4] and whether you are minded to keep faith with God and the holy Roman church by obeying

tale in Sigebert, not a very reliable authority, has led them to be widely assigned to 1080; in any case Gregory's letter is more guardedly expressed than this tradition. Baethgen also argued that Gregory's request for knights to be sent 'ad seruitium beati Petri' fitted 1080 better than the beginning of the struggle between Gregory and Henry. But the case for the more widely accepted date of 1076 remains convincing. Against Baethgen's last point, in ?Apr. 1076 Gregory told the Patarene leader Wifred that he would approach the *fideles sancti Petri* about aid for Milan which may have comprised not only money but also military reinforcements recruited as in this letter: *Reg.* iii. 15, p. 277. Moreover, this letter exactly illustrates the considerations which led Gregory to circulate no. 14 in the summer of 1076.

J.L. 4997. *G.P.* i, p. 402, no. 5. MSS.: Wolfenbüttel, Hzg.–Aug. Bibl. Helmstedt 1024, no. 22, fos. 47ᵛ–48ʳ, twelfth cent. (*W*). *Codex Udalrici*: Zwettl, Stiftsarch. 283, pp. 115–16, twelfth cent. (*Z*); Vienna, Österr. Nationalbibl. 398, fos. 65ᵛ–66ʳ, twelfth cent. (*C*). Printed: *Codex Udalrici*: Eccard, *Corp. hist.* ii, no. 152, cols. 155–6; Jaffé, *Mon. Bamb.* no. 50, pp. 109–10. Ughelli, *Ital. sac.* v. 593–4. Hahn, *Coll. mon.* i. 116–17. *Ep. coll.* no. 13, pp. 534–5.

[1] 1068–82.
[2] No letter or other record of Gregory's approach survives.
[3] i.e. the feast of St. Peter *ad uincula* (1 Aug.).
[4] Cf. Acts 5: 29.

obseruare, quam filiis iniquitatis herendo conculcare censuerit. Rogamus etiam atque inuitamus ut ad seruicium beati Petri pro posse tuo milites mittere studeas, eosque si decreueris mittere Mathilde[1] filie nostre notificare procures, cuius ope conducti securi possint ad nos et sine impedimento, fauente Domino, peruenire.

14

To all the faithful in Germany: in answer to those who doubt the justice of his excommunication of Henry IV Gregory sets out in detail the grounds of his sentence
*(1076, summer)**

Gregorius episcopus[a] seruus seruorum Dei omnibus episcopis ducibus comitibus ceterisque fidelibus[b] in regno Theutonicorum christianam fidem defendentibus[c] salutem et apostolicam[d] bene- dictionem.[e]

Audiuimus quosdam inter uos[f] de excommunicatione quam in regem fecimus dubitare ac querere utrum iuste excommuni- catus sit et si nostra sententia ex auctoritate legalis censure ea qua debuit deliberatione processerit.[g] Quapropter qualiter ad[h] excommunicandum illum adducti sumus, prout uerius potuimus

---

[a] *om.* episcopus *WHZCXY*   [b] *om.* fidelibus *WHZCXY*   [c] dili- gentibus *F*   [d] *om.* apostolicam *L*   [e] *om.* Gregorius episcopus . . . apostolicam benedictionem *M*   [f] Audiuimus inter uos quosdam *ZCXY* [g] progressa est *LPSN*; congressa sit *WH*; progressa sit *MF*; egressa sit *ZCXY* [h] *om.* qualiter ad *WH*; *om.* qualiter *F*

---

* This is amongst the most important of all Gregory's letters, and the extensive MS. attestation in many kinds of source indicates that it circulated widely. Its purpose was to insist that Gregory's deposition and excommunication of Henry IV at his Lent council of 1076 were both canonically correct and fully called for by the king's misconduct since his accession. Many bishops, in particular, who had supported Henry at Worms in Jan. 1076 when he called upon Gregory to step down from the papacy soon began to show hesitation. By vindicating his own actions Gregory sought to rally the German princes and people to his cause, and to ease the way for them to respond. This letter may be compared with *Reg.* iv. 1, 25 July 1076, pp. 289–92, which appears to have been written after it and which echoes some of its themes.

J.L. 4999. MSS.: Paul of Bernried, *Greg. VII uita*: Vienna, Österr. Nationalbibl. 336, fos. 259ᵛ–260ᵛ, twelfth cent. (*V*); Heiligenkreuz, Stiftsbibl. 12, fos. 191ʳ–192ʳ, twelfth cent.; Admont, Stiftsbibl. 24, fo. 137ʳ⁻ᵛ, twelfth cent.; Melk, Stiftsbibl. 492, fos. 102ᵛ–105ʳ, twelfth cent. Bruno, *Sax. bell.*: Leipzig, Universitätsbibl.

righteousness rather than to despise them by cleaving to the children of iniquity. We also ask and summon you to the best of your ability to send knights for the service of St. Peter. If you decide to send them you should inform our daughter Matilda;[1] for by her help they can have safe conduct and, if God wills, they can reach us in safety.

To all the faithful in Germany (1076, summer)

Gregory, bishop, servant of the servants of God, to all bishops, dukes, counts, and other faithful men in the kingdom of Germany who are defending the Christian religion, greeting and apostolic blessing.

We have heard that some of your countrymen have doubts about the excommunication which we have placed upon the king: they question whether he was excommunicated justly and whether our sentence proceeded from due deliberation and had the sanction of lawful authority. We have accordingly been at pains to set forth to the eyes and minds of all as truthfully as we could, upon the

1323, fos. 23ᵛ–25ʳ, c. 1500 (L). *Annalista Saxo*: Paris, Bibl. nat. lat. 11851, fos. 176ʳ–177ʳ, twelfth cent. (P). Wolfenbüttel, Hzg.–Aug. Bibl. Helmstedt 1024, no. 10, fos. 37ʳ–38ʳ, twelfth cent. (W). Hanover Collection: Hanover, Niedersächs. Landesbibl. XI. 671, no. 7, fos. 28ʳ–30ᵛ, sixteenth cent. (H). Manegold of Lautenbach, *Ad Gebeh. lib.*: Karlsruhe, Badische Landesbibl. Rastatt 27, fos. 42ʳ–44ʳ, twelfth cent. (M). Hugh of Flavigny, *Chron.*: Berlin, Deutsche Staatsbibl. Phillipps 1870, fos. 113ᵛ–115ʳ, eleventh cent. (F). Sélestat, Bibl. municip. 13, fos. 58ᵛ–59ᵛ, eleventh cent. (S). *Codex Udalrici*: Zwettl, Stiftsarch. 283, pp. 107–9, twelfth cent. (Z); Vienna, Österr. Nationalbibl. 398, fos. 61ᵛ–63ʳ, twelfth cent. (C); Munich, Bayer. Staatsbibl. 4594, fos. 44ʳ–45ʳ, twelfth cent. (X); Vienna, Österr. Nationalbibl. 611, fos. 31ʳ–32ᵛ, twelfth cent. (Y). Printed: Paul of Bernried, *Greg. VII uita, capp.* 77–8, *Pont. Rom. uitae*, ed. Watterich, i. 517–21. Bruno, *Sax. bell. cap.* 72, edd. Lohmann and Schmale, pp. 288–96. *Annalista Saxo, a.* 1076, *M.G.H. Scr.* vi. 708–9. Hugh of Flavigny, *Chron.* ii, *M.G.H. Scr.* viii. 439–40. *Codex Udalrici*: Eccard, *Corp. hist.* ii, no. 146, cols. 146–9. *Ep. coll.* no. 14, pp. 535–40. Holder-Egger, *N.A.* xxxi (1906), 186–8 (N).[2] Manegold of Lautenbach, *Ad Gebeh. lib. cap.* 28, *M.G.H. L. de L.* i. 359–61. Gerhoh of Reichersberg, *De investigatione Antichristi*, i, *M.G.H. L. de L.* iii. 326–8.[3]

---

[1] Countess Matilda of Tuscany.

[2] Holder-Egger edited this letter from a MS. of c. 1080–1100 of which part survived in the cover of a MS. of Nicholas of Lyra's *Postillae in Euangelia* which was in the University Library at Königsberg (now Kaliningrad): I have been unable to discover anything about its subsequent fortunes. The letter preceded the apologia of an unnamed German prelate, perhaps Archbishop Siegfried of Mainz, for his conduct between Oct. 1076 and the summer of 1077.

[3] This letter is also briefly quoted by Frutolf of Michaelsberg, *Ekkehardi chronicon uniuersale*, *M.G.H. Scr.* vi. 202.

teste consciencia nostra, oculis et intellectibus omnium[i] patefacere curauimus, non tam ut singulas causas, que heu! nimium note sunt, quasi nostro clamore proiciamus in publicum, quam ut eorum opinionibus satisfaciamus qui putant nos spiritalem gladium temere et magis motu animi nostri quam diuino metu et iusticie zelo arripuisse.

Cum adhuc in diaconatus officio positi essemus, perlata ad nos de regis actionibus sinistra et multa inhonesta fama, propter imperialem dignitatem et reuerentiam patris et matris eius necnon[j] propter spem ac desiderium correctionis sue sepe eum per litteras et nuncios[k] admonuimus ut a prauitate sua desisteret et, memor clarissimi generis ac dignitatis sue, uitam suam moribus quibus regem et futurum, Deo donante, imperatorem deceret institueret.[l] Postquam autem ad pontificatus apicem[m] licet indigni uenimus et illius etas pariter cresceret[n] et iniquitas, intelligentes Deum omnipotentem tanto districtius de manu nostra animam illius requisiturum quanto nobis ad increpandum illum pre cunctis libertas data fuisset et auctoritas, multo sollicitius eum modis omnibus 'arguendo obsecrando increpando'[1] ad emenda-tionem uite sue hortati sumus. Qui cum sepe nobis deuotas[o] salutationes et litteras[2] mitteret, excusans se[p] tum ex etate quod fluxa esset et fragilis[3] tum quod ab his in quorum mani-bus curia erat multociens sibi male suasum atque consultum sit, monita nostra de die in diem se promptissime suscepturum uerbis quidem promisit, ceterum re et exaggeratione culparum penitus conculcauit.

Inter hec quosdam familiares suos, quorum consiliis et machinationibus episcopatus et multa monasteria inductis per precium lupis pro pastoribus symoniaca heresi fedauerat, ad penitentiam uocauimus, quatinus et bona ecclesiarum que per interuentum tam scelerati commercii sacrilega manu susceperant uenerabilibus locis ad que pertinerent, cum adhuc locus esset emendandi, redderent,[q] et ipsi de perpetrata iniquitate per lamenta penitudinis Deo satisfacerent. Quos dum ad hec exequenda datas

---

[i] *om.* omnium *W*   [j] *om.* propter imperialem . . . eius necnon *L*
[k] *om.* et nuncios *ZCXY*   [l] desisteret *WH*   [m] officium *VM*; ad ponti-
ficatum *F*   [n] crescere *WH*; creuit *F*; crescere coepit *ZCXY*   [o] *om.*
deuotas *ZCXY*   [p] *om.* excusans se *WH*   [q] *om.* uenerabilibus locis . . .
emendandi, redderent *W*; *om.* redderent *P*

---

[1] Cf. 2 Tim. 4: 2.   [2] *Reg.* i. 29a, Aug.–Sept. 1073, pp. 47–9.

testimony of our conscience, how we were brought to excommunicate him. We have done so not so much to noise abroad as it were by the sound of our own voice the several reasons which, alas! are all too well known, as, rather, to satisfy the misgivings of those who think that we seized the spiritual sword rashly and more from the prompting of our own passions than from fear of God and zeal for righteousness.

While we still exercised the office of deacon, there reached us ill and most shameful tidings of the king's behaviour; on account of the imperial dignity and out of respect for his father and mother, and also on account of our hope and desire for his correction, we frequently admonished him by letters and by messengers to cease from his wickedness and, mindful of his illustrious family and rank, to shape his life in ways which befitted a king and, if God so disposed, an emperor-to-be. After we, though unworthy, succeeded to the papal office, his wickedness increased together with his years. Knowing that Almighty God would require his soul of our hand the more stringently because freedom and authority to reprove him were given to us before all other men, we urged him the more anxiously to amend his life, in every way 'convincing, rebuking, exhorting'[1] him. He often sent us cordial letters of greeting,[2] making excuses for himself on the grounds of his youth because such a time of life was frail and weak,[3] and of his having again and again been badly advised and counselled by those who predominated in his court; however, while he made verbal promises that he would each day most readily heed our warnings, he utterly trampled upon them in what he did and by the multiplication of his offences.

In the meantime we summoned to do penance some of his courtiers, by whose counsels and devices he had polluted with the simoniac heresy the bishoprics and the many monasteries in which, for a price, wolves had been established instead of shepherds. Our intention was that while there was yet scope for amendment they might restore the ecclesiastical property which they had sacrilegiously received through their most pernicious trafficking to the venerable places to which it belonged, and that they might themselves make satisfaction to God by tears of repentance for the evils which they had committed. When we knew that they scorned

---

[3] Cf. Sallust, *Catilina*, i. 4; Gregory also used this phrase in *Reg.* iv. 28, 28 June 1077, p. 345, and vi. 13, 15 Dec. 1078, p. 417, as well as in no. 65 below.

inducias spernere et in consueta nequicia pertinaciter stare cognouimus, sicut dignum erat sacrilegos et ministros ac membra diaboli a communione et corpore totius ecclesie separauimus, et regem ut eos a domo sua, a consiliis, et omni communione sua sicut excommunicatos[r] expelleret admonuimus.[s]

Interim uero, ingrauescente contra regem Saxonum causa, cum uires et presidia regni ex maxima parte a se deficere uelle conspiceret,[t] iterum direxit nobis epistolam supplicem et omni humilitate plenam,[1] in qua omnipotenti Deo ac beato Petro ac nobis ualde se culpabilem reddens[u] preces etiam obtulit ut quod ex culpa sua in ecclesiasticis causis contra canonicam iusticiam[v] et decreta sanctorum patrum deliquisset,[w] nostra apostolica prouidentia et auctoritate corrigere studeremus, atque in eo suam nobis per omnia obedientiam consensum[x] et fidele promisit adiutorium. Hoc idem etiam postea a confratribus et legatis nostris Huberto Prenestino episcopo et Geraldo Ostiensi episcopo quos ad illum misimus[y] ad penitentiam susceptus, in illorum manus per sacratas stolas quas in collo tenebant repromittendo confirmauit.[2] Deinde post aliquot tempus commisso cum Saxonibus prelio[3] rex pro uictoria quam adeptus est tales Deo grates et uictimas obtulit ut uota que de emendatione sua fecerat continuo frangeret, et nichil eorum que nobis promiserat attendens excommunicatos in suam familiaritatem et communionem reciperet et ecclesias in eam quam consueuerat confusionem traheret.

Qua de re graui dolore perculsi, quamquam post contempta celestis regis beneficia pene omnis spes correctionis eius nobis ablata sit, adhuc tamen animum eius temptandum fore decreuimus, magis cupientes eum apostolicam mansuetudinem audire quam[z] experiri seueritatem. Itaque misimus ei commonitorias epistolas ut meminerit quid et cui promiserit,[aa] ne credat se posse fallere Deum cuius quanto prolixior est patientia tanto seuerior est cum iudicare ceperit ira, ne inhonoret Deum honorantem se, ne potentiam suam ad Dei contemptum et apostolicam temptet extendere contumeliam; sciens quoniam 'superbis Deus resistit,

[r] *om.* sicut excommunicatos P   [s] *om. the rest of the letter except the last sentence* W   [t] uideret LP   [u] uidens P   [v] *om.* iustitiam P   [w] factum esset LPSN; factum fuisset HZCXY   [x] consilium HZCXY   [y] *om.* quos ad illum misimus X   [z] *After this word almost the whole of N is lost by mutilation*   [aa] *om.* quid et cui promiserit V

[1] Lost; cf. the final sentence of *Reg.* i. 29a.

the pause which they were allowed to do these things and that they obstinately continued in their accustomed wickedness, we duly cut them off, as sacrilegious and as ministers and members of the devil, from the communion and body of the whole church, and we warned the king to drive them as excommunicates from his household, from his counsels, and from all association with himself.

However, the Saxon cause in the meantime waxed mightily against the king. Seeing that the strength and resources of the kingdom were for the most part likely to desert him, he again sent us a suppliant letter full of all humility,[1] in which he acknowledged himself to be deeply guilty in the sight of Almighty God, of St. Peter, and of ourself. He also besought us to be zealous in correcting by our apostolic provision and authority whatever he had done wrong through his own fault in ecclesiastical matters against canonical righteousness and the decrees of the holy fathers; and in this he promised us his entire obedience, concord, and faithful aid. He was, furthermore, afterwards admitted to penance by our brothers and legates whom we sent to him, Bishop Hubert of Palestrina and Bishop Gerald of Ostia, solemnly confirming his promises into their hands by the holy stoles which they wore about their necks.[2] But after some time the king fought a battle with the Saxons.[3] The only thank-offerings which he presented to God for the victory which he obtained were that he straightway broke the promises of amendment which he had made. Paying no heed to what he had promised us he took the excommunicates back into his household and society and dragged his churches into their accustomed confusion.

What happened struck us with deep grief; but although after his contempt for the blessings of the King of Heaven almost all hope of his amendment was taken away from us, we decided that we should still put his disposition to the test, for we desired that he should hear the call of apostolic mercy rather than that he should experience apostolic severity. We therefore sent him a warning letter, urging him to remember what he had promised and to whom: he should not believe that he could deceive the God whose wrath when he begins to judge is as stern as his long-suffering is abundant; nor should he dishonour God by honouring himself, nor should he try to enlarge his own power in contempt of God and in despite of his apostle St. Peter; he should remember that 'God

---

[2] At Nürnberg, soon after Easter 1074; Gregory's legates were Cardinal-bishops Hubert of Palestrina (1073–82) and Gerald of Ostia (1067–77).
[3] At Homburg-on-the-Unstrut, 9 June 1075.

humilibus autem dat gratiam.'¹ Preterea misimus ad eum tres
religiosos uiros, suos utique fideles,² per quos eum secreto
monuimus ut penitentiam ageret de sceleribus suis, que quidem
horrenda dictu sunt pluribus autem nota et in multis partibus*bb*
diuulgata; propter que eum non solum excommunicari usque
ad condignam satisfactionem sed ab omni honore regni absque*cc*
spe recuperationis debere destitui,*dd* diuinarum et humanarum
legum testatur et iubet*ee* auctoritas. Postremo nisi excommunicatos
a sua participatione diuideret nos nichil aliud de eo iudicare aut
decernere*ff* posse nisi quod, separatus ab ecclesia, in excom-
municatorum consortio foret cum quibus ipse potius quam cum
Christo partem habere delegeret.*gg*³ Sane si nostra monita suscipere
et uitam suam corrigere uellet, testem Deum inuocauimus, et
uocamus, quantum nos de eius salute et honore gauderemus,
quanta caritate eum in gremio sancte ecclesie amplecteremur,
utpote eum qui, princeps populi constitutus⁴ et amplissimi regni
gubernacula tenens, catholice pacis et iustitie defensor esse
deberet.

Verum quanti ipse scripta aut per legatos missa nostra uerba
fecerit eius facta declarant. Qui, indigne ferens se a quoquam
reprehendi aut corripi, non solum a perpetratis criminibus*hh*
reuocari ad emendationem non potuit sed, ampliori conscientie
sue furore arreptus, non prius cessauit donec episcopos pene
omnes in Italia, in Teutonicis uero partibus quodquod potuit,
circa fidem Christi naufragare fecit, dum eos debitam beato
Petro et apostolice sedi obedientiam et honorem a domino
nostro Ihesu Christo concessum abnegare coegit.*ii*⁵

Cum igitur iniquitatem eius ad summum prodisse uidimus, pro
his uidelicet causis, primum quod ab eorum communione qui
pro sacrilegio et reatu symoniace heresis excommunicati sunt se
abstinere noluit, deinde quod pro criminosis actibus uite sue
penitentiam non dico suscipere sed nec promittere uoluit, mentita
ea fide*jj* quam in manus legatorum nostrorum promiserat, necnon

---

bb *add* terrae *ZCXY*   *cc* *add* omni *ZCXY*   *dd* institui *V*   *ee* *om.*
et iubet *LP*   *ff* *om.* aut decernere *P*; aut diuidere *H*   *gg* elegit *LP*;
delegit *F*; elegerit *HSZCXY*   *hh* *om.* criminibus *LPHSZCXY*   *ii* *om.*
dum eos . . . abnegare coegit *F*   *jj* ei penitentia *V*; penitentia *MF*; *om.*
fide *H*

---

¹ *Reg.* iii. 10, 8 Dec. 1075, pp. 263–7. Cf. 1 Pet. 5: 5.
² Radbod, Adelpreth, and Gotteschalk: *Reg.* iii. 10, p. 267.

resists the proud but gives grace to the humble'.[1] We also sent to
him three religious men, faithful followers of his own,[2] through
whom we secretly admonished him to do penance for his sins
which, shameful to say, were known to most men and noised abroad
through many parts; for the authority of divine and human laws
enjoined and commanded that on account of them he should not
only be excommunicated until he had made due satisfaction but
that he should be deprived of his entire dignity as king without
hope of recovery. Finally unless he excluded the excommunicates
from associating with him we could come to no other judgement
or decision about him than that he should be separated from the
church and share the company of the excommunicates with whom
he had chosen to have his part rather than with Christ.[3] However,
should he wish to heed our warnings and amend his life, we called,
and still call, God to witness how greatly we would rejoice for his
salvation and honour, and with how much love we would embrace
him in the bosom of holy church as one whom, being set as a prince
over the people[4] and having the rule of a most far-flung kingdom, it
behoves to be the upholder of catholic peace and righteousness.

Yet how much heed he paid to our words whether as written or
as spoken by our envoys, his own deeds proclaim. He scorned that
anyone should restrain or reprove him; not only would he not be
recalled to repentance from the misdeeds which he had committed,
but he was seized by a still greater fury of mind: he did not pause
until he had made shipwreck regarding the faith of Christ of almost
all the Italian bishops and of as many in Germany as he could,
compelling them to contradict their due obedience to St. Peter and
the apostolic see and the office which was given them by our Lord
Jesus Christ.[5]

We therefore saw that his iniquity had now increased to the full.
For the following reasons, first because he would not keep himself
from the society of men who had been excommunicated for the
sacrilege and crime of the simoniac heresy, secondly because he
would not even promise, let alone perform, penance for the guilty
deeds of his own life (for the faith which he promised into the hands
of our legates was a feigned one), and thirdly because he had not

---

[3] Cf. Acts 8: 21. [4] Cf. Isa. 3: 7.
[5] The assemblies of bishops took place at Worms (24 Jan. 1076) and at
Piacenza soon afterwards.

quod corpus Christi id est unitatem sancte*kk* ecclesie scindere non expauit—pro his, inquam, culpis synodali eum iudicio excommunicauimus,[1] ut quem mites non potuimus uel seueri ad uiam salutis Deo adiuuante*ll* reuocare ualeamus, aut si, quod absit, nec districtionis quidem censuram pertimuerit nostra saltem anima negligentie aut timoris discrimini*mm* non succumbat.

Si quis igitur hanc sententiam iniuste uel irrationabiliter prolatam esse putauerit, si talis est ut sacris regulis intelligentie sensum prebere*nn* uelit, nobiscum inde agat et, non quod nos sed quod diuina auctoritas doceat, quod decernat, quod consona sanctorum patrum uoce*oo* iudicet patienter audiens, acquiescat. Nos tamen non estimamus quemquam fidelium*pp* qui ecclesiastica statuta nouerit hoc errore teneri, ut non hoc, etsi publice non audeat affirmare, uel in corde suo recte factum esse perhibeat. Quamquam etsi nos, quod Deus auertat, non satis de graui causa aut minus ordinate eum huiusmodi uinculo ligauerimus, sicut sancti patres asserunt, non idcirco spernenda esset sententia, sed absolutio cum omni humilitate querenda.

Vos autem, dilectissimi, qui iusticiam Dei non pro regia indignatione*qq* nec pro aliquo periculo deserere uoluistis, fatuitatem eorum qui de execratione et mendacio adnuntiabuntur*rr* in summatione*ss*[2] paruipendentes,*tt* uiriliter state et confortamini[3] in Domino, scientes quod illius partem defenditis qui insuperabilis rex et semper*uu* magnificus triumphator iudicaturus est uiuos et mortuos,[4] reddens unicuique secundum opus suum.[5] De cuius multimoda retributione et uos certi esse poteritis, si usque in finem fideles et inconcussi in eius ueritate perstiteritis. Propter quod et nos incessanter pro uobis*vv* rogamus Deum, ut det uobis uirtutem corroborari per Spiritum sanctum[6] in nomine eius, et conuertat cor regis ad penitentiam,[7] ut et ipse aliquando cognoscat nos et uos multo uerius amare eum quam qui nunc suis iniquitatibus obsecuntur et fauent. Quodsi Deo inspirante*ww* uoluerit resipiscere, quicquid contra nos moliatur semper tamen nos ad recipiendum eum in sanctam communionem, prout uestra caritas nobis consuluerit, paratos inueniet.

---

kk om. sancte *VMF*   *ll* om. Deo adiuuante *F*   *mm* magnitudini *F*
nn add non *LP*   *oo* consona uox sanctorum patrum *LPZCXY*   *pp* om. quemquam fidelium *H*   *qq* dignitate *H*   *rr* om. adnuntiabuntur *LP*
ss om. in summatione *F*   *tt* execrantes *F*   *uu* om. semper *LHFZCXY*
vv om. pro uobis *F*   *ww* donante *W*

feared to rend the body of Christ, that is, the unity of holy church
—for these faults, I say, we now excommunicated him by a conciliar sentence:[1] since we could not recall him to the way of salvation by being merciful we tried, with God's help, to do so by being
severe. Thus if, which heaven forbid, he should not fear even this
punitive sanction, our own soul, at least, would not be subject to
the reproach of negligence or fear.

Should anyone think that this sentence was passed unreasonably
or unjustly, then supposing him to be ready to give due assent to
the true interpretation of the holy laws, let him consider the matter
with us. Patiently hearing what not we but divine authority teaches,
decrees, and judges by the unanimous opinion of the holy fathers,
let him yield his approval. But we do not think that any of the
faithful who knows the ecclesiastical decrees can in truth be so far
in the grip of error that, even though he dares not affirm so much
in public, he does not in his heart of hearts acknowledge that what
has been done was done rightly. And, indeed, even if, which God
forbid, we did impose upon the king such a sanction as we imposed
without sufficient reason or beyond the due course of law, as the
holy fathers insist our sentence should not, accordingly, be ignored:
he should with all humility seek absolution from it.

As for you, dearly beloved, who have not been minded to desert
the righteousness of God in face of the king's anger or of any
danger but have despised the foolishness of those who for their
cursing and lies will be proclaimed fitted for destruction,[2] stand
firm and be strong[3] in the Lord, knowing that you defend the cause
of one who as an invincible king and ever-glorious conqueror will
come to judge the quick and the dead,[4] making recompense to each
as his works deserve.[5] You, too, may be sure of his manifold
rewards if you stand firm to the end, faithful and unshaken in his
truth. We in our turn pray to God unceasingly for you that he may
grant you power to be strengthened by the Holy Spirit[6] in his name
and that he may turn the king's heart to penitence;[7] thus the king
also may at last know that we and you love him far more truly than
those who are now compliant and favourable to his sins. If by
God's grace he should be minded to repent, no matter what he
may attempt against us he will nevertheless always find us ready,
according as you may advise us, to receive him back into the fellowship of the church.

[1] *Reg.* iii. 10*a*, pp. 270–1.   [2] Cf. Ps. 58: 13–14 (59: 12–13).
[3] Cf. 1 Cor. 16: 13.   [4] 2 Tim. 4: 1.
[5] Cf. Rev. 2: 23.   [6] Cf. Eph. 3: 16.
[7] Cf. Ecclus. 8: 3 (2).

15

*To all the faithful in the Roman empire: Gregory adds a
postscript to an earlier letter, warning against Henry IV's
deceit and forbidding anyone to absolve the king without
consulting himself*   (*1076*), *29 Aug.**

Gregorius episcopus seruus seruorum Dei [omnibus in Christo
fratribus, episcopis abbatibus sacerdotibus ducibus et principibus
atque militibus omnibusque christianam fidem et beati Petri
honorem reuera diligentibus in Romano imperio habitantibus,]ᵃ
salutem et apostolicam benedictionem.

Postquam fraternitati uestrae epistolam direximus quae ita
incipit: 'Gratias agimus omnipotenti Deo', a fidelibus sanctae
ecclesiae accepimus quod rex summopere procuret nos ab inuicem
seiungere suaque fraude decipere, modo per spirituales modo per
saeculares personas. Proinde dubitamus ne forte ex nostris fratribus minus cauti pro licentia quam dedimus decipiantur. Et ideo
ex parte beati Petri apostolorum principis praecipimus ut nullus
eum praesumat a uinculo anathematis absoluere quousque
illius satisfactio et penitentia per idoneos uestros nobis fuerit
renuntiata, ut simul decernentes per legatos nostros quod aequum
fuerit ac Deo placitum, omni fraude remota, apostolica auctoritate
statuamus. Vos autem diligenter studete eam promissionem eamque securitatem ab illo accipere ut non uideamur pro columbae
simplicitate serpentis prudentiam¹ negligere. Quodsi inter hec,
quod non optamus, morte praeuentus fuerit, non dubitet uestra
fraternitas quam uera penitentia ueraque satisfactio promeretur
absolutionis medicinam impendere.

Data Tiburisᵇ iiii kal. Septembris.

ᵃ eisdem omnibus *F*, *referring back to Reg. iv. 1 as on fo. 115ʳ, which is here
quoted in square brackets*   ᵇ Triburis *F*

---

* In his earlier letter, *Reg.* iv. 1, 25 July 1076, pp. 289–92, Gregory urged his
followers to do everything in their power to bring Henry to true penitence. The
gradual hardening of Gregory's attitude towards Henry which the present
letter suggests became explicit in *Reg.* iv. 3, 3 Sept. 1076, pp. 297–300, where
Gregory spoke of the possibility of a new election to the kingship should Henry
not repent.

To all the faithful in the Roman empire

(*1076*), *29 Aug.*

Gregory, bishop, servant of the servants of God, [to all his brothers in Christ, bishops, abbots, priests, dukes, princes, and knights, and all living in the Roman empire who in truth love the Christian faith and the honour of St. Peter,] greeting and apostolic blessing.

After we sent you the letter which begins thus: 'We give thanks to Almighty God', we learned from faithful members of holy church that the king is doing all in his power to divide us from each other and to deceive us by his falsity, sometimes through spiritual and sometimes through secular persons. We are therefore anxious lest perchance some of the less prudent of our brothers may be misled by the indulgence that we have shown. So on behalf of St. Peter, the prince of the apostles, we ordain that no one shall dare to free him from the bond of excommunication until tidings of his satisfaction and penance have been brought to us by suitable messengers. Then we may at once decide through our legates, by apostolic authority, leaving no room for deceit, what is just and pleasing to God. You on your part should take every care to receive such assurance and such security from him that we may not seem to have neglected the wisdom of the serpent for the innocence of the dove.[1] If, in the meanwhile, though we do not wish it, he should be overtaken by death, you, my brothers, should not hesitate to dispense the medicine of absolution which true penance and true satisfaction deserve.

Tivoli, 29 August.

J.L. 5001. MS.: Hugh of Flavigny, *Chron.*: Berlin, Deutsche Staatsbibl. Phillipps 1870, fo. 116^r, eleventh cent. (*F*). Printed: Hugh of Flavigny, *Chron.* ii, *M.G.H. Scr.* viii. 442. *Ep. coll.* no. 15, pp. 540-1.

---

[1] Cf. Matt. 10: 16.

16

To King William I of England: Gregory describes to him
the scandalous life of Bishop Juhel of Dol and urges him
to help with his expulsion; Gregory has himself consecrated
a successor for his see   (*1076, after 27 Sept.*)*

Gregorius episcopus seruus seruorum Dei excellentissimo filio W.[a]
glorioso regi Anglorum[1] salutem et apostolicam benedictionem.

Compertum esse celsitudini tuae non dubitamus quod dictus
episcopus Dolensis ecclesiae, quae Britannicae provinciae prin-
cipalis est sedes, suae salutis immemor et sanctorum canonum
decreta conculcans, eamdem ecclesiam per simoniacam haeresim
impudenter inuaserit et prolixo iam tempore oppresserit uiolenter.
Datis namque comiti Alano[2] copiosis muneribus, quae[b] usque
hodie ad probamentum prius[c] nequitiae in propatulo extant, non
per ostium in ouile[d] Christi sed ut fur et latro aliunde irrepsit.[3]
Qui etiam nec hoc scelere contentus iniquitatem super iniquitatem
apposuit et, quasi simoniacum esse parum et pro nihilo deputaret,
nicolaita quoque fieri festinauit. Nam in ipso tam perniciose
adepto episcopatu nuptiis publice celebratis scortum potius
quam sponsam ducere non erubuit, ex qua et filios procreauit;
ut qui iam spiritum suum animarum corruptori[e] per simoniaca
commercia prostituerat,[f] per foedae libidinis incestum corpus
suum ita in contumeliam diabolo consecraret; et sic in eo nullus
locus superesset Conditori quem intus exteriusque obligatum
totum sibi aduersarius non uendicasset. Nec tamen huc usque
conatus malitiae substitit, sed etiam atrocissimum facinus turpis-
simumque flagitium horrendo etiam sacrilegio cumulauit. Nam
adultas ex illicito matrimonio filias, praediis ecclesiae et redditibus
nomine dotis collatis atque alienatis, scelere immanissimo mari-
tauit. His iniquitatibus coopertus, eamdem tamen ecclesiam di-
laceratam dissipatamque, si liceat, incubare molitur. Quibus de

---

[a] *om.* W. B   [b] quo B   [c] *sic* BT; ?prioris   [d] ouili B
[e] corruptorem B   [f] prostituat B

---

* In autumn 1076 William was campaigning in Brittany against the rebellious
Ralph, earl of Norfolk, who had established himself in the castle of Dol. Gregory
sought to secure William's concurrence in his plan to depose Bishop Juhel
(*c.* 1039–76) and to replace him by Ivo (Evenus), abbot of Saint-Melaine,
Rennes. In early Oct., before this letter can have arrived, King Philip I of France

To King William I of England   (*1076, after 27 Sept.*)

Gregory, bishop, servant of the servants of God, to his most excellent son William, the renowned king of England,[1] greeting and apostolic blessing.

We do not doubt that you well know how the so-called bishop of the church of Dol, the principal see of the province of Brittany, being heedless of his salvation and trampling upon the decrees of the holy canons, has shamelessly invaded that church by way of the simoniac heresy and has already for a very long time violently oppressed it. For he gave Count Alan[2] numerous gifts which remain to this day for all to see as a proof of his wickedness from the beginning, and did not enter Christ's sheepfold by the door but crept in by some other way like a thief and a robber.[3] He was not content even with this crime but heaped iniquity upon iniquity: as though he counted it little or nothing to be a simoniac he hastened also to become a nicolaite. For in the very bishopric which he had so destructively obtained he was not ashamed to enter openly into marriage and to take a harlot rather than a wife, by whom he then also begot children, so that he who had already prostituted his soul to the debaucher of souls by his simoniacal trafficking might likewise dedicate his body in shame to the devil by his lewd and foul lust; thus there might be no place left in him for the Creator which the adversary did not claim as being altogether bound to himself both within and without.

Yet his malicious endeavours did not stop short even at this point, but he crowned a most frightful crime and a most shameful disgrace by also adding an abominable sacrilege. For by a monstrous outrage he married off the grown-up daughters of his illicit marriage, bestowing and alienating church lands and revenues by way of their dowries. Covered with these iniquities he is trying, if he is allowed, to get a grip on the church of Dol, torn and ravaged though it is. For these reasons you know that he has already been

moved to the relief of Dol and forced William to withdraw. Ivo succeeded to the see and ruled it until his death in 1081.

J.L. 5005. MS.: Paris, Bibl. nat. franç. 22322, pp. 29–30, seventeenth cent. (*B*). Printed: Martène and Durand, *Thesaurus nouus anecdotorum*, iii. 871–2 (*T*); a revision of Martène, *Veterum scriptorum et monumentorum collectio noua*, i. 57–8. Morice, *Mémoires*, i. 442–3. *Ep. coll.* no. 16, pp. 541–2.

---

[1] King of England (1066–87); duke of Normandy (1035–87).
[2] Alanus III, count of Brittany (1008–40).   [3] Cf. John 10: 1–2.

THE *EPISTOLAE VAGANTES* OF

causis celsitudo tua nouerit illum iam beati Petri apostoli spiculo
perfossum et nisi sceleris^g resipuerit anathemate mortifero esse
damnatum. Quapropter paterna caritate te ammonere et causam
breuiter exponere studuimus, ne fortasse per ignorantiam tam
scelesto homini tandiu in tenebris suis iacenti ulterius auxilium
praebeas neue sceleris eius te participem facias; sed sedi apostolicae nostrisque monitis modeste parendo illum a te repellas,
uel etiam ut tandem aliquando sibi consulat atque ad remedium
paenitentiae confugiat blande suadendo, si poteris, inducas. Nam
tales in malo perseuerantes fouere et adiuuare nihil est aliud quam
iram Domini contra se prouocare. Nos uero supradictae ecclesiae
afflictionem diutius non ferentes, Deo inspirante, uirum uita^h
probabilem et compertae religionis inibi ordinauimus et con-
secrauimus, uidelicet S. Melanii abbatem; qui cum ob alias
causas quas explicare prolixum est ad nos uenisset, pontificatus
onus ex insperato subire compulsus est. De quo confidimus in
Domino quia si, ut desideramus litterisque nostris multipliciter
implorare curauimus,[1] principum terrae bonorum uirorum gratiam
et studia habere meruerit, Domino cooperante, sub beati Petri
patrocinio ecclesiam in melius restaurabit.

17

*To his supporters in Germany: Gregory announces that he is
coming to Germany and hopes to reach Mantua by 8 January;
he asks them to prepare to receive him*   (*1076, Dec.*)*

Gregorius episcopus^a seruus seruorum Dei archiepiscopis episcopis
ducibus comitibus nec non maioribus atque minoribus in regno
Teutonicorum constitutis salutem et apostolicam benedictionem.

Nos^b indigni et inutiles principis apostolorum serui statuimus

^g *sic* BT   ^h vitae BT   17   ^a *om.* episcopus WHZC   ^b *add* et C

---

* At his negotiations with the German princes in Oct. 1076 at Tribur-
Oppenheim Henry IV was compelled to seek a reconciliation with Gregory;
the princes determined to invite Gregory to a *Reichstag* at Augsburg on 2 Feb.,
and to renounce Henry's lordship if he did not secure his release from excommunication. The two sides sent envoys to Gregory, who resolved to travel to
Germany. This and the following letters announced his intention; Gregory was
especially concerned to secure an escort from Mantua across the Alps to Augsburg. For the circulation of these letters in Saxony, cf. the Saxons' letter to

pierced by the dart of St. Peter the apostle, and that unless he repents of his crime he is condemned to a death-dealing anathema. We have accordingly been at pains to warn you with fatherly charity and briefly to set forth his case, lest perchance you should in ignorance further afford help to so wicked a man while he lies in his own darkness, and lest you should make yourself a partaker of his offence. Rather, humbly obeying the warnings of the apostolic see and of ourself you should drive him from you, and also, if you can, by careful persuasion induce him at last to take some thought for himself and to seek refuge in the medicine of penance. For to comfort and help such men while they persist in evil is certainly to provoke the wrath of God against ourselves.

We for our part will no longer tolerate the affliction of this church. Moved by God we have appointed and consecrated for it a man of worthy life and proven religion, the abbot of Saint-Melaine, who when he came to us for other reasons too long to explain was altogether unexpectedly compelled to shoulder the burden of the episcopate. We trust in the Lord concerning him that, if as we ourselves desire and have been at pains many times to implore in our letters[1] he is granted the favour and help of the princes and good men of the land, he will with God's help and under St. Peter's protection restore the church to a better condition.

To his supporters in Germany   (*1076, Dec.*)

Gregory, bishop, servant of the servants of God, to the archbishops, bishops, dukes, and counts, and to both greater and lesser men in the kingdom of Germany, greeting and apostolic blessing.

We, an unworthy and unprofitable servant of the prince of the

Gregory of Apr. 1078 in Bruno, *Sax. bell. cap.* 108, edd. Lohmann and Schmale, p. 356.
J.L. 5013. MSS.: Paul of Bernried, *Greg. VII uita*: Vienna, Österr. Nationalbibl. 336, fo. 261ʳ, twelfth cent. (*V*); Heiligenkreuz, Stiftsbibl. 12, fo. 192ᵛ, twelfth cent.; Admont, Stiftsbibl. 24, fo. 138ʳ, twelfth cent.; Melk, Stiftsbibl. 492, fo. 103ᵛ, twelfth cent. Wolfenbüttel, Hzg.–Aug. Bibl. Helmstedt 1024, no. 12, fo. 38ʳ⁻ᵛ, twelfth cent. (*W*). Hanover Collection: Hanover, Niedersächs. Landesbibl. XI. 671, no. 8 *bis*, fo. 32ᵛ, sixteenth cent. (*H*). Leipzig, Universitätsbibl. 201, fo. 171ᵛ, thirteenth cent. (*U*). *Codex Udalrici*: Zwettl, Stiftsarch. 283, p. 110, twelfth cent. (*Z*); Vienna, Österr. Nationalbibl. 398, fo. 63ʳ, twelfth cent. (*C*). Printed: Paul of Bernried, *Greg. VII uita, cap.* 83, *Pont. Rom. uitae*, ed. Watterich, i. 523–4. *Codex Udalrici*: Eccard, *Corp. hist.* ii, no. 147, col. 149. *Ep. coll.* no. 17, pp. 542–3.

[1] *Reg.* iv. 4–5, 27 Sept. 1076, pp. 300–3, with or soon after which this letter must have been written.

ad uos, diuina auxiliante clementia, uenire et, postponentes pene[c]
omnium fidelium nostrorum consilia, ita profectionem nostram
maturare ut VI[d] Idus Ianuarii uelimus Mantue esse,[e] ea [f] quidem
uoluntate et desiderio ut fiducia probate fidei[g] uestre[h] queque[i]
aspera et si necesse fuerit ipsam sanguinis effusionem pro libertate
sancte ecclesie et salute imperii pura et sincera intentione subire
non dubitemus. Vestri igitur studii sit eos de susceptione[j] et
seruicio nostro premonere quos prudentia uestra id posse et
nobis debere cognouerit. Sit etiam ita studii uestri per partes
uestras pacem firmare ut intentionis nostre propositum nichil
possit impedire.[k] Quod et quantas colluctationes cum nunciis
regis habuerimus et quibus rationibus dictis eius[l] obuiauerimus,
quicquid his litteris deesse uidetur[m] latores earum plenius indi-
cabunt. Quibus sicut de his que per eos[n] beato Petro et nobis
promisistis indubitanter credimus, ita uos de his que ex nostra
uobis parte dixerint[o] credere uolumus.

18

*To all the faithful in Germany: Gregory further seeks
German support for his journey to Augsburg* (*1076, Dec.*)*

Gregorius episcopus[a] seruus seruorum Dei omnibus archiepiscopis episcopis abbatibus ducibus marchionibus comitibus
omnibusque christianam et beati Petri apostolorum principis[b]
fidem et doctrinam defendentibus et obseruantibus in omni regno
Teutonicorum[c] salutem et[d] beatorum apostolorum Petri et Pauli
benedictionem omniumque peccatorum absolutionem.

Ego qualiscumque sacerdos, apostolorum principis seruus,

[c] *om.* pene *WZC*   [d] VII *H*   [e] uelimus esse *W*; apud uos uelimus
esse *ZC*   [f] *om.* ea *WH*; nostra *ZC*   [g] spei *V*   [h] *om.* uestre *ZC*
[i] quecumque *W*; quicquid *ZC*   [j] ereptione *WHU*; exceptione *ZC*
[k] sit nihil quod impedire possit *U*   [l] eorum *WHUZC*   [m] in uno
quicquid deest uidetur litteris *W*; immo quicquid de his deesse uidetur
litteris *H*   [n] *om.* per eos *WHZC*   [o] *add* certissime *WHUZC*

18   [a] *om.* episcopus *V*   [b] *om.* apostolorum principis *VF*   [c] *om.* in
omni regno Teutonicorum *V*; *add* habitantibus *HUF*   [d] habentibus
fidem *W*

* J.L. 5014. MSS.: Paul of Bernried, *Greg. VII uita*: Vienna, Österr. Nationalbibl. 336, fo. 261[r-v], twelfth cent. (*V*); Heiligenkreuz, Stiftsbibl. 12, fo. 192[v],
twelfth cent.; Admont, Stiftsbibl. 24, fo. 138[r], twelfth cent.; Melk, Stiftsbibl.

apostles, have decided with the help of God's mercy to come to you and, disregarding the counsels of almost all our advisers, so to hasten our journey that on 8 January we hope to be in Mantua. For it is our purpose and desire that, trusting in your proven fidelity, we should not hesitate with pure and upright zeal to undergo any hardships and if need be even the shedding of our blood for the liberty of holy church and for the salvation of the empire. You therefore for your part should forewarn those whom you know to be able and obliged to help us that they should be ready to receive and serve us. You yourselves should also so diligently make peace throughout your country that nothing may hinder the purpose upon which we have settled.

About the many and great debates which we have had with the king's envoys and the arguments by which we have resisted his words, and whatever else may seem to be omitted from this letter, its bearers will more fully inform you. As we unhesitatingly trust in what you have promised through them to St. Peter and ourself, so we would have you trust in what they have to say on our own behalf.

To all the faithful in Germany (1076, Dec.)

Gregory, bishop, servant of the servants of God, to all archbishops, bishops, abbots, dukes, marquises, counts, and to all in the whole kingdom of Germany who are defending and keeping the faith and teaching of Christ and of St. Peter, the prince of the apostles, greeting and the blessing of the blessed apostles Peter and Paul, also the absolution of all their sins.

I such as I am, a priest and servant of the prince of the apostles,

---

492, fos. 103ᵛ–104ʳ, twelfth cent. Wolfenbüttel, Hzg.–Aug. Bibl. Helmstedt 1024, no. 11, fo. 38ʳ, twelfth cent. (W). Hanover Collection: Hanover, Niedersächs. Landesbibl. XI. 671, no. 8, fo. 32ʳ, sixteenth cent. (H). Leipzig, Universitäts-bibl. 201, fo. 171ᵛ, thirteenth cent. (U). Hugh of Flavigny, Chron.: Berlin, Deutsche Staatsbibl. Phillipps 1870, fo. 117ᵛ, eleventh cent. (F). Codex Udalrici: Zwettl, Stiftsarch. 283, pp. 109–10, twelfth cent. (Z); Vienna, Österr. National-bibl. 398, fo. 63ʳ, twelfth cent. (C). Printed: Paul of Bernried, Greg. VII uita, cap. 83, Pont. Rom. uitae, ed. Watterich, i. 524. Hugh of Flavigny, Chron. ii, M.G.H. Scr. viii. 444. Codex Udalrici: Eccard, Corp. hist. ii, no. 146 bis, col. 149. Ep. coll. no. 18, pp. 543–4.

contra uoluntatem et consilium Romanorum, confidens de misericordia omnipotentis[e] Dei et de uestra fide catholica, uenio ad uos,
paratus propter honorem Dei[f] et salutem animarum uestrarum
mortem subire, sicut Christus[g] pro nobis animam suam posuit.
In hoc enim positi sumus[h] ut per multas tribulationes tendamus
et perueniamus ad regnum Dei.[i][1] Vos autem, fratres mei karissimi
et desiderantissimi,[2] summopere curate ut uos[j] possim Deo adiuuante adire uobisque in omnibus prodesse. Benedicat uos[k]
ex cuius gratia[l] mihi dictum est ad corpus beati Petri in die ordinationis mee:[3] 'Quodcumque benedixeris benedictum erit, et quodcumque solueris super terram erit solutum et in celis.'[4] Amen.[m]

19

*To all the faithful in Germany: Gregory explains his delay in
coming to Germany, during which he has met the penitent
king and restored him to communion. He speaks of the
wickness of the Lombard bishops, and of his continuing
desire to come to Germany*   (*1077, Feb.–Mar.*)*

Gregorius episcopus seruus seruorum Dei dilectissimis in Christo
fratribus et filiis, archiepiscopis episcopis ducibus comitibus
caeterisque principibus cum omni populo regni Theuthonicorum
christianam fidem et religionem defendentibus, salutem et apostolicam bendictionem.

Sicut in prioribus literis et legatorum uerbis uobis significaui-
mus,[5] intelligentes quod digne Deo defensores iustitiae uos in
uera oboedientia et apostolici principatus reuerentia exibuistis, in
uestra fide et consiliis fiducialiter spem ponentes, contra uoluntatem pene omnium fidelium nostrorum, excepta carissima et
fidelissima beati Petri filia uidelicet Mathilde, iter ad uos non

---

[e] *om.* omnipotentis *WZC*   [f] *om.* Dei *V*   [g] *om.* Christus *V*   [h] *om.*
sicut Christus . . . positi sumus *WHUZC*   [i] ad requiem *WZC*; *om.* Dei *H*
[j] *om.* uos *V*   [k] *add.* ille *ZC*   [l] parte *F*   [m] *om.* Amen *VHF*

---

* Together with *Reg.* iv. 12, late Jan. 1077, pp. 311–14, this letter provides
Gregory's account of his absolution of Henry IV on 28 Jan. 1077. After Tribur-
Oppenheim Henry had at first withdrawn to Speyer, but he decided to travel
to Italy and seek reconciliation with the pope apart from the princes. Because
of the princes' failure to provide an escort across the Alps Henry met Gregory

against the will and advice of the Romans but trusting in the mercy
of Almighty God and in your catholic faith, am coming to you,
ready to suffer death for the honour of God and the salvation of
your souls, even as Christ laid down his life for us. For we are so
placed that through many tribulations we must strive for and
attain to the kingdom of God.[1] For your part, my brothers whom
I love and long for,[2] see to it by all means that I may with God's
help come to you and profit you in all things. May he bless you by
whose grace it was said to me at the body of St. Peter on the day of
my ordination:[3] 'Whatsoever you bless shall be blessed, and whatsoever you loose upon earth shall be loosed in heaven.'[4] Amen.

To all the faithful in Germany   (*1077, Feb.–Mar.*)

Gregory, bishop, servant of the servants of God, to his most beloved brothers and sons in Christ the archbishops, bishops, dukes,
counts, and other princes, together with all the people of the
kingdom of Germany who are defending the Christian faith and
religion, greeting and apostolic blessing.

As we have intimated to you in earlier letters and by the words
of our envoys,[5] because we know that, moved by true obedience
and reverence for apostolic sovereignty, you have shown yourselves
in a manner worthy of God to be defenders of righteousness and
because we confidently repose our hope upon your loyalty and
counsels, we have set out on a journey to you beset by many
dangers as well as difficulties, against the wish of almost all our
advisers except Matilda, that most dear and faithful daughter of

at Canossa, a castle of Countess Matilda of Tuscany. Gregory afterwards remained in north Italy and returned to Rome in June.

J.L. 5019. MS.: Hugh of Flavigny, *Chron.*: Berlin, Deutsche Staatsbibl.
Phillipps 1870, fos. 118ᵛ–119ʳ, eleventh cent. Printed: Hugh of Flavigny,
Chron. ii, *M.G.H. Scr.* viii. 445–6. *Ep. coll.* no. 20, pp. 545–7.

---

[1] Cf. Acts 14: 21.   [2] Cf. Phil. 4: 1.   [3] 29 or 30 June 1073.
[4] A free citation of the Eucharistic Prayer of the order for episcopal ordinations: cf. *The Gelasian Sacramentary*, ed. H. A. Wilson (Oxford, 1894), p. 152.
Ordinations of all Roman clergy were performed in St. Peter's.
[5] Cf. nos. 17 and 18.

solum inter multa incommoda sed et pericula aggressi sumus.
Et peruenisse quidem potuissemus, si ducatum eo tempore, eo loco
quo constitutum erat ex uestra parte habuissemus. Cum autem
ex ipsa suspensione nostrae profectionis regi in Italiam properanti
ad nos perueniendi daretur occasio, uicti eius humilitate et
multimoda penitudinis exibitione, ab anathematis uinculo
absolutum in gratiam communionis eum recepimus, de cetero
nichil secum statuentes nisi quod ad cautelam et honorem omnium
uestrum fore putauimus.

Cumque Langobardorum episcopi totius negocii summam ad
communem conuentum et prudentiae uestrae consultationem
reseruatam esse cognoscerent, nec de suis culpis ea quam spera-
bant impunitate absolutionem consequi potuissent, quantam
superbiam quantosque maliciae conatus contra nos adorsi sint
ad dicendum quidem triste, ad audiendum est abhominabile, cum
illi qui in aecclesia Dei columpnae esse debuerunt non modo
in compage corporis Christi nullum locum teneant sed pertinaciter
impugnatores et quantum ad se destructores existant. De rege
uero, ut in his quae nobis promisit simpliciter aut obedienter
ambulauerit non multum letari possumus, praesertim cum ex
eius praesentia pessimi quique contra nos et apostolicam sedem
plus audaciae quam terroris pro perpetrata iniquitate habeant.

Inter hec uestra consilia expectantes tandem per filium nostrum
Rapotonem,[1] quem ad uos misimus, hoc uos uelle et postulare
cognouimus, si quomodo ad partes uestras transire possimus,
atque id ut cautius fieri possit cum regis consilio et adiutorio
agere studeamus. Nos itaque, sicut uobis mandauimus, uestrae
uoluntati atque consiliis in omnibus secundum beneplacitum
Dei satisfacere cupientes, id ipsum per nuncios nostros cum rege
statuere atque coaptare operam damus. Verum quo animo ipse
nobis et uobis in hac causa consentire debeat, ante missionem
huius legationis, quoniam rex a nobis longe distabat, praenoscere
non potuimus, sed mox ut cognouerimus uobis intimare non
tardabimus.

Scitote igitur quoniam haec est uoluntas et desiderium nostrum,
ut uel consensu regis uel si eo nolente fieri possit ad uos pro
communi utilitate et salute omnium uestrum pertranseamus. Quod
si, peccatis et prauorum studiis obstantibus, fieri nequiuerit,

---

[1] Perhaps the same Radbod as Gregory referred to in *Reg.* iii. 10, 8 Dec.
1075, p. 267. Cf. p. 38 n. 2 above.

St. Peter. We indeed might well have arrived, if we had received an escort from you at the appointed time and place. But the delay of our departure gave the king, as he hastened to Italy, a chance of reaching us. We were overcome by his humility and the manifold tokens of his repentance, and we freed him from the bond of excommunication and restored him to the grace of communion; but we made no other arrangements with him save such as we thought would be for the safety and honour of you all.

When the Lombard bishops learnt that a settlement of the whole question had been reserved for a general convention and for your deliberation, and when they could not secure absolution for their sins with the impunity that they hoped for, the excess of pride and of wicked endeavours with which they rose up against us is sad to relate and shocking to hear: these men who should be pillars in the church of God not only retain no place in the structure of Christ's body but are constantly its attackers and would-be destroyers. As for the king, we cannot greatly rejoice that he should do nothing more than obediently walk in the ways which he has promised us; particularly because by reason of his presence certain most wicked men show boldness rather than fear towards us and the apostolic see for the wickedness which they have committed.

Meanwhile as we awaited your counsels we at length learnt through our son Radbod,[1] whom we sent to you, that you wished us to find means of somehow coming to your country, and that you asked us to endeavour to act with the king's advice and help so that we might do so the more safely. We therefore, desiring as we have told you to fulfil your wishes and counsels in all respects according to God's good pleasure, are endeavouring to make the necessary plans and arrangements with the king through our envoys. How far he may agree with us and you in this matter we are unable to foretell before the completion of this embassy, for the king is far distant from us; but as soon as we know we shall not delay to inform you.

You may be assured, then, that our will and desire is, whether with the king's agreement or if it were still possible even against his will, to travel to you for the common good and for the salvation of you all. If the sins and designs of wicked men hinder us so that this cannot be, I shall though absent continually beseech Almighty God with steadfast prayers that he may confirm your hearts and

absens tamen omnipotentem Deum obnixis semper orabo precibus ut corda uestra et fidem in omni gratia et uirtute confirmet, et ita in omnibus uestra consilia et facta dirigat ut libertatem christianae religionis indefessa uirtute defendere, et ea quae ad statum et gloriam nobilissimi regni uestri Deo dignissima et uobis utilissima sunt prouidere possitis et exequi. Vos autem in proposito defendendae iustitiae quod pro nomine Christi et aeterna retributione incepistis ita persistite ut ad coronam tam sancti tam Deo placiti certaminis, Deo donante, pertingere ualeatis.

Plura uobis per scripta misissemus, nisi quod tales ad uos nuncios direximus quibus indubitanter credere potestis, in quorum ore quidquid in epistola minus continetur et pro uobis uel ad uos cor nostrum habet posuimus. Amen.

20

(To Archbishop Hildolf of Cologne): Gregory exhorts him to restore the vill of Klotten to the monastery of St. Nicholas, Brauweiler   *(1077, Jan.–June)**

Non eget, o fili, Deus offerri quicquam ex iniustitia sibi, quia, ut legimus, sic ei fiunt uictimae ex rapina quomodo si mactet quis filium in patris praesentia.[1] Patratorem quidem multorum bonorum agnouimus fratrem nostrum Annonem archiepiscopum. Sed tamen in hac parte minime defendendus est non errasse, dum quod beato Nicolao praeripuit sanctae genitrici Dei gratum holocaustum aestimauit, dicente Domino per prophetam: 'Quia ego Dominus diligens iudicium, et odio habens rapinam in holocausto.'[a2] Nec fas est a fidelibus credi, matrem discrepare a uoluntate filii; dum id prorsus constet utrisque proprium atque commune, eadem

---

^a holocaustum O

---

* Klotten, on the Moselle, was given to the monastery of Brauweiler, her family burial-place, by Queen Richeza of Poland, daughter of its founder, Palsgrave Ezzo of Lorraine (died 1034). Richeza herself desired to be buried at Brauweiler. However, Archbishop Anno of Cologne (1056–75) sought to undermine Ezzo's family who were his political rivals in the Rhineland. In 1063, when Richeza's body was brought for burial, he caused it to be placed in the church of St. Mary *ad Gradus*, in Cologne, which he had himself founded in 1057. At the same time he transferred the ownership of Klotten from Brauweiler to St. Mary's. Abbot Wolfhelm of Brauweiler (1065–91) began a long struggle to recover it, which continued into the time of Archbishop Hildolf (1076–8) when he appealed directly to Gregory.

faith in every grace and virtue, and that he may so direct your
counsels and deeds in all things that you may defend the liberty of
the Christian religion with unwearied valour, and that you may
both seek and accomplish all that is most worthy of God and bene-
ficial to yourselves for the welfare and glory of your most illustrious kingdom. May you so continue in the course of defending
righteousness upon which you have embarked for the name of
Christ and for an eternal reward that by the gift of God you may
eventually attain to the crown in a contest which is so holy and
pleasing to him.

We would have written more to you had we not sent to you such
envoys as you may without hesitation believe. We have committed
to their words such things as are not contained in this letter and
are in our heart to support and guide you. Amen.

(To Archbishop Hildolf of Cologne)   (*1077, Jan.–June*)

My son, God did not prescribe that anything should be offered to
him from the fruits of unrighteousness, for as we read, if sacrifices
are offered to him from the spoils of robbery it is as if someone
should immolate a son in his father's presence.[1] We indeed know
our brother Archbishop Anno to have been a doer of many good
deeds. But in one respect he can by no means be acquitted of
wrongdoing—I mean when he considered what he seized from
St. Nicholas to be an acceptable offering to the holy Mother of
God; because the Lord says through his prophet: 'For I the Lord
love judgement; I hate robbery for burnt offering.'[2] Nor is it rightly
to be believed by the faithful that the Mother should differ from
the will of the Son, when it is in truth their common property both

The date of this fragment is determined by Conrad's statement in Wolfhelm's
Life that Gregory wrote 'tunc forte consistentem in confinibus Alpium', i.e.
after Canossa: *cap.* 14, ed. Wilmans, p. 187. The *Life* was written at Brauweiler
between 1110 and 1123; no MS. of it survives.

J.L. 5043. MS.: none. Printed: Conrad, *Vita Wolfhelmi abbatis Brunwilarensis*, ed. Surius, *De probatis sanctorum historiis*, ii. 787 (*O*); ed. Wilmans,
cap. 14, *M.G.H. Scr.* xii. 187–8. *Ep. coll.* no. 22, p. 548.

---

[1] Cf. Ecclus. 34: 24 (20).   [2] Isa. 61: 8.

uelle et eadem nolle.[1] At tu, ne defendendo iniustitiam uidearis offendere Deum, tolle de medio quod, alias licet bonus, hic male consultus commisit episcopus Anno, ne et illius detrimentum sit coronae et tibi occasio culpae.

21

To the Christians of Narbonne, Gascony, and Spain: Gregory commends his legate, Bishop Amatus of Oléron

(1077, c. 28 June)*

Gregorius episcopus seruus seruorum Dei omnibus archiepiscopis, episcopis, abbatibus, regibus, principibus, clericis quoque ac laicis, in Narbonensi Gallia, Guasconia, Hispaniaque regione, salutem et apostolicam benedictionem.

Dilectissimi fratres et filii, prudentiae uestrae manifestissime notum est, quod Romana ecclesia hanc consuetudinem habuit ab ipsis suae fundacionis primordiis, ut ad omnes partes quae christianae religionis titulo praenotantur suos legatos mitteret; quatinus ea quae gubernator et rector eiusdem Romanae ecclesiae per suam praesentiam expedire non praeualet, uice sua legatis concessa, monita salutis ac morum honestatem per eos cunctis per orbem terrarum constitutis ecclesiis nunciaret, easque apostolica doctrina in omnibus quae sacrae religioni conueniunt diligenter instrueret. Proinde horum presentium portitorem, uenerabilem confratrem nostrum A. episcopum, ad partes uestras dirigimus ut, quae ibi uicia eradicanda sunt a fundamento euulsis, plantaria uirtutum Deo auctore sollerti uigilantia plantare procuret. Quem sicut nostram immo beati Petri presentiam uos suscipere apostolica auctoritate iubemus; ac sic pro reuerentia apostolicae sedis cuius nuncius est, uos in omnibus sibi*a* obedire atque eum audire mandamus ut propriam faciem nostram seu nostrae uiuae uocis

---

a *Erasure and gap of 22 mm. B*

---

* Amatus, bishop of Oléron (1073–89), was Gregory's standing legate in southern France from 1077. This letter is of especial interest as a statement of Gregory's view of the history and authority of papal legates. It was written with, or soon after, Gregory's letter to the kings and magnates of Spain: *Reg.* iv. 28, 28 June 1077, pp. 547–8.

severally and together to will and not to will the same things.[1] But
as for you, in order that you should not seem to offend God by
defending unrighteousness, you should undo what Bishop Anno,
though he was otherwise a good man, in this case did ill-advisedly,
so that it may neither detract from his heavenly crown nor be for
you a cause of guilt.

To the Christians of Narbonne, Gascony, and Spain
(1077, c. 28 June)

Gregory, bishop, servant of the servants of God, to all archbishops,
bishops, abbots, kings, princes, both clerks and laymen, in Narbonne, Gascony, and the region of Spain, greeting and apostolic
blessing.

Most beloved brothers and sons, you very well know that the
Roman church from the very earliest days of its foundation has
had the custom of dispatching its legates to all regions which are
distinguished by the name of the Christian religion. Thus, matters
which the governor and ruler of the Roman church cannot manage
to deal with by his own presence he can entrust on his behalf to
legates, and through them proclaim the precepts of salvation and
integrity of life to all the churches established throughout the
world; and he can diligently instruct them by apostolic doctrine in
all matters which belong to our holy religion. We are accordingly
sending to your parts the bearer of this letter, our venerable
brother Bishop Amatus, in order that whatever errors should there
be eradicated he may utterly root out, and that by God's grace he
may attend with careful vigilance to planting the seed-beds of the
virtues. We charge you by apostolic authority to receive him as
though we, or rather St. Peter, were present; out of reverence for
the apostolic see whose messenger he is, we charge you to obey
and heed him in all things as though you saw our own face or

J.L. 5042. MS.: Paris, Bibl. nat. lat. 3839*A*, fos. 146ᵛ–147ʳ, twelfth cent. (*B*).
Printed: Marca, *Dissertationes de concordia sacerdotii et imperii*, ed. Baluze, ii.
185.[2] *Ep. coll.* no. 21, pp. 547–8.

---

[1] Cf. Sallust, *Catilina*, 20. 4.
[2] Baluze described the letter as copied 'ex uetusto codice MS. S. Albini
Andegauensis'.

oracula. Scriptum est enim: 'Qui uos audit, me audit'.[1] Agite itaque prudenter ac religiose; et sic uos oboedientes Deo et sancto Petro in omnibus exhibite, quatinus, ipso apostolorum principe interueniente, utriusque uitae gloriam et felicitatem consequi mereamini.

22

To the clergy and people of Tours: Gregory informs them that he has restored Archbishop Ralph to his episcopal and priestly office and provides for legates to visit Tours and hear complaints against him   (*1078, after 9 Mar.*)*

G. episcopus seruus seruorum Dei clero et populo Turonensi salutem et apostolicam benedictionem.[a]

Archiepiscopi uestri diligenter causam discutientes, intelleximus non legali accusatione eum ab officio suspensum fuisse, praesertim cum eadem causa ante praesentiam antecessoris nostri uenerandae memoriae pape Alexandri[2] discussa et determinata fuerit. Quapropter apostolica auctoritate episcopale et sacerdotale officium sibi reddidimus. Verum quia aliqui uestrum contra eum adhuc submurmurant et eadem infamia uigilat, decreuimus legatum nostrum R.[3] cum legato Diensis episcopi[4] ad uos dirigere, quatenus certam et meram ueritatem huius rei a uobis percipiant. Vnde interdicimus ex parte beati Petri apostolorum principis ut nullus uestrum[b] contra eum dubium testimonium aut quod canonice possit improbari proferre praesumat, sed quod uidit et audiuit et certissimum habet ueraciter dicat. Nam si aliter praesumptum fuerit, et testis falsitatis damnabitur et causa illa ulterius in perpetuum non discutietur.

---

[a] The address of this letter also appears in Paris, Bibl. nat. Duchesne 4, fo. 110[v]
[b] nostrum B

---

* This letter was evidently written with or soon after Gregory's letter to Bishop Hugh of Die after the Lent council of 1078 regarding a number of French bishops: *Reg.* v. 17, 9 Mar. 1078, pp. 378–80; it repeats his directions in it about Archbishop Ralph of Tours. Ralph was suspended as a consequence of the council of Poitiers in Jan. 1078; see Hugh of Die's letter to Gregory: *R.H.F.* xiv, no. 80, pp. 615–16.

Not in J.L. MS.: Budapest, Bibl. nat. Széch., lat. med. aeui 5, fo. 9[v],

actually heard us speaking. For it is written: 'He who hears you hears me.'[1] Act, then, prudently and in good conscience. So show yourselves obedient in all things to God and to St. Peter that, by the intervention of the prince of the apostles himself, you may deserve to obtain glory and felicity both in this life and in the next.

To the clergy and people of Tours (*1078, after 9 Mar.*)

Gregory, bishop, servant of the servants of God, to the clergy and people of Tours, greeting and apostolic blessing.

After a careful investigation of the case of your archbishop we have discovered that he was not suspended from office by due process of law, especially since his case had been tried and settled before our predecessor of respected memory, Pope Alexander.[2] We have accordingly by apostolic authority restored to him his episcopal and priestly office. But because some of you are still murmuring against him and ill report remains current, we have decided to send to you our legate Roger[3] with an envoy of the bishop of Die,[4] in order that they may learn from you the plain and simple truth of this matter. Therefore, on behalf of St. Peter, the prince of the apostles, we forbid any of you to dare to bring against him questionable testimony or anything that can be canonically impugned; rather, let each say truthfully what he has seen and heard and is altogether sure about. For if anyone should dare to do otherwise he will stand condemned as a false witness, and this case will never at any time be further discussed.

c. 1100 (*B*). Printed: Morin, *R.B.* xlviii (1936) no. 10, pp. 126–7. Ramackers, *P.U.F.* v, no. 9, p. 71.

---

[1] Luke 10: 16.   [2] Alexander II (1061–73).
[3] Roger, subdeacon of the Roman church: cf. *Reg.* v. 20, 24 Apr. 1074, pp. 383–4.   [4] Hugh.

23

To Archbishop Ralph of Tours: Gregory reminds him of his favourable reception when he came to Rome and communicates his plans to send to his region legates for whom he desires his help   (*1078, summer*)*

G. episcopus seruus seruorum Dei R. Turonensium uenerabili archiepiscopo salutem et apostolicam benedictionem.[1]

Specialem[a] quandam fiduciam, frater dilecte, mater tua sancta Romana aecclesia in fraternitate tua habere promeruit, quippe quam affabiliter et quanta dilectione cum ad se uenisti te susceperit, quam paterne te correxerit, potest et debet prudentia tua recordari, immo haec sic fixa et sic detecta ut euelli et caligari nullo modo possint, ante oculos cordis semper habere; ac ideo decet te ut fructum debitae reuerentiae in omnibus quibus tuo auxilio indiguerit sibi prudenter et ex fide exhibeas, ut talium fructuum flagranti odore mater tua intellegat qua dilectione sibi adhaereas. Recordari debes et uales, frater, cum a nobis recesseris, nos iam ad partes tuas legatos destinasse, quorum unum fore domnum abbatem Cluniacensem,[2] nisi necessarium obstaculum impediret, disposueramus. Verum longe aliter euenit quam excogitaueramus,[b] et multorum hereticorum heresis sole clarius detecta mutare sententiam super legatis extorsit. Vnde nobis uisum est domnum Hugonem Diensem episcopum, ac Hubertum sanctae Romanae aecclesiae et nostrum dilectum filium,[3] cum his quoque domnum Wicardum Bisontiensem clericum,[4] ad partes tuas mittere et uicem curae nostrae illis iniungere. Qui conuocatis ex uobis qui ad aecclesiastica negotia tractanda idonei noscuntur una uobiscum diligenti examinatione perquirant, et inquisitis quibuscumque potuerint iuste determinationis finem imponant. Quod si contigerit aliquam partem spiritu superbiae ductam nolle oboedire iustitiae, ei parti quae iustitiam habet fauere uos uolumus et praecipimus, rebellem autem aecclesiastica censura arceri apostolica auctoritate

---

[a] Speciale *B*   [b] excogitauerimus *B*

* Gregory refers to Ralph's visit to Rome in 1074: cf. no. 3 above, and *Reg.* ii. 19, 15 Nov. 1074, pp. 151–2.
Not in J.L. MSS.: Budapest, Bibl. nat. Széch. lat. med. aeui 5, fos. 8ᵛ–9ʳ, *c.* 1100 (*B*). Paris, Bibl. nat. Duchesne 4, fos. 109ᵛ–110ʳ, seventeenth cent.

To Archbishop Ralph of Tours (*1078, summer*)

Gregory, bishop, servant of the servants of God, to Ralph, the venerable archbishop of Tours, greeting and apostolic blessing.[1]

Beloved brother, your mother the holy Roman church has deserved to enjoy your very special confidence. For in truth you can and should remember how kindly and with how great love she received you when you came to her, and how paternally she corrected you; indeed, you should always keep these things so steadfast and unveiled in the forefront of your mind that they may in no way be eradicated or obscured. It is proper for you so prudently and faithfully to show her the fruits of due reverence in whatever way she may need your help, that by the good savour of these fruits your mother may know how lovingly you cleave to her.

You should and surely do remember, brother, that when you left us we had already determined, unless an unavoidable obstacle prevented us, to send legates to your parts, one of whom would be the lord abbot of Cluny.[2] Matters in fact worked out quite otherwise than we planned, and the error of many heretics, exposed more clearly than daylight, forced us to change our plan as regards our legates. It consequently seemed good for us to send to your parts and to commission on our behalf the lord Hugh, bishop of Die, and Hubert, a beloved son of the Roman church and of ourself,[3] and with them also the lord Wighard, a clerk of Besançon.[4] When they have gathered together those of you whom it is fitting to summon for the discussion of church business, they are to make diligent inquiry in concert with you and, having made inquiry of whomever they can, they are to bring the affair to an end in a just manner. Should it happen that either side is so led by the spirit of pride that it will not obey righteousness, we desire and command you to uphold the side which exhibits righteousness, and we command by apostolic authority that the disobedient party should be

Printed: Ramackers, *Q.F.I.A.B.* xxiii (1931-2), no. 6, pp. 38-40. Morin, *R.B.* xlviii (1936), no. 6, pp. 123-4. Ramackers, *P.U.F.* v, no. 10. pp. 72-3.

---

[1] For the date see Schieffer, *Die päpstlichen Legaten in Frankreich*, p. 109, n. 116.
[2] Hugh (1049-1109).   [3] Subdeacon of the Roman church.
[4] Perhaps the Wighard, *decanus* of Notre-Dame and Saint-Paul, Besançon, mentioned in *M.G.H. Dipl.* vi, no. 196 (1067), pp. 253-4.

praecipimus. Preterea si contigerit aliquo impedimento inter-ueniente praedictos legatos ibi simul esse non posse, eis autem qui fuerint, etiamsi unus tantum, similiter ac si simul essent fraternitatem tuam cauere atque ut mihi si praesens essem oboedire praedicta auctoritate monemus. Vnde praedicto Huberto quem in Brittanniam praemisimus cum ad fraternitatem tuam uenire contigerit in praedictis ut mihi cauere, in praedictis ut mihi oboedire ammonemus et nobis commissa auctoritate iubemus. Si qua uero sibi fuerint necessaria ut homini qui a Roma usque ad Brittanniam elaborauerit et a Brittannia usque Romam, si Deus dederit, modis elaborat uenire, caritas tua sibi impertiri nostri causa et amore non dubitet, ut ex filii intelligatur dilectione quanto matrem amplectaris amore.

24

To Bishop Hugh of Langres: Gregory rebukes him for his part in excommunicating Count Robert of Flanders without the authority of himself or his standing legate, Bishop Hugh of Die, to whom he orders him to explain his action; Gregory further warns him not to hinder pilgrims to Rome

(*1078*, c. *25 Nov.*)*

G. episcopus seruus seruorum Dei H. Lingonensi episcopo salutem et apostolicam benedictionem.

Peruenit ad aures nostras quod tu et Hubertus huius aecclesiae legatus Rodbertum Flandrensium comitem excommunicastis. Vnde mirari satis nequeo quod tale aliquid sine praecepto meo et uicarii mei consensu, Diensis uidelicet episcopi, quia aliter fieri a uobis non debuit, facere praesumpsistis, praecipue cum in talibus aut illis partibus uobis nullas uices meas concesserim. Quapropter apostolica auctoritate tibi praecipio ut ad Diensem episcopum uenias et cur hoc ausus sis facere in ueritate sibi aperias, quatinus Deo largiente quod iustum sibi uisum fuerit super hac tua culpa

---

* This letter was written with, or soon after, *Reg.* vi. 7, 25 Nov. 1078, pp. 407–8, in which Gregory charged Hugh of Die to inquire into the excommunica-tion of Count Robert of Flanders (1071–93) by his legate, Hubert, subdeacon of the Roman church, and Bishop Hugh of Langres (c. 1065–85). See also *Reg.* vii. 1, 23 Sept. 1079, pp. 459–60: this suggests a possible alternative date for

constrained by ecclesiastical censure. If, furthermore, it should happen that by reason of some hindrance the legates whom we have named cannot be present together, we warn you by apostolic authority to obey whoever may be present, even though only one, as if all of them were there, and to show obedience as you would to myself if I were to hand. We accordingly warn and charge you by the authority committed to us that, whenever Hubert whom we have sent to Brittany reaches you, you heed and obey him as you would myself in the matters to which I have referred.

Seeing that he has laboriously journeyed from Rome to Brittany and now if God pleases is likewise returning from Brittany to Rome, should he stand in any need let your charity not hesitate to supply him as a service of love to ourself, so that your care for the son may make clear with how much love you embrace the mother.

To Bishop Hugh of Langres   (1078, c. 25 Nov.)

Gregory, bishop, servant of the servants of God, to Bishop Hugh of Langres, greeting and apostolic blessing.

It has come to our ears that you and Hubert, legate of the Roman church, have excommunicated Count Robert of Flanders. I am beyond measure astonished that you should have dared to do such a thing without my own order and the consent of my vicar, the bishop of Die; for otherwise you had no right to act as you did, particularly as I have given you no authority to act on my behalf in such matters or in those parts. I therefore charge you by apostolic authority to go to the bishop of Die and tell him truthfully why you have dared to do this, so that by God's help he may determine what seems to him just as regards this offence of yours.

the present letter, and Gregory's similarly worded rebuke to Hubert for the presumption of ignoring his standing legate tells in its favour. But the lack of an express reference in *Reg.* vii. 1 to Count Robert's excommunication makes a date following *Reg.* vi. 7 more likely; further, Gregory may have delayed his complaint to Hubert because he expected Hubert's early return to Rome: cf. *Reg.* vii. 1, p. 458.

J.L. 5087. MSS.: Saint-Omer, Bibl. municip. 188, fo. 86ʳ, twelfth cent. Boulogne, Bibl. municip. 72, fo. 271ʳ, twelfth cent. Printed: Duchet, *Additions et corrections*, p. 14. Loewenfeld, *N.A.* vii (1882), 161.

decernat. Monemus quoque te et monendo praecipimus ut pere-
grinis ad limina apostolorum uenientibus uel redeuntibus nullam
omnino iniuriam facere uel fieri in partibus tuis permittas, unde
iam multas contra te querimonias audiuimus, si gratiam Dei et
sanctorum apostolorum et nostram benedictionem et dilectionem
habere desideras.

25

*To the supporters of both parties in Germany: Gregory
announces his intention, following his November council at
Rome, to send legates in order either to establish peace or to
punish those who foster division, and forbids anyone to resist
their work*   (*1078, late Nov.*)*

Gregorius episcopus[a] seruus seruorum Dei omnibus archiepiscopis
et episcopis[b] in Teutonico atque in Saxonico[c] regno commorantibus
omnibusque principibus,[d] cunctis etiam maioribus atque minoribus
qui non sunt excommunicati et[e] obedire uoluerint, salutem et
apostolicam benedictionem.

Quoniam ex lite et dissensione que tandiu inter uos sunt[f]
maximum in sancta ecclesia periculum, maximum undique inter
uos detrimentum[g] fieri cottidie[h] cognoscimus, idcirco uisum est
nobis, uisum est[i] et fratribus nostris in concilio congregatis,
summo desiderio estuare,[j] summa ope elaborare pro uiribus
quatinus idonei nuntii[k] tam religione quam scientia pollentes e
latere sedis apostolice ad partes uestras mitterentur,[l] qui religiosos
episcopos, laicos, etiam pacis amatores et iustitie in partibus
uestris commorantes ad hoc opus ydoneos congregarent, qui,
Domini gratia preeunte, die et loco ab illis statuto tam ipsi quam

---

[a] *om.* episcopus *LP*   [b] *om.* et episcopis *T*   [c] *om.* atque in Saxonico
F   [d] *om.* omnibusque principibus *V*   [e] *om.* omnibusque principibus . . .
excommunicati et; *add* si *F*   [f] *om.* que tandiu inter uos sunt; *add* uestra
P   [g] *om.* maximum undique . . . uos detrimentum *P*   [h] *om.* cottidie *V*
[i] *om.* uisum est *VF*   [j] *om.* summo desiderio estuare *P*   [k] legati *VF*
[l] mitteremus *VT*

---

* On 15 Mar. 1077, as a sequel to Canossa, the German princes met at
Forchheim and elected Duke Rudolf of Swabia as anti-king. Thereafter Gregory
sought to arbitrate between Henry IV and Rudolf into whose parties Germany
was divided. At his Nov. council in 1078 envoys of both kings promised that his

We also both warn and charge you to permit neither yourself
nor others in your parts in any way to harm pilgrims travelling to
and from the threshold of the apostles—for we have already heard
many complaints against you on this score—if you would have the
favour of God and the holy apostles, and our own blessing and
love.

To the supporters of both parties in Germany
(1078, late Nov.)

Gregory, bishop, servant of the servants of God, to all the archbishops and bishops living in the German and the Saxon kingdoms
and to all the princes, also to all both greater and lesser who are
not excommunicated and who are disposed to obey, greeting and
apostolic blessing.

We know that from the dispute and discord which have for so
long prevailed amongst you there daily arise grave danger to holy
church and grave harm to you on all sides. It has therefore seemed
good to us, as it has also seemed good to our brothers assembled in
council, to make every endeavour and to labour to the limit of our
resources by sending to your parts on behalf of the apostolic see
suitable legates, outstanding for religion as for knowledge. Their
task will be to gather together the religious bishops, laymen, and
lovers of peace and righteousness who live in your parts and are
suitable for such a work. By the help of God's grace, at a time and
place which they decide, together with others whom we must still

legates should suffer no hindrance: *Reg.* vi. 5*b*, 19 Nov. 1078, pp. 400–1. Gregory
thereafter sent the present letter in which he reiterated the decrees of his Lent
council of 1078, renewed in Nov.: *Reg.* v. 14*a*, pp. 370–1. For the dispatch of
Gregory's legates, Peter of Albano and Ulrich of Padua, cf. nos. 27 and 31
below.

J.L. 5106. MSS.: Paul of Bernried, *Greg. VII uita*: Vienna, Österr. Nationalbibl. 336, fo. 265ᵛ, twelfth cent. (*V*); Heiligenkreuz, Stiftsbibl. 12, fo. 196ʳ, twelfth
cent.; Admont, Stiftsbibl. 24, fo. 141ʳ, twelfth cent.; Melk, Stiftsbibl. 492, fo. 110ʳ,
twelfth cent. Trier, Bistumsarch. Abt. 95, 93, fo. 62ʳ, eleventh cent. (*T*). Bruno,
Sax. bell.: Leipzig, Universitätsbibl. 1323, fos. 47ᵛ–48ʳ, c. 1500 (*L*). *Annalista
Saxo*: Paris, Bibl. nat. lat. 11851, fo. 183ᵛ, twelfth cent. (*P*). Hugh of Flavigny,
Chron.: Berlin, Deutsche Staatsbibl. Phillipps 1870, fo. 122ʳ, eleventh cent.
(*F*). Printed: Paul of Bernried, *Greg. VII uita, cap.* 105, *Pont. Rom. uitae*, ed.
Watterich, i. 537–8. Bruno, *Sax. bell. cap.* 118, edd. Lohmann and Schmale,
pp. 382–4. *Annalista Saxo, a.* 1080, *M.G.H. Scr.* vi. 717. Hugh of Flavigny,
Chron. ii, *M.G.H. Scr.* viii. 449–50. *Ep. coll.* no. 25, pp. 550–1.

quos ipsis adhuc iungere debemus aut pacem componant aut ueritate precognita super illos qui sunt tanti discidii causa canonicam censuram exerceant. Verum quoniam nonnullos, diabolico instinctu confectos, iniquitatis sue facibus ignitos, cupiditate inductos, discordiam potius quam pacem fieri et uidere desiderantes fore non ignoramus, statuimus in hac synodo ad hanc eandem formam^m sicut et in preterita, ut nulla umquam persona alicuius potentie uel dignitatis, siue magna siue parua, siue princeps siue subiectus, aliqua presumptione presumat legatis nostris obsistere, et postquam ad uos peruenerint de componenda pace contraire, nec postea contra interdictum illorum alter in alterum audeat insurgere, sed usque ad diem ab illis statutam firmam pacem omnes sine ulla occasioneⁿ et fraude obseruent. Quicumque autem hec statuta^o nostra ulla presumptione uiolare temptauerint, anathematis uinculo eos ligamus et^p non solum in spiritu uerum etiam in corpore et in omni prosperitate huius uite apostolica auctoritate innodamus et uictoriam eis in armis auferimus, ut uel sic saltem confundantur et duplici contritione conterantur.

26

To the Anti-king Rudolf and his followers in Saxony: Gregory encourages them to be steadfast in their adversities and instructs them concerning the see of Magdeburg

(*1079, late Feb.*)*

G. episcopus seruus seruorum Dei R. regi omnibusque secum in regno Saxonum commanentibus, tam episcopis quam ducibus et comitibus necnon maioribus et minoribus, peccatorum absolutionem et apostolicam benedictionem.

Cum Veritas ipsa dicat omnium qui propter iusticiam persecutionem paciuntur regnum esse celorum,[1] et Apostolus clamet

---

^m *om.* ad hanc eandem formam *P*   ⁿ sine contradictione *F*   ^o instituta *TPF*   ^p *om.* eos ligamus et *F*

---

* As a sequel to Gregory's council in 1078 the Saxons wrote a letter to him— the fourth of a series of five which Bruno preserves (out of their probable order) in the *Sax. bell.*—complaining about Gregory's long hesitation over the German crown, and about the devastation of Germany: *cap.* 112, cf. *capp.* 108, 114–15, 110. The first part of this letter should be read in their light. The second part relates to the see of Magdeburg, vacant by the death of Archbishop Werner after

associate with them, the legates would be charged either to establish peace or else after finding out the truth to pass canonical sentence upon those who are the cause of this great division. As we know that some, led astray by the devil's promptings, kindled by the torches of his wickedness, and misled by covetousness, long to create and to see discord rather than peace, we have decreed in this council in the same terms as at our last, that no person at all of whatever power or dignity, great or small, prince or subject, should by any boldness dare to resist our legates and work against them after they have reached you to establish peace. Nor thereafter let anyone dare to rise up against his neighbour in defiance of their prohibition, but until the day which they appoint let all men keep unbroken peace without any pretence or deceit. If any should venture to infringe these statutes of ours by their boldness we bind them by the chain of excommunication; by apostolic authority we do so not only in their soul but also in their body and in respect of every success of this life, and we take from them victory in arms, so that by this means at least they may be confounded and consumed by the destruction of both body and soul.

To the Anti-king Rudolf and his followers in Saxony
(*1079, late Feb.*)

Gregory, bishop, servant of the servants of God, to King Rudolf and all his supporters in the kingdom of Saxony, bishops, dukes, and counts, both greater men and lesser, absolution from their sins and apostolic blessing.

Since the Truth himself says that the kingdom of heaven belongs to all who suffer persecution for righteousness's sake,[1] and the

the battle of Mellrichstadt (7 Aug. 1078). According to the *Annalista Saxo* its clergy wished one of their own number, Gunther, to succeed: *a.* 1079, *M.G.H. Scr.* vi. 716–17.

J.L. 5108. MSS.: Wolfenbüttel, Hzg.–Aug. Bibl. Helmstedt 1024, no. 23, fo. 48ʳ⁻ᵛ, twelfth cent. (*W*). Bruno, *Sax. bell.*: Leipzig, Universitätsbibl. 1323, fos. 48ᵛ–49ʳ, *c.* 1500 (*L*). *Annalista Saxo*: Paris, Bibl. nat. lat. 11851, fo. 184ʳ, twelfth cent. (*P*). *Codex Udalrici*: Zwettl, Stiftsarch. 283, p. 116, twelfth cent. (*Z*); Vienna, Österr. Nationalbibl. 398, fo. 66ʳ, twelfth cent. (*C*). Printed: *Codex Udalrici*: Eccard, *Corpus hist.* ii, no. 153, col. 156; Jaffé, *Mon. Bamb.* no. 59, pp. 125–6. Hahn, *Coll. mon.* i. 117–19. *Ep. coll.* no. 27, pp. 553–4. Bruno, *Sax. bell. cap.* 120, edd. Lohmann and Schmale, pp. 384–6. *Annalista Saxo, a.* 1080, *M.G.H. Scr.* vi. 717–18.

---

[1] Cf. Matt. 5: 10.

neminem nisi qui legitime certauerit posse coronari,[1] nolite, filii mei, in hoc qui uos iam multo tempore exagitat bellico furore deficere; nolite per ullius fallentis persone mendacia de nostro fideli adiutorio dubitare; sed magis magisque pro tuenda ueritate ecclesiastica, pro defendenda uestre nobilitatis libertate,[a] labori iam citius[b] finiendo incumbite et ex aduerso ascendendo uos et corpora uestra quasi murum pro domo Dei[c] opponere[2] satagite. Quicquam iam in duabus sinodi nostre conuentionibus de rege R. et de Heinrico statutum sit, quidque ibi de pace et concordia regni etiam cum iuramentis sit diffinitum, per litteras nostras et per legatos uestros[d] nisi forte capti sint apertissime potestis agnoscere;[3] et si quid adhuc remanserit per episcopos Metensem[4] et Patauiensem[e5] et abbatem Augustensem[6] qui nobiscum finem rei prestolando morantur cum ad uos ipsi peruenerint quasi in promptu habetis audire. Postremo hoc uos ignorare nolumus, quia omni qua oportet instantia tum orationis nostre assiduitate tum officii nostri grauitate et prospiciendo consulere et consulendo prospicere uestre necessitati non dubitamus.

Audiuimus[f] de uestro archiepiscopatu Magdeburgensi indisciplinatam quorundam eiusdem ecclesie filiorum pro acquirendo seculari habitu[g] et honore obortam fuisse contentionem et eorundem, quod[h] etiam erubescendo dicimus, bonam et conuenientem ad hoc opus non esse conuersationem. Quos modis omnibus ex precepto[i] Dei omnipotentis et sancti Petri et nostro ne sibi in locum damnationis culmen arripiant regiminis prohibete et Dei dignum dispensatorem prout ius postulat et ordo cum nostra uoluntate et apostolica benedictione et communi omnium bonorum tam clericorum quam laicorum electione disponite. Vos enim ipsi nostis quod in constituendis episcopis neglecta sanctorum patrum instituta hunc qui modo funditur sanguinem genuerunt, et adhuc nisi prouideantur peiores prioribus errores fouendo parturiunt.

---

[a] liberalitate *W*   [b] *om.* iam citius *W*   [c] Israel *LP*   [d] nostros *W*
[e] Papyensem *ZC*   [f] *This paragraph is lacking in LP*   [g] ambitu *W*
[h] qui *W*   [i] excepto *W*

[1] Cf. 2 Tim. 2: 5.   [2] Cf. Ezek. 13: 5.
[3] Cf. the Lent and Nov. councils of 1078: *Reg.* v. 14a, pp. 368–73, vi. 5b, pp. 400–1, 403; also no. 25.
[4] Hermann (1073–90).
[5] Altmann (1065–91). For the presence at the Lent council 1079, of Bishops Altmann of Passau and Hermann of Metz, see Bernold, *Ann. a.* 1079, *M.G.H.*

Apostle declares that no one can be crowned except he strive law-fully,[1] do not be disheartened, my sons, in the storm of war which has now for so long assailed you; do not because of the lies of any deceitful man have doubts about our faithfulness in helping you. Devote yourselves more and more to safeguarding Christian truth and to defending the liberty of your noble race by a labour which must now very soon have an end, and rising superior to your mis-fortunes zealously set yourselves and your bodies as a wall for the house of God.[2] What has already been decided about King Rudolf and Henry in two meetings of our council and what was established there upon oath concerning the peace and concord of the kingdom you can fully learn from our letters and your envoys, unless perchance they were captured;[3] if anything remains still unsettled you will hear more definitely about it from the bishops of Metz[4] and Passau[5] and the abbot of Reichenau,[6] who are remaining with us to await the outcome of the matter, when they come to you. Finally we would have you know that we do not waver in consider-ing and providing for your needs with all due urgency, both by our zealous prayers and by the authority of our office.

With regard to your archiepiscopal see of Magdeburg, we have heard that a disorderly strife has arisen amongst some of the clergy of Magdeburg who would seize its worldly trappings and honour, and—we speak the words with shame—that their manner of life is not good and fitting for such a responsibility. By command of Almighty God, of St. Peter, and of ourself you must by all means forbid them to grasp the highest office for themselves to their own damnation; and, as right and order require, you should provide a steward who is pleasing to God with our consent and apostolic blessing and after public election by all good men, both clergy and lay. For you yourselves know that it was neglect of the rulings of the holy fathers in appointing bishops which led to this present bloodshed and that, unless these rulings are respected, the outcome will be a multiplication of evils still worse than the former ones.

Scr. v. 316. The *Codex Udalrici* refers instead to Bishop Ulrich of Padua (1064–80); cf. no. 31.

[6] Abbot Ekkehard of Reichenau (*Augia*) (1071–88) is intended: cf. *Reg.* vi. 18, 14 Feb. 1079, pp. 429–30. The text refers in error to Augsburg (*Augusta*).

27

To the Anti-king Rudolf and his German supporters:
Gregory explains the difficulty of his negotiations with
Henry IV and gives more detailed counsel about the see of
Magdeburg   (*1079, Mar.–Apr.*)*

G. episcopus seruus seruorum Dei R. regi et omnibus secum christianam religionem defendentibus salutem et apostolicam benedictionem.

Quod regnum Theutonicorum, hactenus inter omnia mundi regna nobilissimum, iam uideo incendiis cedibus et rapinis deuastari confundi et annullari, quam magnus exinde cordi meo dolor insideat, quam continuus in uisceribus meis me gemitus afficiat, testis est ille solus qui omnium hominum corda scrutatur[1] et probat. Deferuntur enim mihi iam sepius legationes H.,[2] cum per proprios nuncios tum per cognatos et aliarum terrarum principes et affines, modo omnem oboedientiam promittendo, modo per uaria ingenia sollicitando id a me summo conamine cupientes efficere quo me ad uotum suum suis partibus ualeant inclinare. Verum quia hinc inde et Romana grauitas et apostolica mansuetudo me per mediam iusticiae uiam incedere cogit, omnibus quibus possum modis hoc oportet intendere, quomodo ueram a falsa iusticiam, perfectam a ficta oboedientiam iudicio sancti Spiritus ualeam discernere et rato ordine ad finem usque perducere. Haec uero et alia, si propitio Deo ad uos sani perueniunt, legati mei[3] melius quam hae litterae uiua uoce testificabuntur et docebunt.[a]

Audiui quidem a legato meo B.[4] metropolim Magdeburgensem iamdiu esse uiduatam[5] et adhuc peruersa quorundam contentione ne desponsari possit fuisse turbatam. His modis omnibus ex praecepto Dei omnipotentis et sancti Petri et meo ne praeualeant resistite, et domui Dei dignum dispensatorem per ostium[6] introducere

---

[a] *The remainder of the letter survives only in T*

* Following closely upon no. 26 this letter deals further with the same topics.
J.L. 5107. MSS.: Trier, Bistumsarch. Abt. 95, 93, fo. 62[r], eleventh cent. (*T*).
Bruno, *Sax. bell.*: Leipzig, Universitätsbibl. 1323, fo. 48[r–v], *c.* 1500. *Annalista Saxo*: Paris, Bibl. nat. 11851, fos. 183[v]–184[r], twelfth cent. Printed: *Ep. coll.* no. 26, pp. 552–3. Bruno, *Sax. bell. cap.* 119, edd. Lohmann and Schmale, p. 384. *Annalista Saxo, a.* 1080, *M.G.H. Scr.* vi. 717.

To the Anti-king Rudolf and his German supporters
(1079, Mar.–Apr.)

Gregory, bishop, servant of the servants of God, to King Rudolf
and all who with him are defending the Christian religion, greeting
and apostolic blessing.

He alone who searches and tries the hearts of all men[1] is witness
of the great grief which dwells in my heart and of the continual
sorrow which vexes my inmost self, because I see the kingdom of
Germany, hitherto the most glorious of all the kingdoms of the
world, now wasted, ravaged, and destroyed by fire, slaughter, and
rapine. Messages have been repeatedly brought to me from Henry,[2]
sometimes by his own envoys and sometimes by his kinsmen or
by princes of other lands or by his neighbours, now promising
full obedience and now trying to inveigle me by various devices,
in their pertinacious attempts to get from me some concession by
which, as he desires, they could bend me to his side. But because
Roman gravity on the one hand and apostolic mercy on the other
compel me to proceed by the middle way of righteousness, I must
by all means in my power see to it that, by the judgement of the
Holy Spirit, I can distinguish true righteousness from false and
perfect obedience from feigned, and continue in the proper course
until the end. These and other matters my legates,[3] if by God's
mercy they reach you safe and sound, will testify and explain more
satisfactorily by word of mouth than I can set down in this letter.

Now I have heard from my legate Bernard[4] that the metropolitan
see of Magdeburg has for long been vacant,[5] and that it is still
troubled by the wicked strife of men who would prevent its being
duly filled. By the commandment of God, St. Peter, and myself
you should resist these men by all means lest they should have their
way, and by the common consent and choice of all religious men—
archbishops and bishops, clerks and laymen—you should take
steps to bring in by the door[6] a worthy steward over the house of

---

[1] Cf. Rom. 8: 27.   [2] Henry IV.
[3] Probably Cardinal Peter of Albano (1072–89) and Bishop Ulrich of Padua,
sent to Germany after the Lent Council of Feb. 1079; but cf. no. 26.
[4] Abbot Bernard of Saint-Victor, Marseilles (1064–79).
[5] By the death of Archbishop Werner.   [6] Cf. John 10: 1.

cum communi omnium religiosorum tam archiepiscoporum quam episcoporum nec non etiam clericorum et laicorum consensu et electione procurate. Quodsi meis uultis adquiescere consiliis, audio enim inter uos esse quosdam boni testimonii uiros, A. scilicet Goslariensem decanum,[1] G. Bertaldi ducis filium,[2] H. Sigifridi comitis filium,[3] quorum unum me praecipiente et consentiente eligite et in archiepiscopum praenominatae aecclesiae ordinate. Si uero in his tribus qui dignus sit non poterit inueniri, in contritione cordis orando et ieiunando ad Deum conuertimini, rogantes ut, sua reuelante gratia, persona quae huic negocio sit conueniens possit ostendi, hoc proculdubio scientes, quia sicut illum qui ambitu saecularis potentiae inordinate intrauerit, uinculo excommunicationis alligabo, ita quoque eum qui canonice intronizatus fuerit a peccatis absoluo et apostolica benedictione benedico.

28

To the monks of Monte Cassino: Gregory reproves their carelessness in allowing the men of Prince Jordan of Capua to rob them of money deposited with them, and places their church under an interdict (*1079, Apr.*)*

Gregorius episcopus seruus seruorum Dei dilectis in Christo filiis sancti Benedicti monachis salutem et apostolicam benedictionem.

Audiuimus, quod sine grauissimo dolore dicere non possumus, quosdam homines a Iordano*a* principe suggestione diaboli missos secretarium uestrum intrasse et quaedam commissa

---

a Iordane *M*

---

* This and the following letter relate to an incident in which men of Prince Jordan of Capua (1078–90), in whose principality Monte Cassino lay, took from the monastic church money deposited there by Bishop Dodo of Grosseto (Roselle) (*c.* 1060–*c.* 1079). In *M* the following explanatory note is added:

Hoc autem accidit pro Rosellano episcopo. Nam idem episcopus non paruam pecuniam huic commendauerat loco. Iordanus autem princeps missis militibus praecepit ut eandem sibi deferrent pecuniam. Fratres autem ad haec, 'Pecuniam quae sancto Benedicto credita est nos alicui uiuencium minime damus, sed eam super corpus eius ponimus: inde qui praesumpserit auferat.' Milites autem tollentes thesaurum de altario ad principem deferunt. Quo

God. If you would follow my advice, I hear that there are amongst you certain men of good report, I mean A. dean of Goslar,[1] Gebhard son of Duke Berthold,[2] and Hartwig son of Count Siegfried:[3] elect one of them by my command and sanction, and consecrate him to be archbishop of the vacant church. But if none of these three be found worthy, you should turn to God in humbleness of heart, praying and fasting, and asking that his grace may so enlighten you that a person who is fitted for this task may be made known. You may be quite sure that, just as I shall bind by the chain of excommunication anyone who climbs in against due order by the devices of worldly power, so I also absolve from his sins and confer an apostolic blessing upon him who shall be canonically enthroned.

To the monks of Monte Cassino (*1079, Apr.*)

Gregory, bishop, servant of the servants of God, to his beloved sons in Christ, the monks of St. Benedict, greeting and apostolic blessing.

We have heard tidings of which we cannot speak without the deepest sadness, that men sent at the devil's prompting by Prince Jordan have entered your sanctuary and with unheard-of boldness

accepto statim idem princeps tanti auctor sceleris lumen amisit et usque ad mortem ita permansit.

Cf. *Chronica Mon. Casinensis*, iii. 46, *M.G.H. Scr.* vii. 736; *Reg.* vi. 5*b*, 18 Nov. 1078, p. 403, and vi. 37, 21 Apr. 1079, pp. 453–4; in the second of these letters Gregory referred to Jordan's sacrilegious action as having occurred 'nouissime'. Gregory no doubt regarded the interdict as in part a punitive measure against the prince and his men, for it deprived them of the intercessory support which, to the eleventh-century mind, was an essential service of monks to temporal rulers and lords. Its effect would in his view be similar to the sanction expressed at the end of no. 25 above and elsewhere in his letters.

J.L. 5129. *I.P.* viii, p. 148, no. 117. MS.: Monte Cassino, Archivio abbaziale, *Petri Diaconi Registrum*, no. 34, fo. 21ᵛ, twelfth cent. (*M*). Printed: Gattula, *Historia abbatiae Cassinensis*, i. 149. Tosti, *Storia della badia di Montecassino*, i. 427–8. *Ep. coll.* no. 29, pp. 555–6.

---

[1] Unknown.
[2] Gebhard, son of Berthold I of Zähringen, duke of Carinthia (1061–77); later bishop of Constance (1084–1110).
[3] Hartwig, archbishop of Magdeburg (1079–1102), son of Count Siegfried of Spanheim.

uobis inaudita temeritate detulisse. In quo facto nimiae negle-
genciae et acriter ulciscendae timiditatis uos et abbatem uestrum[1]
arguere possumus. Et grauius aduersum uos commoueri deberemus
nisi ea qua uos semper caritate dileximus detineremur. Siquidem
tolerabilius nobis uideretur uillas et castella sancti Benedicti
in praedam et direpcionem dari quam ut sanctus locus et per totam,
ut credimus, christianitatem famosus et uenerabilis tante igno-
minie periculo subiaceret. Quapropter, huius temeritatis noxam
inultam esse non ferentes, praesertim cum locum uestrum uiolatum
esse et exemplo huius facinoris deteriora posse uobis contingere
perpendamus, ammonemus ut diuinum officium in ecclesia beati
Benedicti non faciatis, sed altaria omnia que intus sunt de-
tegentes quantum sit huiusmodi uiolacionis periculum quosque
cognoscere faciatis. Si enim in ecclesia sancti Petri humano
sanguine respersa diuinum officium non sine diligenti recon-
ciliatione celebratur,[2] multo magis istud quod in ecclesia beati
Benedicti perniciosius commissum est competenti indiget ex-
piacione. Vos itaque omnipotentem Dominum instanter depre-
camini ut tristiciae mentis nostrae dignetur super hac re nobis
consolacionem impendere, et ad reparandam in omni uestram[a]
dignitatem modis quibus decet nos instruere.

29

To the monks of Monte Cassino: Gregory raises the interdict
which he had placed upon their church and desires their
prayers   *(1079, Apr.)**

Gregorius episcopus seruus seruorum Dei uenerabili congregacioni
Casinensis cenobii salutem et apostolicam benedictionem.

Nuper, dilectissimi fratres, nos uiolencia sacrilegii huic reueren-
tissimo loco illata compulsi uestrae ecclesiae officium ob tantum
facinus irrogatum interdiximus. Verum quia ascensionis Domini
sollempnitas[3] toto uenerabilis orbe nunc imminet, nolentes iam

---

   [a] uestrae *M*

* J.L. 5130. *I.P.* viii, p. 148, no. 118. MS.: Monte Cassino, Archivio
abbaziale, *Petri Diaconi Registrum*, no. 35, fo. 21ᵛ, twelfth cent. Printed: Gattula,
Historia abbatiae Cassinensis, i. 149. Tosti, *Storia della badia di Montecassino*,
i. 428. *Ep. coll.* no. 30, pp. 556–7.

have made off with things which were entrusted to you. As regards
this deed we must reprove you and your abbot[1] for great carelessness and for fearfulness to punish it severely. We should be still
more seriously aroused against you were we not held back by the
charity with which we have always loved you. For it would seem
to us more tolerable that St. Benedict's estates and fortresses
should be given over to plunder and pillage than that a holy place
which is famous and held in honour, as we believe, through the
whole of Christendom, should be exposed to the risk of so great
an outrage. We cannot, therefore, allow an offence of such boldness to pass unavenged, especially when we consider that your
house has been invaded and that the example of this crime may
cause worse things to happen to you. We charge you not to hold
divine service in the church of St. Benedict but to strip all the
altars in it, and so make known to those whom it concerns how
great is the peril of such a profanation. For if, when St. Peter's
church was besprinkled with human blood divine service was not
performed until there had been a careful purification,[2] how much
more does such an outrage as this, performed so sacrilegiously in
the church of St. Benedict, call for proper expiation. Do you therefore earnestly beseech Almighty God that he will mercifully grant
us relief from our sorrow of mind over this matter, and that he
will guide us in fully restoring your honour by whatever means
are appropriate.

To the monks of Monte Cassino   (*1079, Apr.*)

Gregory, bishop, servant of the servants of God, to the venerable
congregation of the monastery of Cassino, greeting and apostolic
blessing.

Recently, most beloved brethren, we were compelled by the
sacrilegious violence which was used against this most venerable
place to lay an interdict upon the services of your church by reason
of the great outrage of which it was the victim. However because
the festival of the Lord's Ascension,[3] which is honoured in all the

---

[1] Desiderius (1058–86).
[2] St. Peter's, Rome. The incident referred to is not otherwise known.
[3] 2 May 1079.

propter alicuius scelus in tanto festo tam religiosum locum officio
pietatis carere, decreuimus et uos et eundem locum interdicto
absoluere. Quapropter apostolica mansuetudine ducti reddimus
et ecclesiae ministerium cultumque religionis et deuocioni
uestrae licenciam celebrandi. Volumus eciam atque rogamus
caritatem uestram ut nostri memores pro nobis preces fundatis
ad Dominum, pro statu quoque sanctae Romane ecclesiae
rectori rerum cotidie supplicetis, nec non tam pro inimicis quam
eciam pro amicis dilectionis affectu omnipotentem Dominum
deprecari sedulo memineritis et studeatis; nec non et pro illo[1]
qui tam sanctissimum locum toto mundo famosum uiolauit
preces effundite, ut Deus det illi cor penitens et sic eum ad se
conuertat ut in hac uita et futura mereatur graciam Dei optinere.

30

*To Bishop Hugh of Die: Gregory instructs him, as his
standing legate, regarding various matters with which he is
to concern himself*   (*1079, Apr.–May*)*

Gregorius episcopus seruus seruorum Dei dilecto in Christo
fratri Hugoni Diensi episcopo salutem et apostolicam benedictionem.

Quod diuina clementia pacem ecclesiae tuae restituit, sciat
fraternitas tua nos haud aliter quam de nostra aut sanctae Romanae
ecclesiae tranquillitate et profectu gaudere.[2] Et hoc in mente tua
semper maneat fixum quod omnipotens Deus, cui fideliter
famulari toto cordis affectu anniteris, et temporalem tibi pacem
competenter conciliabit et sempiternam meritis tuis bonus
remunerator retribuet.

De discordia uero quam inter Lugdunensem archiepiscopum[3]
et abbatem Cluniacensem[4] significasti, nouerit dilectio tua nos non
parum grauari sed, quoniam inter religiosos iurgia sunt, multum
profecto dolere.[5] Quippe quorum concordia multis prodesse

---

* J.L. 5147. MS.: Hugh of Flavigny, *Chron.*: Berlin, Deutsche Staatsbibl.
Phillipps 1870, fo. 101ʳ, eleventh cent. Printed: Hugh of Flavigny, *Chron.* ii,
M.G.H. Scr. viii. 421. *Ep. coll.* no. 32, pp. 559–61.

[1] Jordan of Capua.
[2] Nothing is known of Hugh's dealings in his own diocese at this time.

world, is now at hand and because we are indeed unwilling that at this great feast so sacred a place should on account of anyone's offence be denied the performance of worship, we have decided to free both you and your monastery from the interdict. Accordingly, inspired by apostolic clemency we restore to your church the ministry and service of religion, and to yourselves the right to officiate. We also desire and ask you to be mindful of us and to pray for us to the Lord, and also to intercede daily to the ruler of all things for the well-being of the holy Roman church. Will you always continue diligently to pray with loving devotion to the Almighty Lord not only for your enemies but for your friends as well. Also you should offer your prayers for him who has invaded so holy and world-famous a place,[1] that God may give him a contrite heart and so turn him to himself that he may deserve to have God's grace in this life and in the next.

To Bishop Hugh of Die   (*1079, Apr.–May*)

Gregory, bishop, servant of the servants of God, to his beloved brother in Christ Bishop Hugh of Die, greeting and apostolic blessing.

You may be sure that we rejoice because God's mercy has restored peace to your church no less than we should rejoice for the quiet and benefit of ourself or of the holy Roman church.[2] And let it always remain firmly established in your mind that Almighty God, whom you have sought to serve faithfully with all the love of your heart, will both secure for you a sufficiency of this world's peace and, as one who gives ample recompense, will also reward you with eternal peace according to your merits.

Now concerning the strife of which you have told us between the archbishop of Lyons[3] and the abbot of Cluny,[4] you may be sure that we are in no small way distressed but indeed greatly grieve that there should be contention between these religious men.[5] In truth, just as concord between them could and would

---

[3] Gebuin (1077–82).   [4] Hugh.
[5] The genesis of this quarrel, which arose from complaints by the church of Mâcon about Cluny's invasion of their temporal rights and in which the archbishop supported Mâcon, is also illustrated by *Reg.* vi. 33, 14 Apr. 1079, pp. 446–7; the present letter was probably written soon after it. See Cowdrey, *The Cluniacs and the Gregorian Reform*, pp. 51–3.

poterat et debuerat, non dubium est quin de eorum dissensione plurimis oriatur et futura sit grauis pernicies. Vnde fraternitatem tuam uigilare oportet et curare necesse est religiosos tibi uiros adhibere et ita praefatos ex parte nostra super concordia conuenire. Denique quicumque illorum iustitiae secundum consilia uestra non adquieuerit, nulli sit ambiguum quod nos in eum grauiter, omnis personae acceptione postposita, commouebimur.

Quia uero in partibus praeordinatis concilium celebrare non potuistis utiliter,[1] competens arbitramur ut aptum locum diligentia uestra inueniat ubi synodo congregata Remensis archiepiscopi[2] causa diligenter examinetur. Et quidem si idonei accusatores et testes inuenti fuerint quod obicitur ei canonice comprobantes, quam iustitia dictauerit sententiam dare absque hesitatione uos uolumus. Alioquin si tales personae fuerint quae recipi rationabiliter nequeant, quoniam turpis de eo fama non solum Galliam uerum etiam fere totam repleuit Italiam, sex episcopis quorum uita non notetur infamia assumptis sibi, si potest excuset se, et sic purgatus cum pace in aecclesia sua et propria dignitate remaneat.

Preterea eum[3] quem per saecularem potestatem, id est regiam inuestituram, Cabilonensem aecclesiam intrasse significastis, ab omni regimine et spe ipsius aecclesiae alienum esse, apostolica auctoritate decernimus. Quodsi post huius nostrae interdictionis sententiam ad huius regiminis dignitatem aspirauerit, quid beati Petri gladius ualeat sine dubio experietur et in perpetuum nulla sibi aecclesiastici regiminis fiducia relinquetur. Ad comprimendum etiam multorum conatus illicitos qui obstinatis animis non timent Deum postponere et superbiam suam propalare, diabolum imitantes qui, non contentus sibi concessis, dum illicite nititur ad altiora et quod habebat iuste amisit, uolumus uos in omnibus conciliis uestris uice nostra omnes illos excommunicare quicumque apostolicae sedis decreto super hac re synodaliter constituto obuiare praesumpserit et de manu alicuius layci inuestituram aecclesiarum susceperit,[4] ut his saltim terroribus a spe ambitionis suae reducti non aliunde ut fures et latrones ad ouile dominicum

---

[1] i.e. the proposed council of Troyes.   [2] Manasses I (1069–80).

[3] Uncertain, but possibly the Frotger who witnessed a royal charter of 1085 as bishop of Châlon(-sur-Saône): *Recueil des actes de Philippe Ier, roi de France (1059–1108)*, ed. M. Prou (Paris, 1908), no. 113, pp. 285–7; cf. *G.C.* iv. 886–7.

[4] Besides the lost decree of Gregory's Lent council in 1075 he legislated against lay investiture in Nov. 1078: *Reg.* vi. 5*b*, p. 403.

benefit many, so there is no doubt that serious harm may and will arise to very many people from their disagreement. So you should be vigilant and careful to associate with yourself other religious men and by this means call them together on our behalf to bring about a settlement. But should either of them not yield to righteousness according to your counsels, let no one doubt that, putting aside all respect of persons, we shall be gravely angered against him.

Because you could not conveniently hold a council where it had been intended,[1] we think it requisite that you should find a suitable place for holding another council at which the case of the archbishop of Rheims[2] may be carefully investigated. If suitable accusers and witnesses can be found to provide canonical proof of the allegations against him, we desire you without hesitation to pass the sentence which righteousness requires. If on the other hand they turn out to be such persons as cannot rightly be heard, since an evil report of him has filled not only France but also almost all of Italy let him associate with himself six bishops whose lives are untainted by ill repute and, if he is able, absolve himself; thus purged let him remain peacefully in his church and episcopal office.

Next, as for the man[3] who, as you have informed us, has invaded the church of Châlon by means of the temporal power, that is by royal investiture, we decree by apostolic authority that he is deprived of all rule over and claim to this church. If after this sentence of ours prohibiting him he should still aspire to this office and dignity he will undoubtedly feel the full force of St. Peter's sword and for the future all hope of office in the church will be denied him. Furthermore, to curb the lawless endeavours of the many who with obstinate minds do not fear to ignore God and exhibit their own pride, thereby imitating the devil who, not content with what had been given him, snatched lawlessly at higher things and justly lost what he had, we wish you at all your councils which you hold on our behalf to excommunicate all who dare to ignore the decree of the apostolic see on this matter which was enacted by our council, and who receive the investiture of churches from the hand of any layman.[4] By these sanctions, at least, we would recall them from the prompting of their own ambition so that they do not like thieves and robbers climb into the Lord's sheepfold by another way; we would instead have men summoned

ascendant, sed ex habitatione religiosorum uirorum inuitati, ut boni et idonei pastores per ostium ingrediantur.[1]

Admonemus etiam ut uiscera pietatis tuae dolor et calamitas Linguonensis aecclesiae penetret, et una cum fratre nostro Lugdunensi archiepiscopo modis quibus ualetis, tantis eius periculis consulatis, illud principaliter perficientes ut in decanum qui fere omnia illius aecclesiae officia pessimis studiis arripuit iustam sententiam detis, et officia illa per religiosos et competentes uiros pure deinceps administrentur.[2]

31

To Cardinal Peter of Albano and Bishop Ulrich of Padua: Gregory intimates that he has heard complaints about their conduct as legates, and counsels them about their dealings with Henry IV and with others in Germany

(*1079, July–Oct.*)*

Gregorius episcopus seruus seruorum Dei dilectis in Christo fratribus et coepiscopis Petro Albanensi et Odelrico Patauiensi salutem et apostolicam benedictionem.

Sunt multi, quibus tamen non credimus, qui de legatione uestra murmurare incipiunt, suspicantes uos aliter uelle incedere quam a nobis praeceptum est, et alterum uestrum nimis simpliciter, alterum uero non adeo simpliciter acturum esse causantur.[3] Quapropter diligentissima circumspectione cauendum est uobis ut utramque suspicionem possitis extinguere. Quod ita facile cum Dei adiutorio proueniet, si praecepta nostra ante mentis oculos

---

* Gregory sent these two legates to Germany after his Lent council in 1079 to endeavour to determine which of the two kings truly and which only apparently fulfilled the demands of righteousness (*iustitia*): cf. nos. 25–6 above. For their journey, see *Reg.* vi. 38, 16 June 1079, pp. 454–5; Berthold, *Ann. a.* 1079, *M.G.H. Scr.* v. 318–22. At Whitsun Henry IV received them at Regensburg, and eventually it was agreed that a conference of both parties should take place at Würzburg on 15 Aug. to discuss peace. But the legates' meeting with Henry seems so to have aroused the suspicions of Rudolf and the Saxons that their party did not come. The legates declined Henry's suggestion that they should therefore declare themselves against Rudolf. They returned to Rome in or soon after Oct. with their mission unaccomplished.

Gregory's statement in this letter that Abbot Ekkehard of Reichenau had been captured 'nuper' may indicate a date in July for this letter (Giesebrecht,

from the dwelling of the righteous who may enter by the door like good and worthy shepherds.[1]

Finally we urge you to allow the affliction and adversity of the church of Langres to excite your compassion and, in concert with our brother the archbishop of Lyons, to do everything possible to help it in its great perils. Above all you should see that you pass just sentence upon the dean who by the basest arts has seized almost all the offices of this church, and that these offices may for the future be blamelessly administered by religious and suitable men.[2]

To Cardinal Peter of Albano and Bishop Ulrich of Padua
(1079, July–Oct.)

Gregory, bishop, servant of the servants of God, to his beloved brothers in Christ and fellow bishops Peter of Albano and Ulrich of Padua, greeting and apostolic blessing.

There are some who are—although without convincing us— beginning to complain of your conduct as legates: they imagine that you are minded to act otherwise than we commissioned you, alleging that one of you is likely to behave all too guilelessly but the second by no means so guilelessly.[3] You should accordingly maintain the utmost vigilance if possible to quench either suspicion. With God's help this will easily happen if you always keep

Meyer von Knonau), or in July–Aug. (Miccoli). But *nuper* would permit a lapse of some weeks or even months, and any date up to that of *Reg.* vii. 3 is possible (Jaffé, Fliche): cf. note 3 below.

J.L. 5137. *G.P.* ii, pt. 1, p. 32, no. 14, and ibid., p. 156, no. 24. MS.: Hugh of Flavigny, *Chron.*: Berlin, Deutsche Staatsbibl. Phillipps 1870, fos. 122ʳ–123ʳ, eleventh cent. (*F*). Printed: Hugh of Flavigny, *Chron.* ii, *M.G.H. Scr.* viii. 450–1. *Ep. coll.* no. 31, pp. 557–9.

---

[1] Cf. John 10: 1–2.
[2] Nothing further is known about these matters.
[3] Gregory refers to the possibility of his legates having acted against their instructions in *Reg.* vii. 3, 1 Oct. 1079, p. 462. Henry IV's diploma of 23 July 1079 for the church of Padua suggests that Ulrich may have used his position as legate to secure the king's confirmation of his church's privileges: *M.G.H. Dipl.* vi, no. 312, pp. 410–12. Cf. Berthold's statement that the legates came to Würzburg 'muneribus . . . corrupti' (*Ann. a.* 1079, *M.G.H. Scr.* v. 321).

semper teneatis et nichil aliud praesumatis efficere nisi quod nos uobis noscimur non modo nudis uerbis uerum etiam litteris inculcando mandasse.

Volumus autem ut de causa regum uel regni, siue etiam de Treuirensi[1] uel Coloniensi[2] et Augustensi[3] electis, uel de omnibus istis qui inuestituram per manum laicam acceperunt, nullum praesumatis exercere iudicium, summumque uobis studium sit, si rex adquieuerit uobis de statuendo colloquio et pace firmanda in regno et de restituendis episcopis in sedibus suis, et hec eadem cito ad nos aut per uos ipsos aut per certos legatos annunciare ut tot et tales personas possimus illuc ad constitutum tempus dirigere qui ad tantum negocium determinandum ualeant una uobiscum Deo auxiliante sufficere.

Interim uero sic uos utrique parti communes et ab omni suspicionis neuo, quantum in uobis est, cum diuinae gratiae adiutorio exibete immunes, ut iustitiae semper et nullomodo partibus faueatis sicut habetis formam nostram, qui uidelicet, postquam iudicium tanti huius negocii in manu beati Petri commissum est, nichil aliud uobis testibus intendimus nisi ut per iustitiae semitam incedamus. Ad nullam partem sinceritatem apostolicae discretionis infleximus, nullis promissionibus aut terroribus cessimus, nec aliud umquam Deo protegente acturos nos esse confidimus.[4]

Preterea specialiter uobis de abbate Augiense iniungimus, qui nuper ad apostolorum limina ueniens non solum captus est sed etiam in loco eius quidam est tyrannice subrogatus, ut ea bona sua quibus exspoliatus est, expulso inuasore illo, restitui faciatis.[5] Qui tamen, postquam de his quae perdidit fuerit pleniter inuestitus, si quid contra illum habet aliquis,[a] paratus erit in nostro iudicio respondere; non enim debet ab alio aliquo iudicari qui in apostolica sede scitur a memet consecratus.[6] Et certe grauis fuit praesumptio manum in eum ponere qui tanto erat priuilegio munitus. Quodsi

---

[a] aliquid F

---

[1] Egilbert (1079–1101), nominated 6 Jan. 1079.
[2] Sigewin (1079–89), nominated after Christmas 1078.
[3] Siegfried II (1077–96), invested 8 Sept. 1077.
[4] This paragraph, except the first two words, is quoted without significant variation by Paul of Bernried, *Greg. VII uita*, cap. 103, *Pont. Rom. uitae*, ed. Watterich, i. 536.
[5] In 1079 Abbot Ekkehard of Reichenau was taken prisoner at Borgo San Donnino, near Parma; Henry IV installed as abbot in his place Ulrich, abbot

our commands clearly before your mind's eye and venture to do
nothing save what we are known to have charged you with, not
only in our verbal instructions but also by letter.

It is our will that you should venture to pass no judgement in
the matter of the kings or the kingdom, nor again concerning the
bishops-elect of Trier,[1] Cologne,[2] and Augsburg,[3] nor concerning
all those who have received investiture at lay hands. You should
make every endeavour to see whether the king will agree with you
about holding a conference and establishing peace in the kingdom
and about restoring bishops to their sees, and you should speedily
inform us about these matters either in person or by reliable messengers, in order that we may dispatch there at the appointed time
sufficient suitable persons who may with God's help settle this
great matter in concert with us.

Meanwhile, then, show yourselves so well disposed towards
either side and as far as in you lies with the help of God's grace
so free from any taint of mistrust, that you may always promote
righteousness and in no way partisan interests; thereby you will
be following our own example, for, as you are witnesses, after
judgement in this great matter was entrusted to the hand of St.
Peter we have had no other purpose than to walk in the path of
righteousness. We have not deviated from the integrity of apostolic
judgement towards either side nor have we given way to any promises or threats, and we trust that, under God's protection, we
shall never act otherwise.[4]

We further specially charge you concerning the abbot of Reichenau. Not only was he himself taken captive as he was not long since
coming to the threshold of the apostles, but another was high-
handedly thrust into his place. See that you cause the invader to
be expelled and the possessions of which the abbot has been deprived to be restored.[5] If, after he has been fully invested with the
possession of what he has lost, anyone has a complaint against him,
he must be ready to answer before our own judgement; for anyone
who is known to have been consecrated by me at the apostolic see
must not be judged by anyone else:[6] it was indeed a grave presumption to lay hands upon one protected by so great a privilege. If in

of St. Gall and later patriarch of Aquileia (1086–1121): *Casuum sancti Galli
continuatio ii*, *M.G.H. Scr.* ii. 157.
  [6] Cf. *Reg.* i. 82, 6 May 1074, pp. 117–18; Berthold, *Ann. a.* 1074, *M.G.H.
Scr.* v. 276.

inuasor ille contra interdictum nostrum praedicto fratri sua restituere contempserit, confestim in eum uelut in rebellem et inuasorem ex auctoritate apostolica sententiam excommunicationis intendite. Quidquid autem agitis uel quidquid uobis contigerit litteris semper mandare et frequenter ad nos mittere procurate.

Omnipotens et misericors Deus, a quo bona cuncta procedunt, meritis beatae Dei genitricis Mariae dominae nostrae et beatorum apostolorum suorum Petri et Pauli, ab omni malo uos defendere et in omnem ueritatem inducere dignetur, quatinus quidquid agitis secundum timorem Dei et utilitatem sanctae ecclesiae feliciter[b] peragatis.

Inter omnia studiosissime Wormacensis episcopi mementote qui, cum esset diu ab ecclesia sua expulsus et ob id Romam ueniret ut auxilium apostolicae sedis adquireret, non solum nichil sibi profuit sed modo etiam peius incurrit.[1] Interim uos salutamus et rogamus ut sitis memores nostri memoris uestri apud Deum.

32

To the faithful of Italy and Germany: Gregory forbids them
to accept the ministrations of unchaste clergy and enjoins
obedience to the papacy   (*1079*)*

G. episcopus seruus seruorum Dei per totum Italicum regnum et Teutonicorum debitam sancto Petro obedientiam exhibentibus salutem et[a] apostolicam benedictionem.

Si qui sunt presbiteri uel diaconi uel subdiaconi[b] qui iaceant in crimine fornicationis, interdicimus eis ex parte omnipotentis Dei et auctoritate sancti Petri introitum aecclesiae usque dum peniteant et emendent. Si qui uero in peccato suo perseuerare

---

[b] fideliter; feliciter *interlined above* F   32 [a] *om.* salutem et *LM*
[b] presbiteri diaconi *with a short space and erasure between these words* K

---

* This letter has hitherto been known only from fragments, and is printed in its entirety for the first time. The only indication of its date is its position in Berthold and Marianus Scottus.

J.L. 5109. MSS.: Kremsmünster, Stiftsbibl. 27, fo. 202ᵛ, eleventh cent. (*K*). Florence, Bibl. Med. Laur. Plut. 16. 15, fo. 6ᵛ, eleventh cent. (*L*). Printed: Mansi, xx. 433–4. *Ep. coll.* no. 28, pp. 554–5. Fragments of this letter appear as follows: (i) Berthold, *Ann. a.* 1079: MS.: Sarnen, Kollegsbibl. Muri-Sarnen

defiance of our order the intruder will not restore our brother's possessions to him, you should forthwith by apostolic authority issue a sentence of excommunication against him as a rebel and intruder. But whatever you do or whatever may happen to you see that you always keep us informed by letters and communicate often with us.

May the almighty and merciful God, from whom all good things come, by the merits of our Lady Mary the blessed Mother of God and of his blessed apostles Peter and Paul vouchsafe to keep you from all evil and guide you into all truth, so that whatever you undertake you may happily accomplish according to the fear of God and the welfare of holy church.

In the midst of all these things remember most assiduously the bishop of Worms who, after he had been for long an exile from his church and therefore came to Rome to secure the help of the apostolic see, not only has gained no benefit for himself but now has fallen into still worse trouble.[1] Meanwhile we greet you and ask you to be mindful before God of us who are mindful of you.

To the faithful of Italy and Germany (*1079*)

Gregory, bishop, servant of the servants of God, to all who show due obedience to St. Peter throughout the whole kingdom of Italy and of Germany greeting and apostolic blessing.

As for priests, deacons, and subdeacons who are guilty of the crime of fornication, on behalf of Almighty God and by the authority of St. Peter we forbid them entry into the church until they repent and amend their ways. Should any prefer to remain in

10, fo. 138[r], twelfth cent.[2] Printed: *M.G.H. Scr.* v. 317 (Si qui sunt . . . oratio in peccatum). (ii) Marianus Scottus, *Chron. a.* 1079: MS.: Rome, Vatican Library, Palatino-Vaticanus 830, fo. 166[r], eleventh cent. (*M*). Printed: *M.G.H. Scr.* v. 561 (Gregorius episcopus . . . benedictionibus uestris). (iii) Gerhoh of Reichersberg, *Tractatus in psalmum X*: MS.: Reichersberg, Stiftsbibl. 1, fo. 106[r], twelfth cent. (*R*). Printed: *M.G.H. L. de L.* iii. 417–18 (Si qui sunt . . . obedire contempnit). Cf. *Epistola ad Innocentium papam, M.G.H. L. de L.* iii. 215.

---

[1] Adalbert (1070–1107), expelled from his see in 1074. He was captured after the battle of Mellrichstadt on 7 Aug. 1078 and taken before the king, but he later escaped: Bruno, *Sax. bell. cap.* 96, edd. Lohmann and Schmale, p. 340; *De unit. eccles. cons.* ii. 16, *M.G.H. L. de L.* ii. 231–2.

[2] I am most grateful to Dr. G. Tangl for sending me a photograph of this fragment.

maluerint, nullus uestrum officium eorum auscultare*c* praesumat; quia benedictio illis uertitur in maledictionem et oratio in peccatum, testante Domino per prophetam: 'Maledicam', inquit, 'benedictionibus uestris.'[1] Qui uero huic saluberrimo praecepto obedire noluerit idolatriae peccatum incurrit, testante Samuhele et beato Gregorio astruente: 'Peccatum enim ariolandi est repugnare*d* et scelus idolatriae nolle*e* acquiescere.'[2] Peccatum ergo paganitatis incurrit quisquis, dum Christianum se asserit, sedi apostolicae obedire contempnit. Vos queso apostolicis praeceptis obedite ut ad hereditatem celestis regni mereamini peruenire.

33

To Archbishop Ralph of Tours: Gregory informs him that he has released the bearer of the letter from excommunication and restored him to his office, commending him to the archbishop's care (*1079*)*

G. seruus seruorum Dei dilecto in Christo fratri R. Turonensi archiepiscopo salutem et apostolicam benedictionem.

Visis fraternitatis tuae litteris quibus praesentium litterarum*a* post longum et communem patriae suae errorem sententiam apostolicae sedis non sine condigna paenitentia recognouisse significasti, precibus tuis assensum praebuimus, ita ut paenitentia iniuncta ab excommunicatione absolueremus et officium quo se suspenderat sibi redderemus, si tamen aliud crimen unde ab officio arceri debeat sibi non contradicit, etsi in promissionibus quibus se obligauit, uidelicet sanctae Romanae aecclesiae praeceptis obedire, perseuerauerit. Vnde uolumus ut, quia gratiam et amorem apostolicae sedis consecutus est, consequatur deinceps tuae dilectionis augmentum et ad suum*b* suorumque filiorum exhortationis documentum, tanto quidem diligentius quanto regnum illud a praedicationibus expers et ad deteriora procliue esse dinoscitur; quatinus et ipse de his quae ad episcopalem pertinent

---

c audire *LR*   *d* om. repugnare *L;* non obedire *R*   *e* nulli *L*
33   *a* *Some such word as* portitorem *seems to be missing*   *b* suam *BD*

---

* In all probability the bearer was Bishop Silvester of Rennes (1076–96), suspended from office for simony at the council of Poitiers in Jan. 1078 and restored over a year later: *R.H.F.* xiv. 615; *G.C.* xiv. 745.

their sin let none of you dare to hear their offices. For their blessing is made a curse and their prayer a sin, as the Lord testifies through the prophet who says: 'I will curse your blessings.'[1] Anyone who will not obey this most healthful precept falls into the sin of idolatry, as Samuel witnessed and St. Gregory confirmed: 'For rebellion is as the sin of witchcraft, and stubbornness is as the offence of idolatry.'[2] Therefore anyone falls into the sin of heathenism who, while claiming that he is a Christian, disdains to obey the apostolic see. I beseech you, obey our apostolic precepts so that you may attain to your inheritance in the heavenly kingdom.

To Archbishop Ralph of Tours   (1079)

Gregory, servant of the servants of God, to his beloved brother in Christ, Archbishop Ralph of Tours, greeting and apostolic blessing.

We have seen your letter in which you assure us that, after the prolonged and general error of his countrymen, [the bearer] of this present letter has accepted the judgement of the apostolic see together with the appropriate penance. We have consented to your request by assigning him a penance and freeing him from excommunication, and by restoring him to the office from which he had brought about his own suspension; subject always to his not condemning himself by another crime deserving forfeiture of office and to his persevering in the promises by which he bound himself that he will obey the commands of the holy Roman church. We therefore desire that, because he has received the pardon and love of the apostolic see, he may henceforth receive the increase of your own favour and the guidance of your teaching for himself and for his children; they should be the more assiduously given as his kingdom is notoriously destitute of preaching and liable to lapse into evil ways. By this means he may be instructed in the duties of

Not in J.L. MSS.: Budapest, Bibl. nat. Széch. lat. med. aeui 5, fo. 8ᵛ, c. 1100, (B). Paris, Bibl. nat. Duchesne 4, fo. 109ᵛ, seventeenth cent. (D). Printed: Ramackers, Q.F.I.A.B. xxiii (1931–2), no. 10, p. 42. Morin, R.B. xlviii (1936), no. 4, p. 122. Ramackers, P.U.F. v, no. 14, pp. 75–6.

---

[1] Mal. 2: 2.
[2] Cf. 1 Reg. (1 Sam.) 15: 23; Gregory the Great, Moralia, xxxv. 28, P.L. lxxvi. 765. Cf. no. 10 above.

sollicitudinem informetur et talentum tibi creditum in discussione diuini examinis tibi duplicetur. Quod autem tibi litteras non misimus, non negligentiae nostrae sed, ut uidemur recordari, legatorum festinantiae potes ascribere.

34

To Abbot Anselm of Bec: Gregory encourages him to persist in prayer for himself and for the church, and asks him to remedy a complaint against one of his monks (c. *1079*)*

Gregorius episcopus seruus seruorum Dei Anselmo uenerabili abbati Beccensi[1] salutem et apostolicam benedictionem.

Quoniam fructuum tuorum bonus odor ad nos usque redoluit, quam dignas grates Deo referimus et te in Christi dilectione ex corde amplectimur, credentes pro certo tuorum studiorum exemplis aecclesiam Dei in melius promoueri et tuis similiumque tibi precibus etiam ab instantibus periculis Christi subueniente misericordia posse eripi. Nosti, frater: si iusti apud Deum praeualuit oratio, quid iustorum?[2] Praeualebit equidem, immo impetrabit sine dubio quod petierit.[3] Ipsius etiam ueritatis auctoritate cogimur hoc confiteri: 'Pulsate', inquit, 'et aperietur uobis, petite et accipietis.'[4] Pulsate simpliciter, petite simpliciter, haec etiam quae sibi placeant. Simplex est ostium, simplex dator; uult peti simplicia et quae sibi conueniant. Hoc modo aperietur, hoc modo accipietis, hoc modo iustorum exaudietur oratio. Vnde uolumus tuam tuorumque fraternitatem assidue Deum orare ut aecclesiam suam et nos qui ei licet indigni praesidemus ab instantibus hereticorum oppressionibus eripiat et illos errore dimisso ad uiam ueritatis reducat.

Querimoniam apud nos fecit quidam peregrinus de quodam conuerso tuo. 'Iustus Dominus et iusticias dilexit, aequitatem

---

* J.L. 5149. MSS.: London, Lambeth Pal. 59, no. 111, fo. 53[r-v], early twelfth cent. London, Lambeth Pal. 224, fos. 120[v]-121[r], early twelfth cent. (*A*). Paris, Bibl. nat. lat. 2478, fo. 44[r-v], twelfth cent. Paris, Bibl. nat. lat. 14762, fo. 88[r-v], twelfth cent. Cambridge, Corpus Christi Coll. 135, fo. 41[r-v], twelfth cent. Cambridge, Corpus Christi Coll. 299, fos. 73[r]-74[v], late twelfth cent. (*B*). Printed: Labbe and Cossart, *Sacrosancta concilia*, x. 410. *Ep.* ii. 31, *S. Anselmi opera*, ed. Gerberon, p. 353. *Ep. coll.* no. 33, pp. 561-2. *Ep.* 102, *S. Anselmi opera*, ed. Schmitt, iii. 235.

episcopal care, while when God examines your own stewardship
you may receive back doubled the talent which is committed to
you.

That we have sent you no letter you should put down not to
neglect on our part but, as we think it right to mention, to the haste
of the messengers.

To Abbot Anselm of Bec   (c. *1079*)

Gregory, bishop, servant of the servants of God, to Anselm, the
venerable abbot of Bec,[1] greeting and apostolic blessing.

Because the sweet savour of your good works has reached so far
as ourself we give due thanks to God and we cordially embrace
you in the love of Christ, confidently believing that by the example
of your endeavours the church of God has been led onwards in
virtue and that by the prayers of you and those like you she may
by the help of Christ's mercy also be delivered from the perils
which beset her. Consider, brother: if the prayer of one righteous
man availed with God, what shall that of many righteous do?[2] It
will assuredly avail, nay, will without doubt obtain what it desires.[3]
We are bound to affirm this upon the warrant of the Truth himself:
'Knock', he says, 'and it shall be opened to you; ask and you shall
receive.'[4] Knock in simplicity, ask in simplicity, even for things
which may please him. The door is simple, the giver is simple; he
desires to be asked for simple things and for things which may
beseem him. In this way it shall be opened, in this way you shall
receive, in this way the prayer of righteous men shall be heard. So
we wish you and your brothers to pray to God continually that he
may deliver his church and ourself who, unworthy though we be,
have the care of her, from the menacing attacks of heretics, and
that he may put away their error and restore them to the way of
truth.

A pilgrim has made a complaint to us about one of your monks.
'The Lord is righteous and he loves righteous deeds; his face looks

---

[1] Abbot of Bec (1078–93); archbishop of Canterbury (1093–1109).
[2] Cf. Jas. 5: 16.   [3] Cf. 2 Reg. (2 Sam.) 19: 38.
[4] Cf. Matt. 7: 7.

uidit uultus eius.'[1] Imitare Dominum tuum, imitare magistrum a quo habes doctrinam uitae. Praecipimus et nos ut ei iusticiam facias coram Huberto[a2] dilecto filio nostro et, ut intelleximus, amico tuo.

35

To Archbishop Ralph of Tours: Gregory asks him to investigate complaints made to him by Bishop Quiriacus of Nantes against Abbot William of Saint-Florent and Bishop Silvester of Rennes   (*1073–9, July*)*

G. episcopus seruus seruorum Dei dilecto in Christo fratri R. Turonensi archiepiscopo salutem et apostolicam benedictionem.

Dilectissimus confrater noster Q. Nannetensis episcopus[3] queritur quod abbas monasterii sancti Florentii[4] partem diocesis suae iniuste sibi auferat et alteri episcopatui subdere praesumat. Redonensem etiam episcopum nichilominus de diocesi sua iniuriam maximam intulisse innotuit, et de aliis qui bona aecclesiae suae in Andegauensi episcopatu retinent; uolumus te diligenter operam dare quatenus ipse de his omnibus per te apostolica auctoritate fultum plenam iustitiam consequatur.

36

To Abbot Bartholomew of Marmoutier: Gregory confirms the gifts of Bishop Quiriacus of Nantes to Marmoutier   (*1073–9, July*)†

G. episcopus seruus seruorum Dei B. uenerabili abbati[5] salutem et apostolicam benedictionem.

Quicquid confrater noster Q. Namnetensis episcopus[6] per scriptum monasterio uestro contulit nos priuilegio apostolicae

[a] Hugone *AB*

---

* Not in J.L. MSS.: Budapest, Bibl. nat. Széch. lat. med. aeui 5, fo. 9[r], *c.* 1100. Paris, Bibl. nat. Duchesne 4, fo. 110[r], seventeenth cent. Printed: Ramackers, *Q.F.I.A.B.* xxiii (1931–2), no. 5, p. 38. Morin, *R.B.* xlviii (1936), no. 7, pp. 124–5. Ramackers, *P.U.F.* v. no. 11, p. 73.

upon equity.'[1] Copy your Lord, copy the Master from whom you
have the doctrine of life. We, also, charge you to do what is
righteous regarding him before Hubert[2] our beloved son and, as
we understand, your friend.

To Archbishop Ralph of Tours   (1073–9, July)

Gregory, bishop, servant of the servants of God, to his beloved
brother in Christ, Archbishop Ralph of Tours, greeting and apostolic blessing.

Our most beloved brother Bishop Quiriacus of Nantes[3] complains that the abbot of the monastery of Saint-Florent[4] has unjustly taken away from him a part of his diocese and has dared to
make it subject to another see. He has made complaints to us that
the bishop of Rennes, too, has no less done the gravest wrong to his
diocese, and about others who have seized his church's property in
the diocese of Angers. We wish you to make diligent inquiry so
that he may obtain full justice regarding all these matters through
you, acting with the sanction of apostolic authority.

To Abbot Bartholomew of Marmoutier   (1073–9, July)

Gregory, servant of the servants of God, to the venerable Abbot
Bartholomew,[5] greeting and apostolic blessing.

We confirm both to you and to your successors by a privilege of
the apostolic see whatever our brother Bishop Quiriacus of Nantes[6]

† Not in J.L. MS.: Paris, Bibl. nat. Baluze 77, fo. 133, 1713, (Q).[7] Printed:
Ramackers, *P.U.F.* v, no. 12, pp. 73–4.

---

[1] Cf. Ps. 10 (11): 8.
[2] Subdeacon, frequently Gregory's legate to the Anglo-Norman kingdom.
[3] 1060–30 July 1079.
[4] Abbot William (1070–1118) of Saint-Florent-lès-Saumur (dioc. Angers).
[5] Abbot Bartholomew (1064–83) of Marmoutier (dioc. Tours).
[6] Cf. his charter of 1075 founding and giving to Marmoutier the priory of
Henor: Morice, *Mémoires pour servir de preuves à l'histoire de Bretagne*, v. 443–4.
[7] This folio consists of a copy made by Baluze of material stated to be 'Ex
chartulario Britannico Majoris monasterii Turonensis', fo. 16.

sedis confirmauimus tam tibi*ᵃ* quam successoribus tuis,*ᵇ* et per eandem auctoritatem monasterium uestrum, salua iustitia eiusdem episcopi, omnia uobis ab eo collata in perpetuum tenere atque possidere sancimus.

37

To Archbishop Ralph of Tours: Gregory assures him of his esteem and of his willingness to help the church of Tours. In order to settle the matter of Count Fulk of Anjou he is awaiting the arrival of Abbot Hugh of Cluny who will act as his legate in consultation with the archbishop and with Bishop Hugh of Die   (*1078–9*)*

G. episcopus seruus seruorum Dei dilecto in Christo R. confratri et coepiscopo Turonensi salutem et apostolicam benedictionem.

Visis dilectionis tuae litteris manifeste intelleximus quae sit tibi deuotio et qui amor erga matrem tuam sanctam Romanam aecclesiam. Doluisti enim atque compassus es eidem matri tuae ac nobis, non utcumque sed ut caritas exigit et sanctum membrum decet amplecti suum uenerabile caput, prout litterae ipsae testantur; et quia iuste ac digne doluisti, concessit tibi Deus inde cito uenire ad gaudium. Quapropter certus esto, quod pro hac digna iustaque deuotione quam sancto pectore geris, a Romana aecclesia et nobis eam uicissitudinem semper omnibus diebus uitae nostrae habebis, ut in omnibus aecclesiae tuae honori prouidere semper simus parati, et ad quascumque ipsius utilitates nostrum auxilium imploraueris, impromptos nos ad succurrendum siue subueniendum aecclesiae tuae uel tibi habere minime poteris. De caetero de causa comitis Fulconis quia ad uotum tuae fraternitatis minime ad praesens forsitan respondemus, non miretur religio tua seu aliquo modo perturbetur; praestolamur enim Cluniacensem abbatem ad nos in proximo peruenturum, propiciante Domino, cui omne negotium uestrum superimponere decreuimus, ut ipse communicato tecum atque cum Diensi

---

ᵃ sibi *in the text, corrected to* tibi *in the margin Q*   *ᵇ* suis *in the text, corrected to* tuis *in the margin Q*

---

* For the excommunication of Count Fulk cf. no. 3 above.

has given to your monastery by written grant, and by the same authority we lay down that, saving the bishop's jurisdiction, your monastery shall have and possess in perpetuity all that he has given you.

To Archbishop Ralph of Tours (1078-9)

Gregory, bishop, servant of the servants of God, to his beloved in Christ, Ralph, his brother and fellow bishop of Tours, greeting and apostolic blessing.

Having seen your letter we clearly apprehend what devotion and love you have towards your mother the holy Roman church. For you have been sorrowful and afflicted for your mother and for us not in small measure but, as your letter itself testifies, according to the demands of charity and as a holy member should embrace her venerable head. Because you have been rightly and duly sorrowful God has granted you to pass quickly from sorrow to joy. You may accordingly be assured that in return for the right and proper love which you bear in a holy heart you will always, for all the days of our life, have this return from the Roman church and from ourself, that in all things we shall ever be ready to provide for the honour of your church. For whatever of its necessities you may ask our help you will find us in no way slack to help and to succour your church and yourself.

For the rest, do not wonder or be in any way disturbed that for the present we happen to make no answer to your request in the affair of Count Fulk. For we are awaiting the abbot of Cluny who, with God's favour, will soon come to us, and we have decided to place your whole business upon his shoulders: with due regard for righteousness, after taking counsel with you and the bishop of

---

Not in J.L. MSS.: Budapest, Bibl. nat. Széch. lat. med. aeui 5, fo. 9ʳ⁻ᵛ, c. 1100. Paris, Bibl. nat. Duchesne 4, fo. 110ʳ⁻ᵛ, seventeenth cent. Printed: Ramackers, *Q.F.I.A.B.* xxiii (1931–2), no. 7, pp. 40–1. Morin, *R.B.* xlviii (1936), no. 8, p. 125. Ramackers, *P.U.F.* v, no. 13, pp. 74–5.

episcopo iusticia salua consilio quod melius fuerit inde diffiniat, ita tamen ut aecclesia tua ab infestationibus eiusdem comitis refrigerio pociatur.

38

To Bishop Landeric of Mâcon: Gregory reproves him for declining to obey his legate Cardinal Peter of Albano when he confirmed Cluny's privileges, charges him to show that he accepts them, and urges him to maintain peace with Abbot Hugh of Cluny (*1080, early Mar.*)*

Gregorius episcopus seruus seruorum Dei dilecto in Christo fratri Landrico Matisconensi episcopo salutem et apostolicam benedictionem.

Mirari ualde compellimur quomodo fraternitas tua, persuasione clericorum sicut audiuimus, in confirmatione priuilegiorum Cluniensis ecclesiae episcopo Albanensi legationem nostram ferenti inobediens extiterit, praesertim cum etiamsi aliquid, quod non credimus, inconsultius tibi irrogare uoluisset, quidquid esset pro reuerentia apostolicae sedis ferre decuisset. Itaque propter bonam uitam et pastoralem uigilantiam qua circa ecclesiam tibi commissam desudas, hanc culpam supportantes, praecipimus tibi quatenus, uocatis de melioribus monachis Cluniensis ecclesiae, ad communem locum inter Matisconem et Cluniacum uenias, ut in praesentia illorum praedictum priuilegium confirmes, et sic in episcopali officio restitutus adiuuante Domino populum tuum ualeas consolari. De caetero fraternitatem tuam paterno affectu quo eam amplectimur admonemus ne improbitati uel leuitati clericorum tuorum ulterius credulus existas, sed meis, qui te non tua diligo, potius quam illorum consiliis acquiescas. Quod si feceris scias profecto quod nos ecclesiam tibi commissam praeiudicium sustinere nullatenus patiemur. Interim autem sine omni inquietudine et discordia uos et abbas Cluniensis pacifice

---

* This letter adumbrates the turn subsequently taken by the quarrel between Cluny and the church of Mâcon, of which no. 30 above concerns the beginning. Archbishop Gebuin of Lyons and Bishop Landeric took certain steps in infringement of Cluny's privileges, and Abbot Hugh appealed to Rome. Gregory dispatched Cardinal Peter of Albano to Cluny where he fully upheld the monks and condemned the bishops. The bishops continued to resist, and in this letter

Die, he is to decide what shall be for the best, so that your church may obtain relief from the count's attacks.

To Bishop Landeric of Mâcon (*1080, early Mar.*)

Gregory, bishop, servant of the servants of God, to his beloved brother in Christ, Bishop Landeric of Mâcon, greeting and apostolic blessing.

We cannot but marvel greatly that, as we have heard at the prompting of your clerks, you have shown yourself disobedient to the bishop of Albano when he was acting as our legate to confirm the privileges of the church of Cluny. We marvel especially because even if, as we do not believe, he had wanted to impose something upon you ill-advisedly, you should have accepted whatever it was out of respect for the apostolic see. On account of your good life and of the pastoral vigilance with which you labour for the church which is committed to you we bear with your fault; but we charge you that you go to a public place between Mâcon and Cluny to which some of the graver monks of the church of Cluny shall also be summoned, and in their presence you are to confirm Cluny's privileges. Thus you may be restored to the episcopal office and, with God's help, be a consolation to your people. For the rest we warn you, with the fatherly affection in which we hold you, that you should never again be deceived by the impudence and irresponsibility of your clerks, but that you follow my counsels, not theirs; for I love you, not just your possessions. If you do this you may assuredly know that we shall never allow the church which is committed to you to suffer any loss. In the meanwhile, without any murmuring and discord, let you and the abbot of Cluny

Gregory insists upon his legate's rulings, leaving the matter for final settlement by Bishop Hugh of Die or if necessary by himself at Rome. The attack upon Archbishop Warmund of Vienne (1077–81) took place after, at Abbot Hugh's invitation, he carried out ordinations at Cluny in order to demonstrate its exemption: see *Charta Petri Albanensis episcopi et cardinalis Romani de immunitate Cluniaci*, in *Bibliotheca Cluniacensis*, cols. 511–14. For a discussion of the whole quarrel see Cowdrey, *The Cluniacs and the Gregorian Reform*, pp. 51–7.

J.L. 5182. MS.: none. Printed: *Bullarium Cluniacense*, p. 21. Severt, *Chronologia historica*, ii. 113–14. *Ep. coll.* no. 37, pp. 564–5.

maneatis, donec coram uicario Diensi episcopo huiusmodi lis religiosarum personarum consilio terminetur, aut, si illud non potuerit fieri, nos utraque parte uocata et causa diligenter discussa, auxiliante gratia Dei, finem congruum imponere ualeamus. Clerici autem qui spiritu superbiae ducti contra legatum nostrum Albanensem episcopum turbam fecerunt et archiepiscopum Viennensem a Cluniaco reuertentem ablatis rebus suis contumeliose inuaserunt, apud Cluniacum nudis pedibus ante altare sancti Petri satisfaciant, et sic emendatis moribus absoluantur.

39

Allocution in praise of Cluny   (*1080, early Mar.*)*

Domnus ac beatissimus papa Gregorius VII anno pontificatus sui septimo in basilica Lateranensi quae et Constantiniana dicitur in honore Saluatoris et beati Iohannis Baptiste consilium generale celebrans, indicto cunctis silentio, surrexit et dixit*a*:

Noueritis, fratres et consacerdotes nostri, immo tota*b* haec sancta synodus cognoscat et sciat, quia cum ultra montes multa sint monasteria ad honorem Dei omnipotentis et beatorum apostolorum Petri et Pauli*c* nobiliter et religiose fundata, inter omnia quoddam*d* in illis partibus habetur, quod quasi peculiare et proprium beato Petro et huic aecclesiae speciali iure adheret, Cluniaticum uidelicet, ad honorem et tutelam huius sanctae et apostolicae sedis ab ipsis primordiis principaliter adsignatum, et faciente*e* diuina clementia sub religiosis et sanctis abbatibus ad id usque dignitatis et religionis peruenit, ut ceteris monasteriis, quamuis multis antiquioribus, quantum ipse cognosco, in Dei seruitio et spiritali feruore praecellat, et nullum in terra illa quod ego sciam huic omnino ualeat adaequari. Nullus enim abbas

---

a *add* in hunc modum B   *b* *om.* tota B   *c* *om.* Petri et Pauli B
d *add* monasterium quod B   *e* fauente B

---

* This allocution illustrates the procedure of Gregory's Lent and Nov. councils at the Lateran. It contains his own vindication at Rome of the immunity and exemption of Cluny, the challenge to which by the archbishop of Lyons and the bishop of Mâcon was the subject of no. 38.

J.L. 7 Mar. 1080. MSS.: Rome, Vatican Library, lat. 1208, fos. 125ᵛ–126ᵛ, twelfth cent. (*V*).¹ Paris, Bibl. nat. Moreau 283, fos. 39ᵛ–40ʳ, copy made in 1773

behave peaceably until this dispute is settled before our vicar the bishop of Die with the counsel of religious persons, or, if this cannot happen, until we ourselves can summon both parties and having thoroughly examined the matter can with the help of God's grace bring it to a proper conclusion. As for the clerks who, led by the spirit of pride, made a tumult against our legate the bishop of Albano and plundered and shamefully attacked the archbishop of Vienne as he was returning from Cluny, let them make satisfaction barefooted before the altar of St. Peter at Cluny, and so when they have mended their ways let them be absolved.

Allocution in praise of Cluny   (*1080, early Mar.*)

The most blessed lord Pope Gregory VII held a general council during the seventh year of his pontificate in the Lateran basilica of our Saviour and St. John the Baptist, which is also called the basilica of Constantine. In the course of it he rose and called all to silence, and said:

Our brothers and fellow priests, you know, indeed all this holy council knows and understands, that, although there are many monasteries beyond the mountains which have been nobly and religiously founded to the honour of Almighty God and of the blessed apostles Peter and Paul, there is one amongst the others in those parts which belongs to St. Peter and to this church by an especial right as a peculiar possession—I mean Cluny, which from the very first was principally given over to the honour and protection of this holy and apostolic see. By God's mercy it has come to such a height of excellence and religion under its religious and holy abbots that it surpasses all other monasteries, even much older ones, as I well know, in the service of God and in spiritual fervour. I know of no other in that part of the world to which it can at all be compared. For there has never been an abbot of it who was not

from a lost fifteenth-cent. copy, (*B*).[2] Printed: Baronius, *Annales eccles.* xi. 551–2. *Bullarium Cluniacense*, pp. 21–2. Duckett, *Charters and Records*, ii. 206–8. Cowdrey, *The Cluniacs and the Gregorian Reform*, pp. 272–3.

---

[1] With the rubric 'Decretum domni Gregorii pape de Clunicensi monasterio'.
[2] For a description of this transcript made by Lambert de Barive, see Cowdrey, *The Cluniacs and the Gregorian Reform*, p. 271, n. 1.

umquam ibi fuit qui sanctus non fuisset. Quod abbates et monachi huius semper aecclesiae filii in nullo degeneres*f* extiterunt, nec curuauerunt genua sua ante Bahal nec Bahalim,[1] nec Geroboam,*g*[2] sed huius sanctae Romanae sedis libertatem dignitatemque imitantes,*h* quam ab origine traxerunt, nobiliter sibi per successionis seriem auctoritatem seruauere. Non enim alicui umquam*i* alienae uel terrenae potestati colla subdiderunt, in sola beati Petri et huius aecclesiae subiectione defensioneque*j* permanentes. Et idcirco uolumus atque apostolica auctoritate firmamus et contradicimus,*k* ut nulla umquam persona, parua uel magna, siue potestas aliqua, non archiepiscopus, non episcopus, nullus regum, ducum, marchionum, principum, comitum, nec etiam aliquis legatus meus, supra illum locum et monasterium umquam buccam suam aperiat aliquamue exerceat potestatem. Verum iuxta tenorem priuilegii nostri[3] et antecessorum nostrorum auctoritatem, et libertatis immunitatem sibi ab hac sede concessam integram perpetuamque omnino possideat, ut tantummodo sub alis apostolicis ab omni aestu et turbine inpugnationis respiret, et in gremio huius sanctae*l* aecclesiae, ad honorem omnipotentis Dei et beatorum apostolorum Petri et Pauli in perpetuum dulcissime quiescat.

Et ita uertens se domnus papa ad dextram partem*m* sinodalis conuentus, percunctatus est eos dicens: 'Placet ita uobis? laudatis?' Responderunt: 'Placet, laudamus.' Vertens se iterum in sinistram eodem modo interrogauit.*n* Eodem quoque modo responsum est a sancto conuentu: 'Placet, laudamus.' Post haec uerba stando in throno pontificali perorata domnus papa assedit.*o*

---

f degenere *V*   *g* ne hieroboam *underscored with dots to indicate an uncertain reading B*   *h* *The first two syllables made deliberately illegible and underscored with dots B*   *i* *om.* umquam *B*   *j* *om.* defensioneque *B*   *k* contendimus *B*   *l* *add* matris *B*   *m* *om.* partem *B*   *n* eodem interrogatum *V*   *o* *om. the last sentence B*

---

[1] Cf. 3 Reg. (1 Kgs.) 19: 18.   [2] Cf. 3 Reg. (1 Kgs.) 12: 25–33.
[3] For Gregory's privilege of 1075, see Santifaller, *Q.F.* no. 107, pp. 95–100.

a saint; its abbots and monks have never in any way dishonoured
their sonship of this church nor bowed the knee to Baal[1] and the
Baalim [like] Jeroboam.[2] They have always copied the liberty and
dignity of this holy Roman see which they have enjoyed from the
beginning, and from generation to generation they have nobly preserved for themselves its authority. For they have never bent their
necks before any outsider or earthly power, but they have remained
under the exclusive obedience and protection of St. Peter and this
church. We accordingly will and by apostolic authority we affirm
and lay down that no person whatsoever, small nor great, and no
power whatsoever, no archbishop nor bishop, no king, duke, marquis, prince, count, nor even any legate of mine, may ever open
his mouth nor exercise any power against this place and monastery.
According to the terms of our privilege[3] and the authority of our
predecessors, it is altogether to possess fully and perpetually the
immunity and liberty which have been granted to it by this see.
Covered by apostolic wings and by them alone, it is to breathe
freely, away from all commotion and from every attacking storm.
It is to enjoy perpetual and pleasant peace in the bosom of this
holy church, to the honour of Almighty God and of the blessed
apostles Peter and Paul.

So the pope turned to the right side of the council and asked
them, 'Does this please you? do you approve?' They answered,
'It pleases us, we approve.' He turned to the left and asked again
in the same way. The holy council gave the same answer, 'It pleases
us, we approve.' After these words which he spoke standing at the
papal throne, the lord pope took his seat.

40

To the clergy, vicomte, and people of Narbonne: Gregory urges them to obey their archbishop and to pay due heed to papal censures (*1080, before 23 Dec.*)*

Gregorius episcopus seruus seruorum Dei clero, vicecomiti Aymerico,[1] nec non uniuerso populo Narbonensi.

Apostolicam benedictionem libenter mandaremus si in apostolicae sedis reatum incurrisse uos non cognosceremus. Verum, ubi ab eadem uos resipuisse excommunicatione cognouerimus et archiepiscopalem patri uestro Dalmatio obedientiam exhibere, benedictionem beati Petri mandabimus. Sicut nouit prudentia uestra, inimicus humani generis ecclesiam uestram malis et simoniacis pastoribus inuasam quasi ius proprium longo tempore possedit. Sed condolentes necessitati ac periculo uestro, bonum et legalem pastorem uobis praeficiendum censuimus, non aliunde sed per ostium, id est per Christum, intrantem.[2] Qui enim aliter, id est sine Christo, ingrediuntur, fures sunt et latrones, ad hoc constituti, ut gregem dominicum mactent et perdant.[3] Hic itaque, apostolicae sedis benedictione et auctoritate confirmatus, per exemplum laudandae conuersationis suae et documentum praedicationis quidquid culpa et iniuria malorum pontificum inter uos commissum est, Deo auxiliante, poterit corrigere uosque bonus pastor summo pastori deuotissime commendare. Admonemus itaque prudentiam uestram ut eum quem legaliter ecclesia Romana uobis constituit honeste et cum beneuolentia recipiatis et ei sicut spirituali patri et archiepiscopo obedientiam et reuerentiam impendatis, memores dominici sermonis fideles suos commendantis: 'Qui uos audit, me audit; et qui uos spernit, me spernit.'[4] Neque enim uos ignorare uoluimus quod si quis uestrum, quod non speramus, obedientiam sibi contradixerit, iram Dei et uindictam beati Petri ad periculum suum prouocabit; et sententiam

---

* This letter was written before *Reg.* viii. 16, 23 Dec. 1080, pp. 537–8, in which Gregory referred to his own nominee for the see of Narbonne, Archbishop Dalmatius (1081–96), as having been accepted by the people though not yet put into possession of the see: cf. Fliche, *La Réforme grégorienne*, ii. 254 n. 4. Gregory's concern for the see was a long-standing one. He had taken measures against Archbishop Wifred (*c.* 1019–79): *Reg.* iii. 10*a*, 14–20 Feb. 1076, p. 269; v. 14*a*, 27 Feb.–3 Mar. 1078, p. 370; vi. 17*a*, 11 Feb. 1079, p. 429. In 1079 Bishop Peter of Rodez (1046–79) simoniacally obtained the see, and he was

To the clergy, vicomte, and people of Narbonne
(1080, before 23 Dec.)

Gregory, bishop, servant of the servants of God, to the clergy, to vicomte Aymeric,[1] and also to the whole people of Narbonne.

We would gladly have sent our apostolic blessing, did we not know that you have incurred guilt against the apostolic see. When we learn that you have been restored from your excommunication and that you are showing such obedience to your father Dalmatius as is due to your archbishop, we shall send you St. Peter's blessing. As you know, the enemy of the human race has for long possessed your church as if it were his own property, for it has been invaded by wicked and simoniacal shepherds. But because we are troubled by your plight and danger, we have thought it good to set over you a good and lawful shepherd entering in not by another way but by the door, that is, by Christ;[2] for those who enter otherwise, that is, apart from Christ, are thieves and robbers appointed to the end that they should destroy and disperse the Lord's flock.[3] Thus, strengthened by the blessing and authority of the apostolic see, with God's help he will be able by the example of a praiseworthy life and by the pattern of his preaching to set right whatever wrong has been done amongst you by the fault and evildoing of wicked bishops, and as a good shepherd to commit you most faithfully to the Chief Shepherd.

Therefore we charge you to receive honestly and with a good will him whom the Roman church has lawfully appointed for you, and to pay him obedience and reverence as befits your spiritual father and archbishop, remembering the Lord's saying when he commended his disciples: 'He who hears you hears me, and he who rejects you rejects me.'[4] Nor would we have you ignorant that if any of you, which we hope will not be the case, should refuse him obedience, he will call down the wrath of God and the punishment of St. Peter to his own destruction, and we shall confirm by

condemned at the council of Toulouse (1079), probably held by the legates Bishops Hugh of Die and Amatus of Oléron: cf. Schieffer, *Die päpstlichen Legaten in Frankreich*, p. 114. Gregory deposed and excommunicated Peter at his Lent council in 1080, and nominated Dalmatius: *Reg.* vii. 14*a*, 7 Mar. 1080, p. 481; cf. *Reg.* viii. 16.

J.L. 5192. MS.: none. Printed: Catel, *Mémoires de l'histoire du Languedoc*, 782–3. Labbe and Cossart, *Sacrosancta concilia*, x. 410–11. *Ep. coll.* no. 35, pp. 563–4. The text is that of Labbe and Cossart.

---

[1] Vicomte of Narbonne (*c.* 1080–1105/6).   [2] Cf. John 10: 1.
[3] Cf. John 10: 10.   [4] Luke 10: 16.

excommunicationis in Tolosa synodo a legatis nostris promulga-
tam apostolica auctoritate confirmabimus. Qui uero obediens
fuerit, gratia et benedictione eiusdem apostolicae sedis gaudebit.

41

*To Bishop Hubert of Thérouanne: Gregory rebukes him for
his connivance at clerical unchastity, orders him to remedy
the disorders of his church, and summons him to his Lent
council* (*1080, late*)*

G. episcopus seruus seruorum Dei H. Teruanensi episcopo
salutem et apostolicam benedictionem, si decretis apostolicae
sedis scienter non resistit.

Clamor et querimonia filiorum aecclesiae tuae peruenit ad aures
nostras te contra decreta nostra immo sanctorumque patrum
consensisse fornicationi clericorum, addentes etiam quod pueris
illorum qui nolunt consentire huic iniquitati interdicis babtismum
et mortuis sepulturam. Quod nos graue ferentes auctoritate
apostolorum Petri et Pauli tibi praecipimus, ut hoc ita a te emen-
detur ut amplius ex hac re querela ad nos non ueniat. Insuper
tibi praecipimus ut ad synodum quam Deo auctore in prima
ebdomada quadragesimae celebraturi sumus[1] omni occasione
postposita uenias.

42

*To the monks of la Grasse: Gregory assures them that he
gave his legate Richard no permanent dominion over them
but only authority to reform them on his behalf, and charges
them to obey Archbishop Dalmatius of Narbonne* (*1081*)†

G. episcopus seruus seruorum Dei omnibus fratribus in monasterio
sanctae Mariae Vrbionensi constitutis salutem et apostolicam
benedictionem.

De controuersia que inter uos et consacerdotem nostrum

---

* This letter was probably written some time after Gregory's letter to Bishop
Hubert of Thérouanne (1078/9–81): *Reg.* vii. 16, 26 Mar. 1080, pp. 489–91;
a comparison of their salutations, in the light of the additional sentence printed

apostolic authority the sentence of excommunication which our legates published at the council of Toulouse. But whoever is obedient will rejoice in the favour and blessing of the apostolic see.

To Bishop Hubert of Thérouanne   (*1080, late*)

Gregory, bishop, servant of the servants of God, to Bishop Hubert of Thérouanne, greeting and apostolic blessing, if he does not knowingly resist the decrees of the apostolic see.

A cry and complaint of the sons of your church has reached our ears that, contrary to our own decrees and those of the holy fathers, you have been consenting to fornication by the clergy and that in addition you forbid baptism to the children, and burial to the dead, of those who will not tolerate such an iniquity. We regard this matter most seriously and by the authority of the apostles Peter and Paul we charge you so to put it right that no further complaint about it reaches us. Furthermore we charge you that, laying aside every excuse, you come to the council which under God's guidance we shall hold during the first week of Lent.[1]

To the monks of la Grasse   (*1081*)

Gregory, bishop, servant of the servants of God, to all the brethren living in the monastery of Sainte-Marie, la Grasse, greeting and apostolic blessing.

With God's help we shall put a final end to the dispute which

on p. 491, suggests that sufficient time had elapsed for Hubert to clear himself of an earlier accusation of simony.

J.L. 5188. MSS: Saint-Omer, Bibl. municip. 188, fos. 86ᵛ–87ʳ, twelfth cent. Boulogne, Bibl. municip. 72, fo. 272ʳ, twelfth cent. Printed: Duchet, *Additions et corrections*, pp. 14–15. Loewenfeld, *N.A.* vii (1882), 162.

† On 18 Apr. 1081 Gregory entrusted the monastery of Sainte-Marie, la Grasse, for reform to Richard, abbot of Saint-Victor, Marseilles (1079–1108) and papal legate, together with that of Montmajour, 'quae ad huius sedis defensionem pertinere propriique iuris eius esse noscuntur, iamdudum secularium monachorum culpa a religionis tramite deuiasse intelleximus': Santifaller, *Q.F.* no. 198, pp. 229–31. For Archbishop Dalmatius, cf. no. 40 above; he was abbot of la Grasse from *c.* 1069 and retained this office for several years after he became archbishop of Narbonne. At his Lent council in 1081 Gregory again confirmed the deposition of the simoniacal Archbishop Peter: *Reg.* viii. 20*a*, p. 544.

J.L. 5223. MS.: Paris, Bibl. nat. lat. 933, fo. 110ᵛ, eleventh cent.[2] Printed: *B.É.C.* xxxv (1874), 433–4.

[1] 21–7 Feb. 1081.
[2] This MS. is a *Rituale ad usum monasterii sanctae Mariae Crassensis.*

R. orta est, Deo auxiliante, certum finem componemus, ita ut nullam contra eum murmurationis occasionem habeatis. Certum siquidem sit uobis nos nullam in monasterio uestro praedicto legato nostro R. contra libertatem aecclesiae uestrae dominationem dedisse, sed hoc sibi concessisse ut, si uos ab monastica discederetis religione, liceret ei uice nostra corrigere. De cetero admonemus et apostolica auctoritate praecipimus ut confratri nostro Dalmatio archiepiscopo debitam solitamque impendatis obedientiam et eum benigne et honeste suscipientes in patrem et abbatem habeatis ut, sicut ante episcopalem ordinationem subditi sibi fuistis, ita deinceps regimini et magisterio suo subdamini. Cum autem, Deo annuente, archiepiscopatum suum habuerit in pace, ipse ad nos ueniet adducens quosdam ex uobis, et aecclesia uestra ad honorem et uestram libertatem ordinabitur.

43

To Abbot Peter of Fucecchio and Prior Rudolf of Camaldoli: Gregory explains why he cannot accede to their request that he absolve Ughiccio the son of Bulgarelli   (?1081)*

G. episcopus seruus seruorum Dei P. abbati Ficeclensi et R. praeposito Campomaldi salutem et apostolicam benedictionem.

Petiuit religio uestra quatinus Vgicionem Bulgarelli filium de reatu suo non resipiscentem neque culpam suam confitentem sic absoluamus. Vos autem satis nouistis quia carum ipsum habere usque ad hoc graue facinus suum soliti fuimus, et certe ultra caeteros sui ordinis principes Tusciae antehac eum dileximus, eo quod ipse more patris sui bonos defendere et religionem in potestate sua plantare prae caeteris studuit. Vnde si quomodo rationabiliter postulationi uestrae possemus annuere, profecto tum propter praedictam bonitatem suam et preces uxoris suae, tum propter petitiones uestras eum libenter absolueremus. Verum

---

* Gregory writes to the heads of two Tuscan monasteries. San Salvatore, Fucecchio, was in the diocese of Lucca. Rudolf was prior of San Salvatore, Camaldoli (dioc. Arezzo), a hermit community founded by St. Romuald of Ravenna (*c.* 950–1027), the constitution of which was later settled by Pope Alexander II, *Ep.* lxxxix (1072), *P.L.* cxlvi. 1373–5. Rudolf appears as prior in charters dating from 1074 to 1087: *Regesto di Camaldoli*, ed. L. Schiaparelli and F. Baldasseroni, i (Regesta chartarum Italiae, ii, Rome, 1907), 159–218. Camaldoli

has arisen between you and our fellow priest Richard, so that you may have no occasion for complaint against him. You may rest assured that we gave Richard, our legate, no dominion over your monastery which infringes the liberty of your church, but gave him this authority, that if you had fallen away from monastic devotion he might correct matters on our behalf. Furthermore we warn and by apostolic authority command that you show proper and customary obedience to our brother Archbishop Dalmatius, and that, receiving him readily and as is fitting, you acknowledge him as father and abbot: as you were subject to him before his episcopal consecration, so you should thereafter be subject to his rule and authority. So soon as, by God's help, he holds his archiepiscopal see in peace, he will himself come to us bringing some of your number, and your church's affairs will be ordered as befits your honour and liberty.

To Abbot Peter of Fucecchio and Prior Rudolf of Camaldoli (?1081)

Gregory, bishop, servant of the servants of God, to Abbot Peter of Fucecchio and Prior Rudolf of Camaldoli, greeting and apostolic blessing.

You have asked us to absolve Ughiccio the son of Bulgarelli, although he has neither repented of his guilt nor confessed his fault. Now you well know that before this great outrage of his we used to hold him dear; indeed, we previously loved him above the other Tuscan princes of his rank because, following his father's example, he strove more than they to defend good men and to establish religion in his lands. If, therefore, we could by any means properly agree to your request we would indeed gladly absolve him, on account both of his own past goodness and his wife's prayers and of your own requests. But neither reason nor the

was called Campus Maldoli after Count Maldolus who in 1012 gave buildings and land to its founder.

Ughiccio, son of Count William Bulgarelli, of the Cadolingi family, was excommunicated at Gregory's Lent council in 1078 for invading the property of the church of Lucca: *Reg.* v. 14a, p. 371. He was also implicated in the expulsion from his see in Oct. 1080 of the staunchly Gregorian Bishop Anselm II of Lucca (1073–86): cf. E. Kittel, 'Der Kampf um die Reform des Domkapitels in Lucca', *Festschrift Albert Brackmann* (Weimar, 1931), pp. 233–7.

J.L. 5219. *I.P.* iii, p. 482, no. 3. MS.: Rome, Vatican Library, Barberinus lat. 538, fos. 58ᵛ–59ʳ, c. 1100, (V). Printed: Thaner, *N.A.* iv (1878), 402–3.

neque ratio aut consuetudo sanctae aecclesiae hoc habet neque
sanctorum patrum nos ad hoc inducit exemplum, ut iuste et
canonice excommunicatus culpam suam non agnoscens nec ex
corde ueniam petens mereatur absolui. Nisi enim quis ex intimo
corde penitens reatum suum confiteatur, inutilis est absolutio
nec dicenda nisi deceptio. Quod autem ipse comes ad malitiae
suae defensionem se iniuste et ob alicuius gratiam dicit excommunicatum, perpendat et ex sanctorum patrum sententiis diligenter inquirat quid de conspiratoribus ipsi statuerint, et cum
se in sacrilega conspiratione Lucensium fuisse meminerit, desinat
ad augmentum*a* mali flagitium suum maximeque defendere.
Adhuc enim quod non minus est graue, quia episcopum Lucensem
legaliter et canonice ordinatum de aecclesia sua expelli consensit
uel permisit, merito in se anathematis gladium prouocauit.
Enimuero nollemus nos ullam uel minimam personam pro qua
Christus sanguinem suum fudit non dictante iustitia excommunicare, si sciremus ob id oportere nos aut exilium subire aut
usque ad sanguinis effusionem deuenire. Permaxime*b* autem ut*c*
praefatus comes ad paenitentiam sicut Christianum oportet de
tanto facinore conuerteretur, optaremus profecto grande in-
commodum uel infirmitatem personae nostrae accidere. Proinde
sanctitatem uestram inuitamus atque rogamus ut specialiter pro
eo ad Dominum preces effundere cotidie memineritis, quatinus
diuina pietas cor et mentem illius uisitet, compungat, et ad
penitentiam conuertat, ut de culpis suis resipiscens gemens et
indulgentiam poscens in reliquum per bonorum operum exercitia
in membris sanctae aecclesiae digne possit connumerari.

44

To Bishop Hugh of Die and Abbot Richard of Marseilles:
Gregory instructs them to settle a dispute between the clergy of
Dax and their opponents about certain churches (*1081–2*)*

G. episcopus seruus seruorum Dei V. Diensi episcopo et R.
cardinali et abbati[1] salutem et apostolicam benedictionem.

Aquensis archidiaconus A. queritur quod archiepiscopus

---

a suum *erased* V   *b* Permaxme V   *c* aut V

* J.L. 5241. MS.: none. Printed: *R.H.F.* xiv. 186.[2] *Ep. coll.* no. 43, p. 570.

custom of holy church allows this, nor does the example of the holy fathers afford a precedent for absolving one who has been justly and canonically excommunicated, who does not acknowledge his fault, and who does not seek pardon with his whole heart. For unless a man repents in his inmost heart and confesses his guilt, his absolution is without effect and only fit to be called a deception. Since the count himself defends his own wickedness by saying that he was excommunicated unjustly and to curry someone else's favour, let him consider and diligently inquire from the writings of the holy fathers what they have laid down on the subject of plotters; let him remember that he was involved in the sacrilegious plot of the citizens of Lucca, and cease to aggravate his wickedness by striving to defend his outrage. In addition he deservedly called forth the sword of anathema against himself for a no less serious matter, because he encouraged or allowed the lawfully and canonically instituted bishop of Lucca to be driven from his church. We of a truth are not willing to excommunicate against the dictates of righteousness any person, however insignificant, for whom Christ shed his blood, even if we knew that we ourselves must therefore either suffer exile or be placed in danger of bloodshed. Rather, in order that the count should be persuaded to do penance as befits a Christian for so great a crime, we would gladly choose that some great misfortune or harm should happen to our own self. Therefore we urge and beseech you to remember especially to pour out your prayers daily for him to the Lord, imploring God's mercy to visit, soften, and turn to penitence his heart and mind, so that repenting, bewailing, and asking pardon for his sins he may in the future by his performance of good works prove worthy to be reckoned amongst the members of holy church.

To Bishop Hugh of Die and Abbot Richard of Marseilles
(1081–2)

Gregory, bishop, servant of the servants of God, to Bishop Hugh of Die and Richard, cardinal and abbot,[1] greeting and apostolic blessing.

Arnald, archdeacon of Dax, complains that Archbishop

---

[1] Of Saint-Victor, Marseilles.

[2] The letter is from a document entitled 'Controuersia de limitibus Aquensis et Olorensis episcopatuum', described as 'ex collectaneis Baluzii in Biblioth. nat. Paris. nunc primum edita': ibid., p. 183.

W.[1] et A. legatus noster[2] nec non episcopus Vasantensis[3] insurgunt
aduersus ecclesiam suam et ecclesias quasdam eiusdem episcopatus
sui auferunt et uiolenter inuadunt. Ausciensis quoque archiepiscopus et Amatus episcopus literis suis nobis significauere[a]
ab Aquensibus easdem ecclesias proprietati Olorensis ecclesiae ab
antiquo tempore pertinuisse. Vnde fraternitati uestrae iniungimus
ut, si potestis ambo, sin autem unus in competenti loco eorum
negotium audiat atque, canonicis rationibus diligenter utrimque
perscrutatis, Deo placentem et iustitiae congruum finem imponat.

45

To Count Robert of Flanders: Gregory warns him to have
no more to do with the promotion of a simoniacal clerk named
Lambert to the see of Thérouanne   (*1082*)*

G. episcopus seruus seruorum Dei R. glorioso Flandrensium
comiti salutem et apostolicam benedictionem.

Notum tibi esse non dubitamus quantum nos hactenus nobilita-
tem tuam dilexerimus, cuius[a] industriam inter ceteros Franciae
principes satis honesta fama commendabat. Vnde quia bonis
studiis tuis congratulamur, cum contraria de te referuntur multum
profecto dolemus. Audiuimus nuper te cuidam clerico sacrilegio
Lamberto, qui publice Taruanensem episcopatum mercatus est,
contra uoluntatem clericorum illi ecclesiae imposito imo ab eis
omnino iampridem repudiato assensisse, eique adiutorium et
potestatem ecclesiam inuadendi praestitisse. De qualibus ipsa
Veritas dicit: 'Qui non intrat per ostium in ouile ouium sed
ascendit aliunde, ille fur est et latro',[4] et beatus papa Leo: 'Non
habeatur inter episcopos qui non fuerit a clero electus et a populo
expetitus.'[5] Oportet ergo prudentiam tuam diuinae maiestatis
omnipotentiam et districtionem prae oculis incessanter habere,
nulliusque mortalium gratiam uel timorem illi praeferre cui et
uitam et salutem et honorem tuum non ambigis te debere. Ergo

----

   [a] *Some words appear to be lacking*   45   [a] cui *G.*

   * In 1082 Lambert was intruded into the see of Thérouanne in succession to
Bishop Hubert (cf. no. 41 above) by Count Robert I of Flanders and King Philip
I of France (1060–1108): cf. Simon, *Gesta abbatum sancti Bertini Sithiensium*,
ii. 53, *M.G.H. Scr.* xiii. 646.

William,[1] our legate Amatus,[2] and the bishop of Bazas[3] are assailing his church and are seizing and forcibly invading some churches of his diocese. The archbishop of Auch and Bishop Amatus have also informed us in their letters . . . by the men of Dax that these churches have belonged from ancient times to the church of Oléron. We therefore charge you that if possible both of you, but if not one, should hear their dispute in a convenient place and, after carefully weighing the canonical arguments on both sides, should make a settlement which is pleasing to God and according to righteousness.

To Count Robert of Flanders   (1082)

Gregory, bishop, servant of the servants of God, to Robert, the renowned count of Flanders, greeting and apostolic blessing.

We have no doubt that you know how much we have hitherto loved you whose zeal a most honest report has singled out amongst the other princes of France. Just because we applaud your good works, we greatly grieve when we hear adverse things of you. We have heard that you have recently shown approval of a sacrilegious clerk, one Lambert, who publicly bought the see of Thérouanne, who was forced upon that church against the clergy's will, and who, indeed, has long since been utterly rejected by them; and that you have provided him with help and resources to invade the church. It is of such as he that the Truth himself says: 'He who does not enter the sheepfold by the door but climbs in by another way, that man is a thief and a robber';[4] and that the blessed Pope Leo says: 'Let him not be numbered among the bishops who is not elected by the clergy and desired by the people.'[5] You should accordingly keep ever before your eyes the omnipotence and severity of God's majesty, and you should not place the fear or favour of any mortal man before him to whom, as you well know, you owe your life, safety, and honour.

J.L. 5242. MS.: none. Printed: *G.C.* x, *Instrumenta ecclesiae Boloniensis*, no. 1, cols. 393–5 (*G*).[6] *Ep. coll.* no. 40, pp. 567–8.

---

[1] William of Auch (1068–96).   [2] Bishop of Oléron.
[3] Raymond (1057–84).   [4] John 10: 1.
[5] Pope Leo I; cf. *Ep.* clxvii, *P.L.* liv. 1203.
[6] This letter and nos. 46–7 are said to be copied 'ex schedis Martenii'.

quia te audiuimus admonitu fidelitatis quam regi Philippo feceras
ad id periculose esse inductum, ex parte omnipotentis Dei praecipimus ut, si praedictus Lambertus tam nefariis modis ad episcopatum prorupit, nullatenus ei sacerdotalem obedientiam uel
reuerentiam exhibeas, sed a male mercata et inuasa sede alienum
et extorrem facere praefatis clericis amminiculando procures. Non
enim te decet aestimare illa te adiuratione ad tam grauissimum
scelus adstringi, quia perniciosius est illum per quem iuratur
quam cui iuratur, et Deum quam hominem offendere. Simul ipse
satis perpendis quia plus debetur animae quam corpori, et tunc
profecto fidelitas perspicue magis seruatur iubenti quando salus
animae eius corporeis commodis et iniquis praelata iussis magis
attenditur. Age ergo ut non pro homine supplicium sed pro Dei
timore expectare debeas praemium; atque sic praedictis clericis
qui promotioni illius libere ex parte Dei contradixerunt opitulari
eosque defendere procures, ut quanto te gratia diuina altius
sublimauit, tanto magis et bonis fiduciam et prauis terrorem
praebeas, ceterisque principibus te imitabilem reddas.

Plumbeo sigillo idcirco signari literas istas noluimus, ne si
forte caperentur ab impiis eodem sigillo posset falsitatis quippiam
fieri.

46

To the clergy and people of the church of Thérouanne, and
especially Count Robert of Flanders: Gregory blames them
for their part in promoting Lambert to the see of Thérouanne
and urges them to seek his expulsion   (*1082*)*

G. episcopus seruus seruorum Dei clero et populo Taruanensis
ecclesiae, praecipueque nobili comiti R., salutem et apostolicam
benedictionem, si obedierint.[a]

Sicut aliis literis misimus, non ignorat solertia tua nos iamdudum te satis diligere propterea quod te bonis studiis inter ceteros
Franciae principes, fama ferente, audiuimus eminere. Nam potioris

---

[a] obierint *G*

---

* This letter, which was evidently written soon after no. 45, reinforces its
pleas and arguments. The change from the plural in the address to the singular

We have heard that it was under colour of the fealty which you have performed to King Philip that, to your peril, you were persuaded to do this. We therefore charge you in the name of Almighty God that, if this Lambert has seized the episcopate by such wicked means, you show him nothing whatever of the obedience and reverence which are due to a priest, but that you support the local clergy by ensuring that he is deprived of and excluded from the see which he has so evilly bought and invaded. For you should not think that your oath of fealty binds you to perform so heinous a crime: it is more perilous to offend him by whom we swear than him to whom we swear, that is, God rather than man. You should likewise well consider that we owe a greater debt to the soul than to the body, so that a man certainly the better keeps fealty to a superior when he attends first to the salvation of his own soul, preferring it to bodily goods and wrongful orders. Act, then, with an eye not to the punishment which men can inflict, but to the reward which follows from fearing God; and be zealous to help and support the clerks who on God's behalf have boldly resisted Lambert's promotion. Thus the higher God's grace has raised you up, the more you may inspire confidence in good men and terror in the wicked, and make yourself a model for other princes.

We would not allow this letter to be sealed with a leaden seal, lest if perchance it were captured by the ungodly some forgery might be attempted by using the seal.

To the clergy and people of the church of Thérouanne, and especially Count Robert of Flanders.   (1082)

Gregory, bishop, servant of the servants of God, to the clergy and people of the church of Thérouanne, and especially to the excellent Count Robert, greeting and apostolic blessing, if they are obedient.

As we have said in another letter, you are not ignorant that we have for long greatly loved you on account of the reports which we heard of your pre-eminence in good works amongst the other

in the letter indicates that separate copies were prepared for the count and for the clergy and people.

J.L. 5250. MS.: none. Printed: *G.C.* x, *Instrumenta ecclesiae Boloniensis*, no. 2, col. 395 (*G*). *Ep. coll.* no. 41, pp. 568–9.

erga te dilectionis habendae causa nobis haec extitit, quia te christianae religionis amatorem ecclesiasticaeque disciplinae et honoris suffragatorem ac defensorem in quibusdam cognouimus. Vnde cum a solita probitate contraria forte audiuimus, quantum doleamus prudentia tua satis perpendit. Nuper uero de te quoddam nobis innotuit, quod, sicut a priscis moribus tuis alienum, ita quoque penitus credere uisum fuit indignum, uidelicet quod contradicentibus Taruanensis ecclesiae clericis renitentibusque, tua protectione auxilioque fretus, quidam Lambertus illius ecclesiae sedem inuaserit. Qui publice simoniacus, aperte*b* diuini muneris emptor, quanto se in tali negotio turpiorem et impudentiorem ostendit, tanto tuum non fauorem sed zelum, non opem sed repulsionem experiri debuit. Verum quia obstante rege, sub specie timoris ne peierares, ad id mali inductus fuisse diceris, idcirco iampridem et nunc literis te admonere censuimus quatinus, uanum timorem abiiciendo, quod iure metuendum uidetur attenderes. Nouerit ergo prudentia tua fidelitatem terreno domino tunc non recte seruari cum coelestis Domini et Creatoris gratia per illam probatur offendi, et si corpori multo amplius animae, si mortali homini multo maxime sempiterno Deo fidem et deuotionem deberi. Proinde tam nobilitati tuae quam et praefatae ecclesiae clero et populo ex parte beati Petri praecipimus ut praedicto Lamberto nullam episcopalem reuerentiam exhibeatis, sed ipsum uelut furem et latronem existimantes ab inuasa sede propellere, fautoresque ipsius donec resipuerint cohibere procuretis. Quod si se praedictus inuasor ferre praeiudicium dixerit et de re sua non ita esse*c* ut dicitur, se posse probare existimauerit, audientiam legati nostri Diensis immo Lugdunensis archiepiscopi[1] petat, quatenus per competentem illius discussionem iustumque iudicium obtinere quod postulat aequitas ualeat.

b a parte *G*   *c* esset *G*

---

[1] Hugh's translation from Die to Lyons, evidently very recent, took place in 1082.

princes of France. For we had this reason for showing the greater love towards you, that we knew you to be in many ways a lover of the Christian religion and a supporter and defender of the church's discipline and honour. So when we chanced to hear of things which were contrary to your usual uprightness, you will readily appreciate how grieved we were. For we recently had tidings of you which seemed as foreign to your former ways as they were also altogether shameful to believe: that in spite of the protests and remonstrations of the clergy of the church of Thérouanne, a certain Lambert supported by your protection and aid invaded the see of this church. He is notoriously a simoniac and openly a purchaser of the gift of God. The baser and the more shameless he has shown himself in this traffic, the more he should have experienced your anger and resistance, not your favour and help. Now you may say that you were brought to do this evil since the king opposed you, and from fear lest you should therefore perjure yourself. But both formerly and now in our letter we have thought fit to warn you to cast aside vain fear and give heed to what you should rightly dread. Thus you will be well aware that fealty to an earthly lord is not rightly observed when we manifestly offend the grace of the heavenly Lord and Creator, and that if we owe faith and devotion in respect of the body and to mortal men we owe them much more in respect of the soul and to the eternal God.

So on behalf of St. Peter we command both you and the clergy and people of the church of Thérouanne that you show this Lambert no reverence as a bishop but that, holding him to be a thief and a robber, you see that you drive him from the see which he has invaded and harry his supporters until they repent. Should this intruder say that he is suffering an injustice and should he think that he can prove what is reported of him to be untrue, let him seek a hearing of our legate the bishop of Die—or rather the archbishop of Lyons,[1] so that by proper trial and just judgement at his hands he may duly receive what justice demands.

47

*To Count Robert of Flanders: Gregory again urges him to
rid the church of Thérouanne of Lambert, and to restore
certain clerks whom he has sent into exile*   (*1082–3*)*

G. episcopus seruus seruorum Dei R. glorioso Flandrensium
comiti dilecto in Christo filio salutem et apostolicam benedictionem.

Iam saepius excellentiae tuae scripsimus super causa clericorum
Taruanensis ecclesiae E. praepositi,[1] S. decani,[2] I. diaconi[3] et
reliquorum quos, malignorum mortiferis suggestionibus, bonis
propriis priuatos in exilium pro obedientia apostolica detrusisti, ut
eos ad integrum sicut iustum est restaurares, et illum haereticum
L. depositum et excommunicatum amplius non sustentares sed
magis ecclesiam captiuatam de eius tyrannide et oppressione
liberares. Quod quia, sicut illi adhuc lacrymabiliter conqueruntur,
nondum pleniter peregisti, crebris querimoniis eorum fatigati
adhuc nobilitati tuae mandamus et ex parte Dei et apostolorum
principis praecipimus ut ecclesiam de praedicto antichristi
membro eripias, clericisque praefatis sua omnia clementer
restituas, et gratiam tuam pristinam eis habere permittas, ut
Deus omnipotens tibi suam gratiam hic et in futuro saeculo
tribuat, et beatus Petrus ad cuius praesentiam confugium fecerunt
ianuas coeli post huius uitae felicem terminum tibi aperiat.

---

* The background of this letter is supplied by *Reg.* ix. 35, pp. 623–4, which
Gregory dispatched simultaneously to the bishops and magnates of Flanders.
Lambert had been excommunicated by Gregory's legates Archbishop Hugh of
Lyons and Bishop Amatus of Oléron at the council of Meaux (Oct. 1082) but
had defied the sentence by securing consecration at the hands of suspended
bishops. With the support of Count Robert he had violently entered his church
and the count had condemned the clerks who opposed him to banishment and
forfeiture of goods. In the present letter Gregory called for their restoration and
for the count to abandon Lambert.

For the later course of the affair, the chronology of which is very uncertain,
cf. *Reg.* ix. 13, pp. 591–2, ix. 31, pp. 617–18, ix. 33–4, pp. 619–22, ix. 36, pp.
628–9.

J.L. 5247. MS.: none. Printed: *G.C.* x, *Instrumenta ecclesiae Boloniensis*, no. 3,
cols. 395–6. *Ep. coll.* no. 42, pp. 569–70.

---

[1] The 'Arnulfus (Ernulfus) Morinorum archidiaconus et ecclesiae b. Audo-
mari prepositus' referred to in Hariulf, *Vita S. Arnulfi Suessonensis episcopi*,
R.H.F. xiv. 59; cf. *Reg.* ix. 35, p. 623.

To Count Robert of Flanders   (*1082–3*)

Gregory, bishop, servant of the servants of God, to Robert, the renowned count of Flanders, his beloved son in Christ, greeting and apostolic blessing.

We have already written to you very often about the matter of the clerks of the church of Thérouanne—of the provost E.,[1] the dean S.,[2] the deacon I.,[3] and the others whom by the deadly suggestions of wicked men you have sent into exile and deprived of their property on account of their obedience to the apostolic see. We have urged you fully to restore them as is right and no longer to support the heretic Lambert who has been deposed and excommunicated, but rather to free the captive church from his tyranny and oppression. The clerks are still miserably complaining that you have not yet fully done so, and we are wearied by their frequent complaints. Therefore we charge you and on behalf of God and of the prince of apostles we command you, that you deliver the church from this member of Antichrist, that you graciously restore to the clerks all their property, and that you vouchsafe your favour to them as of old. Then Almighty God may grant you his grace here and in the world to come, and St. Peter in whose presence they have taken refuge may open to you the gates of heaven when you have happily completed this present life.

[2] Unknown.
[3] Perhaps the Ingelrannus, canon of Saint-Omer, of *Reg.* ix. 33, p. 620, cf. *Reg.* ix. 35, p. 623.

48

To Archbishop Ralph of Tours: Gregory reproves him for delaying to consecrate Bishop Hoel of le Mans from fear of Count Fulk of Anjou and urges him to perform his duty
(*1082*)*

G. episcopus seruus seruorum Dei R. uenerabili Turonensi archiepiscopo, salutem et apostolicam benedictionem.

Audiuimus quod Cenomanensi electo, cuius consecratio ad ius tuae ecclesiae pertinet, consecrari per te cupienti tua fraternitas mundani timoris intuitu imponere manum renuerit, metuens scilicet ne propter hoc comes Andegauensis offenderetur; quae res a sacerdotali, praecipue pontificali, sublimitate quam procul esse debeat beatus Gregorius in septimo libro Moralium de ueritate loquens id quod de iustitia nihilominus intelligi conueniat his uerbis ostendit: 'Iste namque ueritatem iam libenter defendere appetit, sed tamen in ipso suo appetitu trepidus indignationem potestatis humanae pertimescit, cumque in terra hominem contra ueritatem pauet, eiusdem ueritatis iram coelitus sustinet.'[1] Proinde prudentiam tuam monemus et apostolica auctoritate praecipimus ut praelibatum electum consecrare nisi canonica ratio contradicat, postposita saecularis offensionis occasione, non ulterius recuses aut negligas. Denique potius tibi timendum est ne, si magis pauori quam iustitiae obsequi deliberaueris, et ille sicut aequum fuerit ab alio consecretur, et Turonensis ecclesia per tuam segnitiem, quod absit, honoris sui detrimentum sentire incipiat.

---

* After the death on 1 Dec. 1081 of Bishop Arnald of le Mans (1066–81) Hoel was elected bishop with the support of William I of England: Orderic Vitalis, *Hist. eccles.* iv. 11, ed. le Prévost, ii. 248–50. Count Fulk of Anjou prohibited his consecration by Archbishop Ralph of Tours; in this letter Gregory urged the archbishop to proceed with it. Ralph could not comply (cf. no. 52 below), so Hoel was consecrated on 21 Apr. 1085 by Archbishop William of Rouen. Hoel died in 1096.

J.L. 5226. MS.: Angers, Bibl. municip. 368, fo. 1ʳ, eleventh cent. Printed: Delisle, *B.É.C.* 6th ser. i (1865), 559. *Ann. iur. pont.* x, no. 55, cols. 417–18.

---

[1] *Moralia*, vii. 26, *P.L.* lxxv. 783.

To Archbishop Ralph of Tours   (*1082*)

Gregory, bishop, servant of the servants of God, to Ralph, the venerable archbishop of Tours, greeting and apostolic blessing.

We have heard that from worldly fear you have refused to lay hands upon the bishop-elect of le Mans, who wishes to be consecrated by you and whose consecration is the right of your church, because you are afraid of antagonizing the count of Anjou by your action. How far such a thing should be from the high office of a priest and particularly a bishop St. Gregory declares in these words from the seventh book of his *Morals* concerning truth—for what he says no less holds good concerning righteousness: 'See, here is a man who would now gladly defend truth, but he is fearful in his own heart and dreads the wrath of human power; while upon earth he resists the truth through fear of man, he incurs from heaven the anger of the truth which he resists.' We therefore urge and by apostolic authority command you that you put aside the pretext of giving worldly offence, and that unless some canonical reason forbids it you no longer refuse or delay to consecrate the bishop-elect. For your real terror should be that, if you decided to be the servant of fear rather than righteousness, he might, as would be just, be consecrated by someone else; and that by reason of your neglect the church of Tours would, which heaven forbid, begin to find that its honour was suffering diminution.

49

*To Hugh and the other clerks of Sainte-Radegonde, Poitiers:
Gregory insists upon his legates' earlier rulings in the clerks'
dispute with the monastery of Sainte-Croix, Poitiers, about
their respective rights*   (*1082*)*

Gregorius episcopus, seruus seruorum Dei, Hugoni et caeteris
sanctae Radegundis clericis, salutem et apostolicam benedictionem.

Peruenit ad audientiam nostram quod, apostolicae sedis authoritate calcata, priuilegia sanctae Radegundis monasterio sanctae
Crucis ab antiquo concessa infringere conemini, dum neque
debitum clericalis officii pensum praefato monasterio reuerenter,
ut decet et priuilegiorum scripta testantur, exhibetis, et ecclesiam
beatae Radegundis cum ordinationibus suis absque abbatissae
licentia et authoritate tenere uelitis. Quam litem inter uos[a] et
abbatissam anno priore legati nostri, priuilegiorum tenore diligenter perspecto, episcoporum qui aderant iudicio canonice data
sententia deciderunt, scilicet ut concessione et authoritate abbatissae sanctae Crucis, sicut firmiter in priuilegiis cautum est, sanctae
Radegundis ecclesia cum suis ordinationibus omni uenalitate et
spe quaestus procul remota, a uobis teneatur, et utrique ecclesiae
competens seruitium persoluatur, ut neque uos ius ecclesiae
sanctae Crucis nullatenus imminuatis, aut abbatissa aliquid uos
cogat quod canonum autoritate respuere ualeatis. Qua definitione
uos contentos esse opportere iudicamus, et ut neutrius partis
transgressione conuellatur, beati Petri authoritate uehementer
prohibemus quod, si deinceps de causa ulla ad nos proclamatio
peruenerit, noueritis procul dubio ut obedientiae contemptores
grauiore censura faciendos, et eos potissimum qui rectorum sedis
apostolicae priuilegiorum authoritatem uiolare ausu temerario
moliuntur. Valete.

---

[a] eos *M*

---

* Gregory refers to the settlement made by his legates Bishops Amatus of
Oléron and Hugh of Die at the council of Saintes (1081): *R.H.F.* xiv, no. 4,
p. 767; *Ann. iur. pont.* x. 413–14.
    J.L. 5227. MS.: Paris, Bibl. nat. Moreau 31, p. 73, eighteenth cent. (*M*).[1]
Printed: *Anal. iur. pont.* x, no. 51, col. 413. Pflugk-Harttung, *Acta pont. Rom.
ined.* i, no. 53, p. 52.

To Hugh and the other clerks of Sainte-Radegonde, Poitiers (*1082*)

Gregory, bishop, servant of the servants of God, to Hugh and the other clerks of Sainte-Radegonde, greeting and apostolic blessing.

It has reached our hearing that, trampling upon the authority of the apostolic see, you have attempted to infringe the privileges regarding Sainte-Radegonde which were anciently granted to the monastery of Sainte-Croix. For you have not reverently performed at this monastery the clerical duties to which you are bound in a fitting manner and as the terms of the privileges lay down, and you have sought to hold the church of Sainte-Radegonde with its offices without the abbess's licence and authority. Last year our legates carefully examined the contents of the privileges and, after the bishops who were present had canonically passed judgement, they composed the dispute between you and the abbess thus: by the permission and authority of the abbess of Sainte-Croix and as it is firmly stipulated in the privileges, putting aside all greed and hope of gain you are to hold the church of Sainte-Radegonde with its offices and you are to render proper service to both churches. Thus you are in no way to diminish the rights of the church of Sainte-Croix, while the abbess may not compel you to do anything which you can refuse by canonical authority. We think it right that you should rest content with this ruling, and in order that it may not be overthrown by the fault of either party we firmly lay down by St. Peter's authority that if in the future any complaint about the matter should reach us, you may know beyond doubt that those who refuse to be obedient will merit a grave penalty, and those most of all who rashly seek to violate the authority of the rightful privileges of the apostolic see. Farewell.

[1] A MS. note follows: 'Cette charte a été extraite de l'abbaye de Ste Croix de Poitiers, et transcrite sur une copie de l'écriture du 12 siècle. Elle se trouve encore dans le rouleau en parchemin connu dans cette abbaye sous le nom de Testament de Ste Radegonde.'

50

To Abbot Richard of Marseilles: Gregory rebukes his legate because he has excommunicated monks of Moissac who had taken over the church of Saint-Sernin, Toulouse, after they have obeyed the abbot of Cluny's command to withdraw from it (? *1082*)*

G. episcopus seruus seruorum Dei R. uenerabili sanctae Romanae aecclesiae cardinali et abbati Massiliensi salutem et apostolicam benedictionem.

Peruenit ad nos quod monachos illos qui aecclesiam sancti Saturnini non sine licencia proprii abbatis acceperant ac deinde compellente eos iussu maioris abbatis Cluniacensis eandem dimiserant, tua fraternitas illos postea quam satisfacientes exierint excommunicauit. Quod si ita est non parum de prudencia tua miramur. Vnde uolumus atque praecipimus ut tam illos ab excommunicationis uinculo soluas quam et de cetero ne tam leuiter in religiosos uiros huiusmodi sentenciam feras summopere cauere procures. Quid est enim aliud quam auctoritati derogari, indiscrete uel temere in quasque honestas personas auctoritatis licentia uti? Quod ut de futuro uigilanter attendas solliciteque prouideas, iterum iterumque monemus.

---

* The incidents to which this letter refers happened in the course of attempts by Bishop Isarnus of Toulouse (1071–1105) to reform the ancient suburban church of Saint-Sernin. In 1082 these attempts culminated in his expulsion of the canons and their replacement by monks from the Cluniac monastery of Moissac, under the authority of their abbot, Hunald (1072–95). Abbot Hugh of Cluny appears to have had no foreknowledge of the plan and to have responded favourably to Gregory's request that he secure the withdrawal of the monks of Moissac. For a fuller discussion, see Cowdrey, *The Cluniacs and the Gregorian Reform*, pp. 113–18.

J.L. 5239. MS.: Paris, Bibl. nat. lat. 8625, fo. 37ʳ, twelfth cent. Printed: Baluze, *Miscellanea*, vii. 127. *Ep. coll.* no. 39, p. 566.

To Abbot Richard of Marseilles (? *1082*)

Gregory, bishop, servant of the servants of God, to the venerable Richard, cardinal of the holy Roman church and abbot of Marseilles, greeting and apostolic blessing.

We have heard a report concerning the monks who took over the church of Saint-Sernin with the consent of their own abbot but later left it when they were so ordered by their superior the abbot of Cluny, that you have excommunicated them after they had made satisfaction and gone away. If this is so we wonder greatly concerning your prudence. We will and command that you release them from the bond of excommunication, and also that in future you take every precaution not so lightly to pass a sentence of this kind against religious men. To exercise authority intemperately or rashly against men of good report must assuredly detract from its force. We insistently warn you that for the future you keep this truth clearly in mind and that you carefully act upon it.

51

To the archbishops, bishops, and abbots of France [and Germany]: Gregory reproves them because they have not helped the Roman church in her necessity and summons them to his November council at Rome   (1083, summer)*

G. episcopus*ᵃ* seruus seruorum Dei archiepiscopis episcopis et abbatibus*ᵇ* in Gallia*ᶜ* constitutis, qui in gremio sanctae Romanae ecclesiae permanere uidentur, salutem et apostolicam benedictionem.

Quantas tribulationum angustias et persecutionum procellas ac pondera periculorum uniuersalis mater sancta Romana ecclesia temporibus istis perpessa sit quia credi uix potest ex maiori parte latet scientiam uestram. Ad haec*ᵈ* quoque*ᵉ* quid consolationis*ᶠ* quidue suffragii per uos suos filios debitae compassionis perceperit, uos ipsi cognoscitis. Quod enim sine dolore uix possumus uel reminisci, ita caritas pene cunctorum*ᵍ* circa eam refrixit*ʰ* ut haec tempora per euangelium praesignata quodam modo specialiter uideantur ubi dicitur: 'Quoniam abundauit iniquitas refrigescet caritas multorum.'¹ Vnde quid aliud dixerim, nisi quod uos qui aut segniter neglexistis*ⁱ* aut pauide refugistis matri uestrae in tanta pressura solatiari nomine filiorum indignos et caritatis uisceribus alienos uos ostendistis? Quem uero pudorem uel potius quantum dolorem quisquis est sanae mentis non sentiat, cum consideret persecutores christianae religionis tanta factionis conspiratione sic omnimodis annisibus non solum res suas profundendo sed etiam se ipsos morti tradendo ad explendam animi atrocitatem huc usque desudasse, neminem autem uel uix paucissimos iustitiae fautores aut corporis laborem subire aut rerum dispendia pati aut de suis bonis opem matri*ʲ* ecclesiae ferre curauisse. Verum

---

ᵃ om. episcopus ZC   *ᵇ* et abbatibus *illegible in K, where the text is here uncertain*   *ᶜ* Teutonico regno K   *ᵈ* hoc K   *ᵉ* quamque V
ᶠ consilii ZC   *ᵍ* multorum ZC   *ʰ* refrigescit ZC   *ⁱ* nexglexistis V
ʲ add suae ZC

---

* This letter has hitherto been known only from the *Codex Udalrici*; the present text is based directly on the form in which it circulated in France and Germany. It contains a summons to Gregory's Nov. council of 1083 and may have been dispatched at the same time as *Reg.* ix. 29, pp. 612–13 (but for the difficulties which this last letter presents, see Fliche, *La Réforme grégorienne*, ii.

To the archbishops, bishops, and abbots of France [and Germany] (1083, summer)

Gregory, bishop, servant of the servants of God, to the archbishops, bishops, and abbots of France who seem to remain in the bosom of the holy Roman church, greeting and apostolic blessing.

It is largely hidden from your knowledge, for it is almost past belief, how severe are the straits of distress, the storms of persecution, and the burdens of danger which the mother of us all, the holy Roman church, has endured in these times. And what comfort and what help she has received through you, her sons, as the due return of your sympathy, you in your own hearts know. For, as we can hardly even call to mind without sorrow, the love of almost all men towards her has grown so cold that these times of ours seem to have been after a manner specially foretold in the gospel where it is said: 'Because wickedness is multiplied most men's love will grow cold.'[1] So what else am I to say but that you who have either slothfully neglected or else cravenly shunned to bring your mother relief in such distress show yourselves undeserving of the name of sons and strangers to the promptings of love? What shame, or rather how much grief, must anyone of sound mind not feel, when he sees how the assailants of the Christian religion, in such partisan concord, have hitherto laboured to effect their frightful purposes by all manner of exertions, not only lavishing their goods but also giving themselves up to death; while no one, or at most only a very few upholders of righteousness, have cared to undertake active service, or to suffer the loss of their possessions, or to bring help to their mother the church at cost to themselves.

27, n. 1, 418, n. 4). For the Nov. council and for a complaint about Henry IV's obstructiveness, see *Reg.* ix. 35a, pp. 627–8, which also summarizes the Roman view of Henry's *persecutio* of the papacy since his second excommunication at the Lent council of 1080.

J.L. 5259. MSS.: Rome, Vatican Library, lat. 1974, fo. 121ʳ⁻ᵛ, eleventh cent. (*V*). Kremsmünster, Stiftsbibl. 27, fo. 203ᵛ, eleventh cent. (*K*). *Codex Udalrici*: Zwettl, Stiftsarch. 283, pp. 116–17, twelfth cent. (*Z*); Vienna, Österr. National-bibl. 398, fo. 66ʳ⁻ᵛ, twelfth cent. (*C*). Printed: *Codex Udalrici*: Eccard, *Corp. hist.* ii, no. 154, cols. 156–7; Jaffé, *Mon. Bamb.* no. 58, pp. 123–5. *Ep. coll.* no. 23, pp. 548–50.

---

[1] Matt. 24: 12.

utcumque uestra fraternitas sese habuerit, 'benedictus Deus et pater
domini nostri Ihesu Christi, pater misericordiarum et Deus
totius consolationis, qui consolatur nos in omni tribulatione
nostra',[1] qui nos ab aduersariorum manibus et persecutorum
uiolentia protegens, hactenus in manu nostra iustitiam secundum
testimonium conscientiae nostrae defendit atque potentiae suae
uigore humanae infirmitatis imbecillitatem nostram corroborans,
ad iniquitatem peruerti nos nullis promissionum blandiciis,[k]
nullis uexationum[l] terroribus sinit. Ipsi ergo immensas gratias
referimus qui nos infractos hucusque in pressurae tempestate
conseruans ad quandam spem tranquillitatis sic liberis incessibus
duxit, ut non nos contra principalem iustitiae intentionem egisse
aut propria conscientia aut religiosorum uirorum[m] qui nouerunt
examinatio reprehendat.

De caetero, fratres, ut causa iurgiorum et discordia quae inter
apostolicam sedem et regnum iamdudum agitatur, annuente
Domino, communi diligentia[n] ualeat congruum finem[o] sortiri,
uos ad sinodum quam in medio Nouembri celebrare disposuimus
praesentium litterarum conuocatione ex parte beati Petri apostolorum principis praecipientes inuitamus. Hoc etiam uestram
fraternitatem[p] scire uolumus quia, ut secure et ad nos uenire et
in uestram patriam[q] Deo protegente possitis redire, fideles nostri
a maioribus qui nunc erant[r] in curia Heinrici dicti regis iura-
mento securitatem receperunt. Desideramus enim una uobiscum
tractare, diuino fulti[s] auxilio,[t] qualiter possimus pacem Dei[u]
firmare atque ad gremium[v] matris ecclesiae scismaticos uia regia
incedendo[w2] reuocare.

---

[k] blandimentis K   [l] uexantium ZC   [m] *om.* uirorum ZC   [n] *om.*
communi diligentia ZC   [o] *om.* finem K   [p] *The rest of the text is
lacking in K*   [q] potentiam ZC   [r] sunt ZC   [s] iudicio *deleted* C
[t] officio *deleted and* iudicio *interlined above* Z   [u] *om.* Dei ZC   [v] *add*
sanctae ZC   [w] *om.* uia regia incedendo; *add* Deo auxiliante ZC

---

[1] 2 Cor. 1: 3–4.
[2] Cf. Num. 21: 22. The phrase 'pacem Dei' in the Vatican MS. interestingly
synchronizes with the spreading into Germany of the French 'pax Dei': cf.
Cowdrey, 'The Peace and the Truce of God in the Eleventh Century', *Past and
Present*, no. 46 (Feb. 1970), esp. pp. 64–5. In the collection of 32 canons drawn
up in the south of France soon after Gregory's death and wrongly ascribed to
him, which is preserved in the *Liber Tarraconensis*, Gregory was represented as
legislating for the Peace of God at one of his Roman councils: see canon xiv
as printed in Pflugk-Harttung, *Acta pont. Rom. ined.* ii, no. 161, p. 126.

But however the matter may stand with you, 'blessed be the God and Father of our Lord Jesus Christ, the Father of mercies and God of all comfort, who comforts us in all our afflictions',[1] who by protecting us from the hands of our enemies and from the violence of our persecutors has until now, as our conscience testifies, defended righteousness by the work of our hands, and who by strengthening the weakness of our human infirmity by the energy of his power has not allowed us at all to be led away into wickedness by any enticing promises nor by any hostile threats. Therefore we return our thanks without number to him who so far has kept us unharmed from the attacking storm, and has so led us by the way of liberty towards the hope of calm that neither our own conscience nor the scrutiny of religious men who know us well accuses us of having acted contrary to the overruling purposes of righteousness.

Finally, brothers, in order that, if the Lord is willing, a fit conclusion may by our common diligence be reached to the disputes and discord which have for long been rife between the apostolic see and the kingdom, we summon and call you by this letter on behalf of St. Peter, prince of the apostles, to a council which we plan to hold in the middle of November. We would have you know that our envoys have received from the leading men at the court of Henry the so-called king a sworn guarantee that you may come to us in safety and, with God's protection, return to your own country. For, supported by divine help, we desire to take counsel with you about how we may establish the peace of God and how we may recall those in schism to travel by the royal way[2] to the bosom of their mother the church.

52

To the canons of Saint-Martin, Tours: Gregory exhorts them to return to Archbishop Ralph's obedience and to heed the directions of Gregory's legates, while they should avoid the excommunicated Count Fulk (*1082–3*)*

G. episcopus seruus seruorum Dei canonicis sancti Martini Turonensis.

Quia legatis nostris et archiepiscopo uestro uos non obedire sed insuper eum expulisse audiuimus et ab eis uos esse excommunicatos ob culpam uestram didicimus, iccirco salutem et apostolicam benedictionem mittere uobis ausi non fuimus; cuius rei uos indignos existere, profecto plus uobis ipsi dolemus. Nam si animarum uestrarum curam gereretis, omnino nec illud praesumere nec post flagitium tamdiu in impenitudine manere consilium haberetis. Quapropter paterna uos alloquutione monentes ex parte beati Petri praecipimus ut de tanto facinore digne satisfacientes praedictum fratrem nostrum archiepiscopum ad ecclesiam suam cum honore reducere procuretis, ac deinceps ei paternalem sicut decet*a* reuerentiam exibentes obedire nullatenus detrectetis. Praecipimus etiam uobis ut res tam ipsius archiepiscopi quam canonicorum sancti Mauricii in integrum restituatis, atque legatis nostris de cetero debitam obedientiam exibentes, et ab ipso comite excommunicato Fulcone et ab omnibus excommunicatis uos custodire uigilanter studeatis. Quod si nec his etiam mandatis salubribus obedire uolueritis, sententiam anathematis in uos confirmantes apostolice ultioni uos subiacere decernimus.

a *add* oboedientiam et M

---

* This letter was written with *Reg.* ix. 24, pp. 605–7, and illustrates the growing tension between the archbishop and the count which followed their difference over Bishop Hoel of le Mans: no. 48 above. In 1082 Archbishop Ralph was driven from his see at the instance of King Philip I by Count Fulk, who was supported by the canons of Saint-Martin, Tours. The ultimate cause of this most obscure happening appears to have been the king's displeasure at Bishop Hugh of Die's translation to the primatial see of Lyons: Ralph was expelled because of his past collaboration with the standing legate, and the canons of Saint-Maurice, Tours, were loyal to their archbishop. The bishops of the province of Lyons excommunicated the count: *R.H.F.* xiv, no. 11, pp. 673–4.

To the canons of Saint-Martin, Tours   (*1082–3*)

Gregory, bishop, servant of the servants of God, to the canons of Saint-Martin, Tours.

Because we have heard that you have not obeyed our legates and your archbishop but rather have driven the archbishop out, and because we have learnt that for your fault you have been excommunicated by them, we have not ventured to send you our greeting and apostolic blessing. That you do not deserve them indeed grieves us more than it grieves you. For if you cared for your own souls you would surely have seen to it that you neither dared to do what you did nor remained for so long impenitent after the outrage. Therefore we address a fatherly warning to you, and on behalf of St. Peter we command you, to make due satisfaction for so great a crime and to take steps to restore our brother the archbishop with honour to his church. For the future you must not in any way fail to show him the reverence due to a father nor to obey him. We also command you to restore in full the property of the archbishop and of the canons of Saint-Maurice, for the future to pay due reverence to our legates, and to be vigilant and zealous to keep yourselves away from the excommunicate Count Fulk and from all excommunicates. If you will not obey even these healthful mandates, we confirm the sentence of anathema against you and decree that you are subject to apostolic punishment.

The legates who are referred to were Archbishop Hugh of Lyons and Bishop Amatus of Oléron.

J.L. 5232. MS.: Angers, Bibl. municip. 368, fo. 1ʳ, twelfth cent. Printed: Mabillon, *Annales ordinis sancti Benedicti*, v. 176 (*M*). *Ep. coll.* no. 38, pp. 565–6.

53

To Archbishop Hugh of Lyons: Gregory strongly condemns the imprisonment of Bishop Odo of Bayeux by King William I of England (*1082–3*)*

G. episcopus seruus seruorum Dei dilecto in Christo fratri H. Lugdunensi archiepiscopo salutem et apostolicam benedictionem.

Ad notitiam tuam peruenisse non dubitamus qualiter Anglorum rex in fratrem et coepiscopum nostrum Baiocensem contra fas et honestum ausus est manum mittere eumque contra regiam modestiam reuerentiamque sacerdotalem impudenter captum et impudentius adhuc in custodia . . .

54

To all the faithful: Gregory sets forth the plight of the church and appeals for help against her enemies

(*1084, July–Nov.*)†

Gregorius episcopus seruus seruorum Dei omnibus in Christo fidelibus apostolicam sedem reuera diligentibus salutem et apostolicam benedictionem.

Peruenit, fratres karissimi, peruenit ut estimamus ad notitiam uestram quia nostro tempore innouatum est quod in psalmis inquirendo dicitur: 'Quare fremuerunt gentes, et populi meditati sunt inania? Astiterunt reges terrae, et principes conuenerunt in unum aduersus Dominum et aduersus christum eius.'[1] Principes

---

* This fragment should be read with Gregory's far milder letter to William himself about the same matter: *Reg.* ix. 37, pp. 630–1. According to the E version of the *Anglo-Saxon Chronicle* William seized his half-brother Bishop Odo I of Bayeux (1049–97), who was also earl of Kent, in 1082; he seems to have been still a captive at the king's death in 1087. The reasons for his arrest are not clear, but Orderic Vitalis and William of Malmesbury spoke of his sending money to Rome and recruiting knights for an expedition to go there: Ordericus Vitalis, *Historia ecclesiastica*, vii. 8, ed. A. le Prévost, iii (Paris, 1845), 188–92; William of Malmesbury, *Gesta regum*, iii. 277, ed. W. Stubbs, ii (London, Rolls Series, 1889), 334. Odo may have planned to intervene at Rome in Gregory's defence; while William would not tolerate the recruiting in England of knights upon whose service he relied.

J.L. 5253. MS.: Paris, Bibl. nat. 1458, fo. 161ᵛ, twelfth cent. Printed: *Ep. coll.* no. 44, pp. 570–1.

To Archbishop Hugh of Lyons   (1082–3)

Gregory, bishop, servant of the servants of God, to his beloved brother in Christ, Archbishop Hugh of Lyons, greeting and apostolic blessing.

We do not doubt that you have heard how the king of England has dared to lay hands upon our brother and fellow bishop of Bayeux against what is lawful and right, and against proper kingly restraint and the respect which is due to the priesthood has shamelessly captured him and, yet more shamelessly, still [holds him] captive. . . .

To all the faithful   (1084, July–Nov.)

Gregory, bishop, servant of the servants of God, to all the faithful in Christ who verily love the apostolic see, greeting and apostolic blessing.

Dearest brothers, we think it must assuredly have struck you that in our times the psalmist's question and answer have found renewed meaning: 'Why do the nations rage, and the peoples plot vain things? The kings of the earth stand up and the rulers take counsel together against the Lord and against his anointed.'[1] For

† After Gregory had been forced to withdraw with the Normans from Rome to Salerno in July 1084 he held a council at which he renewed his excommunication of Henry IV and the Anti-pope Clement III, whom Henry had nominated at Brixen in 1080 and who crowned him emperor at Rome on 31 Mar. 1084. Gregory prepared this letter for general circulation and dispatched it by his legates—by Cardinal Odo of Ostia to Germany, by Cardinal Peter of Albano and Prince Gisulf of Salerno to France, and by Abbot Jarento of Saint-Bénigne, Dijon, to Portugal: Bernold, *Chron. a.* 1084, *M.G.H. Scr.* v. 441; Hugh of Flavigny, *Chron.* ii, *M.G.H. Scr.* viii. 464. For the very probable suggestion that *Reg.* viii. 23, pp. 565–7, may have embodied Gregory's instructions for the legates to France at this time, see Borino, 'Può il Reg. Vat. 2 (Registro di Gregorio VII) essere il registro della cancellaria?', ii, *S.G.* v (1956), 399–401. Odo of Ostia arrived in Germany by Christmas 1084.

J.L. 5271. MS.: Hugh of Flavigny, *Chron.*: Berlin, Deutsche Staatsbibl. Phillipps 1870, fo. 131ʳ⁻ᵛ, eleventh cent. Printed: Hugh of Flavigny, *Chron.* ii, *M.G.H. Scr.* viii. 464–5. *Ep. coll.* no. 46, pp. 572–5.

[1] Ps. 2: 1–2.

enim gentium et principes sacerdotum cum magna multitudine conuenerunt in unum aduersus Christum, omnipotentis Dei filium, et aduersus apostolum eius Petrum, ut christianam religionem extinguerent et hereticam prauitatem propagarent. Sed Deo miserante illos qui confidunt in Domino nullo terrore nullaque crudelitate uel mundanae gloriae promissione ad suam potuerunt deflectere impietatem. Pro nulla quippe alia qualibet ratione contra nos inique conspirantes manus erexerunt nisi quia periculum sanctae ecclesiae noluimus silentio praeterire et his qui eandem sponsam Dei non erubescunt in seruitutem redigere. In omnibus enim terris licet etiam pauperculis mulierculis suae patriae lege suaque uoluntate uirum accipere legitime; sanctae uero ecclesiae, quae est sponsa Dei et mater nostra, non licet secundum impiorum uotum et detestabilem consuetudinem diuina lege propriaque uoluntate suo sponso legaliter in terris adherere. Non enim pati debemus ut filii sanctae ecclesiae hereticis, adulteris, et inuasoribus quasi patribus subiciantur atque ab eis uelut adulterina infamia notentur. Hinc multa mala, diuersa pericula, et inaudita crudelitatis scelera qualiter sint exorta a nostris legatis luce clarius ueraque relatione potestis addiscere, et si reuera doletis et contristamini de ruina christianae religionis et confusione eique uultis manum praebere adiutorii, intrinsecus certo tacti dolore, ab eisdem instrui satis potestis. Sunt enim beato Petro fidelissimi et inter primos domus eius unusquisque in suo ordine adnumerati, qui nullo terrore nullaque temporalium rerum promissione potuerunt in aliquo ab eius fidelitate et defensione auelli et a gremio sanctae matris ecclesiae separari.

Sed quia, sicut nouit uestra fraternitas, licet indigno et peccatori diuinitus per prophetam dicitur: 'Super montem excelsum' et reliqua,[1] et iterum: 'Clama, ne cesses',[2] uelim nolim, omni postposita uerecundia, timore quoque uel alicuius terreno amore, euangelizo, clamo, clamo, et iterum clamo[3] et adnuncio uobis quia christiana religio et uera fides quam filius Dei de caelo ueniens per patres nostros nos docuit in secularem uersa prauam consuetudinem, heu pro dolor! ad nichilum pene deuenit et, immutato antiquo colore, cecidit non solum in diaboli uerum etiam

---

[1] Isa. 57: 7. [2] Isa. 58: 1; cf. *Reg.* vii. 14a, 7 Mar. 1080, p. 483.
[3] Gregory may have had in mind Gregory the Great, *Homiliarum in Ezechielem*, i, *Homil.* xi. 5, *P.L.* lxxvi. 907–8. (I am grateful to Dr. B. Smalley for this suggestion.)

the princes of the nations and the princes of the priests have indeed taken counsel together with a vast throng against Christ, the Son of Almighty God, and against his apostle Peter, to destroy the Christian religion and to spread their depraved heresy. But by God's mercy there is no fear or cruelty, nor any promise of worldly glory, by which they can pervert to their own ungodliness those who trust in the Lord. They have wickedly conspired and lifted up their hands against us for absolutely no reason whatsoever save that we would not silently disregard the danger which beset holy church nor the men who did not scruple to reduce to slavery the bride of Christ. For in every land even the poorest and least of women are allowed to take a husband according to the law of their country and to their own good pleasure; yet the will of godless men and an abominable custom do not allow holy church, which is the bride of Christ and our mother, lawfully to cleave to her spouse in all lands according to divine law and her own good pleasure. We may not allow the sons of holy church to be made subject to heretics, adulterers, and intruders as though such men were their fathers, nor to be stigmatized through them as by the reproach of adulterous birth. What numerous evils, what various dangers, and what unheard-of crimes of cruelty have arisen from such a state of affairs you may learn more clearly than daylight from the true report of our legates: if you truly grieve and sorrow for the destruction and confounding of the Christian religion and are willing to bring it a helping hand because you are inwardly touched by true compunction, you may receive full instructions from them. For they are most faithful servants of St. Peter and, each of them in his own order, they are amongst the leading men of his household; no fear or promise of temporal goods could in any way turn them from his loyalty and service nor separate them from the bosom of holy mother church.

Because, as you well know, God spoke to me, unworthy and a sinner though I am, through the prophet's words: 'Upon a high mountain' and so on,[1] and again: 'Cry aloud, spare not',[2] whether I wish to or not, laying aside all reluctance, fear, and earthly love of anyone, I preach, I cry, cry, and cry again,[3] and I proclaim to you that the Christian religion and the true faith which the Son of God who came down from heaven taught us through the fathers, have been turned into the evil custom of this world and, shame to say! have almost been brought to naught. Their ancient character has so changed that they have been reduced to a laughing-stock not

in Iudeorum Sarracenorum atque paganorum derisionem. Illi enim leges suas, licet hoc tempore ad nullam animarum salutem utiles, nullisque miraculis, sicut lex nostra aeterni regis frequenti attestatione, clarificatas et corroboratas, prout credunt obseruant. Nos autem seculi inebriati amore et uana decepti ambitione, omni religione et honestate cupiditati atque superbiae postpositis, exleges et quasi fatui uidemur, quia praesentis uitae et futurae salutem et honorem sicut patres nostri non habemus nec etiam sicut oportet speramus. Et si sunt aliqui licet rarissimi qui Deum timeant, pro se utcumque non pro communi fratrum salute decertant prompta uoluntate. Qui uel quot sunt qui pro timore uel amore omnipotentis Dei, in quo uiuimus, mouemur, et sumus,[1] tantum desudent uel usque ad mortem laborent, quantum seculares milites pro dominis suis uel etiam pro amicis et subditis? Ecce multa milia hominum secularium pro dominis suis cotidie currunt in mortem; pro caelesti uero Deo et redemptore nostro non solum in mortem non currunt, uerum etiam quorumdam hominum inimicitias subire contepmnunt. Et si sunt aliqui, immo Deo miserante sunt licet perpaucissimi, qui in faciem impiis usque ad mortem resistere pro amore christianae legis contendunt, non solum a fratribus ut dignum est non adiuuantur sed etiam imprudentes et minus discreti ut dementes habentur.

Sed quia hec et his similia specialiter imminent nobis ut uobis, indicemus quatenus Deo largiente uicia possimus a cordibus fratrum auellere et uirtutes in eis plantare. Rogamus et obsecramus in domino Ihesu, qui nos sua morte redemit, ut tribulationes et angustias quas patimur ab inimicis christianae religionis, cur et qualiter patiamur diligenter inuestigando intelligatis. Ex quo enim dispositione diuina mater aecclesia in trono apostolico me ualde indignum et Deo teste inuitum collocauit, summopere procuraui ut sancta aecclesia, sponsa Dei, domina et mater nostra, ad proprium rediens decus libera, casta, et catholica permaneret. Sed quia hosti antiquo hec omnino displicent, armauit contra nos membra sua ut omnia in contrarium uerteret. Ideo in nos immo in apostolicam sedem tanta fecit, quanta facere a tempore Constantini Magni imperatoris nequiuit. Nec ualde mirum, quia quanto plus

[1] Cf. Acts 17: 28.

only of the devil but also of Jews, Saracens, and pagans. For these men, so far as faith is given them, observe their own laws, even though in this age they are of no avail for the salvation of souls and are not given lustre and confirmation by such miracles as those by which the Eternal King frequently gives his testimony to our law. We, on the other hand, are so drunk with love of this world, we are so deceived by empty ambition, and we so subordinate religion and honour to greed and pride, that we seem to be without law and like fools; for we do not possess our fathers' uprightness and honour regarding this life and the life to come, nor do we even hope for them as we ought. If there are some, however pitifully few, who fear God, they have a ready will to contend only for themselves, not for the general salvation of their fellows. Who are the men, or how many are they, who exert themselves and toil to the death for the fear or love of Almighty God, in whom we live and move and have our being,[1] as do secular knights for their lords or even for their friends and clients? Lo! many thousands of secular men go daily to their death for their lords; but for the God of heaven and our Redeemer they not only do not go to their death but they also refuse to face the hostility of certain men. And if there are some—for by God's mercy there are some, though very few— who for love of Christ's law are determined to stand firm to the death in the face of the ungodly, they are not only not helped as is proper by their fellows but they are also considered to be foolish and of unsound judgement as if they were out of their minds.

But since these things and others like them especially threaten us as they threaten you, we shall briefly show how, by God's grace, we may tear out the vices from our brothers' hearts and plant virtues in them. We ask and beseech you in the Lord Jesus, who redeemed us by his death, to consider diligently and to understand why and how we should suffer the distresses and afflictions which we suffer at the hands of the enemies of the Christian religion. Ever since by God's providence mother church set me upon the apostolic throne, deeply unworthy and, as God is my witness, unwilling though I was, my greatest concern has been that holy church, the bride of Christ, our lady and mother, should return to her true glory and stand free, chaste, and catholic. But because this entirely displeased the ancient enemy he has armed his members against us in order to turn everything upside down. He has accordingly done such things against us, or rather against the apostolic see, as he has not been able to do from the time of the Emperor Constantine the Great. And truly it is no wonder, for the

antichristi tempus appropinquat tanto amplius christianam religionem extinguere decertat.

Nunc autem, fratres mei karissimi, diligenter quae uobis dico audite. Omnes qui in toto orbe christiano censentur nomine et christianam fidem uere cognoscunt, sciunt et credunt beatum Petrum, apostolorum principem, esse omnium christianorum patrem et primum post Christum pastorem, sanctamque Romanam aecclesiam omnium aecclesiarum matrem et magistram. Si ergo hoc creditis et indubitanter tenetis, rogo uos et praecipio ego, qualiscumque frater et indignus magister uester, per omnipotentem Deum, adiuuate et succurrite praedicto patri uestro et matri, si per eos absolutionem omnium peccatorum et benedictionem atque gratiam in hoc seculo et in futuro habere desideratis.

Omnipotens Deus, a quo bona cuncta procedunt, mentem uestram semper illuminet eamque sua dilectione ac proximi fecundet, ut mereamini praefatum patrem uestrum et matrem certa deuotione debitores uobis facere et ad eorum societatem sine uerecundia peruenire. Amen.

55

To all the faithful: Gregory sets forth the misfortunes of the Roman church   *(? 1084)**

Gregorius episcopus seruus seruorum Dei omnibus qui christiana fide censentur et beati apostolorum principis sedem aecclesiarum omnium matrem recognoscunt salutem et absolutionem omnium peccatorum per benedictionem et merita beati Petri et Pauli principum apostolorum.

Notum uobis fieri uolumus, fratres karissimi, quia sancta Romana aecclesia, communis mater, omnium gentium magistra et domina, non solum splendore sanctae religionis uniuersum mundum illuminauit sed etiam multis indigentibus per diversas partes terrae necessaria pietate distribuit. Modo uero peccatis non tantum nostris sed etiam multarum gentium exigentibus, et in religione friguit et terrenas opes maiori ex parte amisit.[1] Non-nulli enim imperatores reges et principes aliorumque ordinum

---

* J.L. 5273. MS.: Angers, Bibl. municip. 368, folio inserted inside back cover, eleventh cent. Printed: *B.É.C.*, 6th ser. i (1865), 560. *Anal. iur. pont.* x, no. 57, col. 418.

nearer the time of Antichrist approaches the more violently he strives to destroy the Christian religion.

So now, my dearly beloved brothers, listen carefully to what I say to you. All who in the whole world bear the name of Christian and truly understand the Christian faith know and believe that St. Peter, the prince of the apostles, is the father of all Christians and their first shepherd after Christ, and that the holy Roman church is the mother and mistress of all the churches. If, then, you believe and unshakably hold this, such as I am, your brother and unworthy master, I ask and command you by Almighty God to help and succour your father and mother, if through them you would have the absolution of all your sins, and blessing and grace in this world and in the world to come.

May Almighty God, from whom all good things come, always enlighten your minds and make them fruitful in love of himself and of your neighbour, that you may by your unwavering devotion make your father and mother your debtors and that you may attain to their fellowship free from shame. Amen.

To all the faithful   (? 1084)

Gregory, bishop, servant of the servants of God, to all who are reckoned as Christians and who acknowledge the see of the blessed prince of apostles to be the mother of all the churches, greeting and the absolution of all their sins by the blessing and merits of St. Peter and St. Paul, the princes of the apostles.

Dearest brothers, we would have you consider that the holy Roman church, our universal mother, the mistress and lady of all peoples, has not only enlightened the whole world by the lustre of her holy religion but also by her mercy has ministered necessities to many who were in need in different parts of the world. But now, by reason not only of our own sins but also of many peoples', she has both grown cold in religion and in large part she has lost her worldly substance.[1] For many—emperors, kings, princes, and other

---

[1] The reference may well be to the apostasy of numerous members of the curia, including thirteen cardinals, in 1084.

personae misera cupiditate capti, maternam maledictionem in-
currere non timentes, eius possessiones inuaserunt, distraxerunt,
et in proprios usus redegerunt; qui etiam gladio anathematis
percussi et more infelicis Iudae sacrilegii uinculo strangulati, ne ad
penitentiam redirent, disipuerunt. Hinc igitur inopia, deuastationes,
latrocinia, rapinae contra ipsum aecclesiae caput, beatum uidelicet
Petrum, et in eius quasi uisceribus exorte sunt. Proinde propria
eius aecclesia et beati Pauli quae illorum[1] . . .

56

To Count Hoel of Brittany: Gregory urges him to restore
and safeguard the possessions of the monastery of Sainte-
Croix, Quimperlé (*1073–84*)*

Gregorius episcopus seruus[a] seruorum Dei Hoelo glorioso
principi salutem et apostolicam benedictionem.

Sicut relatione quorundam didicimus, pater tuus diuino amore
accensus monasterium sanctae Crucis nonnullis bonis ditauit,
quae si aliquis auferre uel minuere praesumit non paruae negligentiae poteris arguere et animas patris et matris minus diligere.
Quapropter si quid a te uel ab aliquo de his quae praedicto
monasterio oblata sunt subreptum esse atque alienatum cognoscis,
uolumus immo ex parte Dei et sancti Petri praecipimus omni
diligentia te recuperare atque ad utilitatem eiusdem uenerabilis
loci modis omnibus tueri atque defendere. Quod si feceris anima-
bus parentum permaxime uideris proficere et tibi apud Deum
maximum lucrum et in saeculum bonam famam optinere. Si
enim hoc unicuique aecclesiae debes, multo magis circa salutem
huius quam pater tuus dilexit et cui diuina prouidentia fratrem
tuum carnalem uoluit prouidere oportet te inuigilare.

[a] *om.* seruus *E*

* Sainte-Croix, Quimperlé, was founded in 1029 by Alan Cagnart, count
of Cornouailles (d. 1058), husband of Judith, daughter of Count Judhael of
Nantes. This letter is written to their son Count Hoel II of Brittany (1066–84),
formerly count of Cornouailles.

J.L. 5265. MSS.: London, Brit. Mus. Egerton 2802, fo. 150[r-v], twelfth cent.
(*E*).[2] Paris, Bibl. nat. Baluze 41, fo. 19[r-v], seventeenth cent. Paris, Bibl. nat.
Baluze 74, fo. 24[r], *c.* 1700. Printed: Loewenfeld, *N.A.* vii (1882), 163. *Cartulaire*

ranks of men—made captive by their wretched greed and not
fearing to incur their mother's curse, have invaded her possessions,
rent them asunder, and plundered them for their own uses. Even
when they were smitten by the sword of excommunication and
strangled like unhappy Judas by the rope of their sacrilege, they
were so foolish that they did not return to penance. Hence arose
scarcity, ravagings, robberies, and rapines, against the very head
of the church, St. Peter himself, and as it were in his own bowels.
Thus his own church and St. Paul's which[1] . . .

To Count Hoel of Brittany   (1073–84)

Gregory, bishop, servant of the servants of God, to the renowned
prince Hoel, greeting and apostolic blessing.

As we have learnt from certain men's report, your father was
inspired by love of God to endow with many goods the monastery
of Sainte-Croix. Should anyone dare to steal or to violate them you
may accuse him of no small disrespect and of insufficient concern
for the souls of your father and mother. Wherefore if you know that
you or anyone else have seized or alienated anything that has
been offered to this monastery, we will, or rather we command
on behalf of God and of Saint Peter, that you restore it with all
diligence, and that you in every way guard and protect it for the
benefit of this venerable place. If you do so you will manifestly
bring the greatest advantage to your parents' souls and win for
yourself exceeding riches with God and a good report in this world.
For if you have such a duty to every church, how much more
should you be watchful for the safety of one which your father
loved and for which by divine providence your own brother
desired to make provision.

de l'abbaye de Sainte-Croix de Quimperlé, ed. Maître and de Berthou, no. 127,
pp. 284–5.

---

[1] This incomplete sentence perhaps alludes to Henry IV's attacks upon
the churches of St. Peter and St. Paul-without-the-Walls: cf. *Reg.* ix. 35a,
pp. 627–8.

[2] Cartulary of Sainte-Croix, Quimperlé. For permission to print the text of
this and the following letter I am grateful to the Trustees of the British Museum.

57

To Toirdhealbhach Ó Briain, king of Ireland, and all the Irish: Gregory proclaims the authority of the vicars of St. Peter and encourages the Irish to have recourse to it (1074–84), 24 or 25 Feb.

Gregorius episcopus seruus seruorum Dei Terdeluacho inclito regi Hiberniae archiepiscopis episcopis abbatibus proceribus omnibusque christianis Hiberniam inhabitantibus salutem et apostolicam benedictionem.

Per orbem uniuersum domini Ihesu doctrina refulsit, quoniam is qui de thalamo suo tanquam sponsus exiuit tabernaculum suum in sole constituit, et nemo est qui caloris eius fulgorem effugere possit.¹ Huius auctoritas sanctam aecclesiam in solida petra fundauit et beato Petro a petra uenerabile nomen habenti eius iura commisit; quam etiam super omnia mundi regna constituit, cui principatus et potestates et quicquid in seculo*a* sublime*b* uidetur esse subiecit, illo Ysaiae completo oraculo: 'Venient', inquit, 'ad te qui detrahebant tibi et adorabunt uestigia pedum tuorum.'² Beato igitur Petro eiusque uicariis, inter quos dispensatio diuina nostram quoque sortem annumerari disposuit, orbis uniuersus obedientiam similiter et reuerentiam debet, quam mente deuota sanctae Romanae aecclesiae exhibere reminiscimini. Vos autem ut karissimos filios exhortamur iustitiam exercere, catholicam aecclesiae pacem tueri et diligere, ipsamque diligentes ulnis caritatis uobis adiungere. Siqua uero negotia penes uos

---

a caelo *L*   *b* sublime *C*

---

* Toirdhealbhach (Turlough), king of Munster, was able in 1073 to establish his authority over Meath and Connaught. Although he failed to secure the submission of the North he remained until his death in 1086 the most powerful Irish ruler since the death in 1014 of his ancestor Brian Boru. The date of the letter raises a problem. Gregory is not known to have been at Sutri on 24–5 Feb. in any year of his reign. But if Marino—some 15 km. distant from the Lateran—is the correct reading, any year in which he was then at Rome is possible, i.e. 1074–6, 1078–84; 24 or 25 Feb. 1076 and 24 Feb. 1083 are the most likely dates.

J.L. 5059. MSS.: London, Brit. Mus. Cotton Claudius A.I, fo. 38ʳ, *c.* 1200 (*C*). London, Brit. Mus. addit. 4791, fo. 152ʳ, seventeenth cent.³ London, Brit. Mus. Sloane 1449, fo. 42ᵛ, seventeenth cent.⁴ Oxford, Bodleian Library, Laud Misc. 611, fo. 5ᵛ, seventeenth cent. (*L*). Dublin, Trinity College, 578, p. 9,

To Toirdhealbhach Ó Briain, king of Ireland, and all the Irish   (1074–84,) 24 or 25 Feb.

Gregory, bishop, servant of the servants of God, to Toirdhealbhach, the illustrious king of Ireland, to the archbishops, bishops, abbots, magnates, and to all Christians who dwell in Ireland, greeting and apostolic blessing.

The teaching of the Lord Jesus has shone through all the world; for he who has come forth from his chamber like a bridegroom has set his tabernacle in the sun, and there is no one who may escape from the brightness of its heat.[1] His authority founded the holy church upon a solid rock and committed her government to St. Peter who owed his venerable name to the rock. He also set her over all the kingdoms of the world and made subject to her principalities and powers and whatsoever in the world is seen to be exalted, thus fulfilling Isaiah's prophecy: 'They shall come to you who despised you', he says, 'and shall bow down at your feet.'[2] Therefore to St. Peter and to his vicars, amongst whom divine providence has appointed that our lot should also be numbered, the whole world owes obedience and likewise reverence: these things you should remember to show the holy Roman church with a faithful mind. Thus we exhort you as most dear sons to perform righteousness, to keep and love the catholic peace of the church, and loving it to bind it to you with the arms of charity. Should any

seventeenth cent.[5] Printed: Ussher, *Veterum epistolarum Hibernicarum sylloge*, no. 29, pp. 75–6.[6] Gwynn, *S.G.* iii. 115. *Pontificia Hibernica*, ed. Sheehy, no. 2, pp. 7–8.

---

[1] Cf. Ps. 18: 6–7 (19: 4–6).   [2] Cf. Isa. 60: 14.

[3] Stated to be taken 'ex MS. Bibliothecae Cottonianae'.

[4] Stated to have been 'copied out of a booke of Sir Robert Cottons'.

[5] This text, in Ussher's hand, is stated by him to be 'ex MS. Bibliothecae Cottonianae'.

[6] Ussher says that he had seen copies of this letter appended to MSS. of the Pseudo-Isidorian Decretals in Cambridge University Library and in Cotton's Library: p. 138. It is hard to understand this statement, for all the surviving copies appear to stem from *C*. I can trace no other MS. of it.

emerserint quae nostro digna uideantur auxilio, incunctanter ad nos dirigere studete, et quod iuste postulaueritis Deo auxiliante impetrabitis.

Data Sutrii*c* vi kal. Mar.

58

To Bishop Altmann of Passau: Gregory answers an inquiry about the orders of sinful clergy   (*1073–85*)*

Gregorius episcopus seruus seruorum Dei dilecto in Christo fratri A. Patauiensi episcopo salutem et apostolicam benedictionem.

Interrogauit nos religio uestra de sacerdotibus in fornicationem lapsis aliisque criminibus irretitis, consulens quidnam de illorum gradu foret censendum . . .

59

To Bishop Altmann of Passau: Gregory urges him and his followers to promote the liberty of the church   (*1073–85*)†

Gregorius episcopus seruus seruorum Dei dilecto in Christo fratri A. Patauiensi episcopo salutem et apostolicam benedictionem.

Quia te credo sincero corde amare pro Deo sancte ecclesie honorem et libertatem, uolo et precipio ut summopere cum clericis his uel laicis qui ad hoc apti uidentur procures ut sponsa Christi amplius non habeatur ancilla . . .

---

c Marino *interlined above in the same hand* C; *add* Marina L

---

* This letter may have been written in connection with Altmann's council of Dec. 1075: *Vita Altmanni, cap.* 11, *M.G.H. Scr.* xii. 232–3.

J.L. 5275. *G.P.* i, p. 169, no. 31. MSS.: *Vita Altmanni*: Heiligenkreuz, Stiftsbibl. 13, fo. 88ᵛ, twelfth cent.; Munich, Bayer. Staatsbibl. lat. 18526*b*, fos. 234ᵛ–235ʳ, fifteenth cent. Printed: *Vita Altmanni, cap.* 30, *M.G.H. Scr.* xii. 238. *Ep. coll.* no. 47, p. 575.

† J.L. 5274. *G.P.* i, p. 169, no. 32. MSS.: *Vita Altmanni*: Heiligenkreuz, Stiftsbibl. 13, fo. 88ᵛ, twelfth cent.; Munich, Bayer. Staatsbibl. lat. 18526*b*, fo. 235ʳ, fifteenth cent. Printed: *Vita Altmanni, cap.* 30, *M.G.H. Scr.* xii. 238. *Ep. coll.* no. 48, p. 575.

matters of business arise among you which seem to call for our aid, be sure straightway to have recourse to us, and whatever you rightly ask you will with God's help obtain.

Sutri, 24 or 25 Feb.

To Bishop Altmann of Passau   (*1073–85*)

Gregory, bishop, servant of the servants of God, to his beloved brother in Christ, Bishop Altmann of Passau, greeting and apostolic blessing.

You inquired of us about priests who have fallen into fornication and who have become ensnared in other sins, asking what should be thought about their orders . . .

To Bishop Altmann of Passau   (*1073–85*)

Gregory, bishop, servant of the servants of God, to his beloved brother in Christ, Bishop Altmann of Passau, greeting and apostolic blessing.

Because I believe that with an upright heart and for the sake of God you love the honour and liberty of holy church, I desire and charge you that, together with these clergy or with such laity as seem proper for the task, you do all possible to see that the bride of Christ is no longer treated as a slave . . .

60

To Bishop Altmann of Passau: Gregory gives his ruling about certain priests who were unwittingly ordained by an excommunicated bishop   (1073–85)*

G. episcopus seruus seruorum Dei dilecto in Christo fratri Patauiensi episcopo salutem et apostolicam benedictionem.

Praesentium latores ad nos uenientes se ab episcopo excommunicato tamen id nescientes presbyteros esse ordinatos confessi sunt. Qua de re nos nuper in litteris quas fraternitati tuae remisimus non plene respondimus. Super hoc itaque dirigimus ut, si eos tunc temporis nesciuisse praefatum episcopum excommunicationi*ᵃ* subiacere constiterit et cetera quae ex eorum uita et moribus perquirenda sunt non impedierint, gradu presbyteratus fungi misericorditer permittas per manus impositionem, et Spiritus Sancti gratiam quam habere non potuerunt alterius praesumptione obtineant ex nostra deuotione.

61

To the archbishop of Tours and the bishop of Angers: Gregory charges them to settle certain complaints of the abbot of Vendôme concerning his property   (1073–85)†

G. episcopus seruus seruorum Dei fratribus et coepiscopis Turonensi et Andegauensi salutem et apostolicam benedictionem.

Admonemus atque praecipimus fraternitati uestrae ut plenam iustitiam faciatis Vindocinensi abbati de ecclesia Ripere,[1] unde queritur, et de Maziaco,[2] et ita studeatis clamoribus suis finem imponere ut de cetero necesse non habeat propterea ad apostolicam sedem recurrere uel nos fatigare.

ᵃ excommunioni *V*

---

* The letter is almost certainly addressed to Altmann of Passau, but might possibly be to Ulrich of Padua. It may be a sequel to no. 58 above, or else to *Reg.* ix. 10, 1081, p. 587 or the letters referred to in it.

Not in J.L. *I.P.* vii, pt. 1, pp. 158–9, no. 5. MS.: Vienna, Österr. Nationalbibl. 2198, fo. 19ᵛ, *c.* 1100 (*V*). Printed: Krause, *N.A.* xvii (1891–2), 296.

To Bishop Altmann of Passau   (*1073–85*)

Gregory, bishop, servant of the servants of God, to his beloved brother in Christ the bishop of Passau, greeting and apostolic blessing.

The bearers of this letter came to us and acknowledged that they were ordained priests by a bishop who was excommunicated, though they were ignorant of this. In the letter which we formerly sent you we did not fully deal with this circumstance. We therefore rule that, if it is the case that they were at the time unaware of the bishop's excommunication and if after due inquiry no other impediment is discovered concerning their life and morals, you may out of mercy admit them to exercise the order of priesthood by the laying on of hands. Thus by our faith they may receive the gift of the Holy Spirit which they could not have by reason of the bishop's audacity.

To the archbishop of Tours and the bishop of Angers
(*1073–85*)

Gregory, bishop, servant of the servants of God, to his brothers and fellow bishops of Tours and Angers, greeting and apostolic blessing.

We urge and charge you to do full justice for the abbot of Vendôme concerning the church of Rivière,[1] about which he has complained, and concerning Mazé,[2] and so endeavour to put an end to his complaints that for the future he may have no need to resort to the apostolic see with regard to them, or to trouble us.

† Gregory writes to Archbishop Ralph of Tours and Bishop Eusebius (1047–81) or Geoffrey (1081–93) of Angers; the abbot of Vendôme is Odericus (1046–82) or David (1083–5).
J.L. 5285. MS.: Angers, Bibl. municip. 368, fo. 1ʳ, eleventh cent. Printed: Delisle, *B.É.C.* 6th ser. i (1865), 560. *Ann. iur. pont.* x, no. 56, col. 418.

---

[1] Indre-et-Loire; cf. *Cartulaire de l'abbaye cardinale de la Trinité de Vendôme*, ed. C. Métais, 4 vols. (Paris, 1893–7), no. 399 (*c.* 1040–5), ii. 150–3.
[2] Maine-et-Loire; cf. ibid., no. 1 (1007–50), i. 5; no. 36 (1040), i. 66; no. 38 (*c.* 1056–60), i. 81; no. 44 (1006–40), i. 95–7; no. 80 (1046–9), i. 150–1; no. 146 (1061), i. 258, for the earlier history of Vendôme's proprietorship.

62

To Abbot Albert: Gregory acknowledges his devotion and assures him of his help; he leaves the settlement of a request to the abbot's discretion (*1073–85*)*

Gregorius papa seruus seruorum Dei Alberto abbati salutem et apostolicam benedictionem.*a*

Deuotionem uestram circa apostolatum nostrum litterae uestrae prodiderunt. Vnde si uobis umquam quicquam nostri adiutorii fuerit necesse, sperate nos libenter impendere. Illud uero quod dixistis relinquimus in uestra uoluntate. Valete.

63

To Archbishop Ralph of Tours: Gregory charges him to investigate a problem regarding a marriage (*1073–85*)†

G. episcopus seruus seruorum Dei R. Turonensi archiepiscopo salutem et apostolicam benedictionem.

Miles iste, harum scilicet portitor litterarum, apud apostolicam sedem conquestus est quod male sibi sociata consanguinea ex iudicio sui episcopi dimissa, coniugem quam sibi per legem coniunxerat sine legali iudicio perdidit.*a* Quapropter super hoc fraternitatem tuam caritate apostolica conuenimus ut cum Pictauensi episcopo[1] colloquium habeas, et nostra apostolica auctoritate ei praecipias ut hoc quod iniuste actum est iuste emendare procuret, sciens quia si res aliter quam debeat agatur, a sede apostolica inultum nullomodo relinquetur.

---

a The sign ✠ precedes the salutation P   63   *a* perdiderit B

---

* The abbot cannot be identified; since the MS. formerly belonged to the dukes of Milan he may well have been from north Italy.
J.L. 5286. MS.: Paris, Bibl. nat. lat. 275, fo. 142ᵛ, eleventh cent. (*P*). Printed: Loewenfeld, *Epist. pont. Rom. ined.* no. 119, p. 58.
† Not in J.L. MSS.: Budapest, Bibl. nat. Széch. lat. med. aeui 5, fo. 8ʳ, *c.* 1100, (*B*). Paris, Bibl. nat. Duchesne 4, fo. 109ʳ, seventeenth cent. Printed:

To Abbot Albert   (*1073–85*)

Gregory, pope, servant of the servants of God, to Abbot Albert, greeting and apostolic blessing.

Your letter proves your devotion towards our apostolic office. Therefore if you ever stand in need of any help from us you may be sure that we will gladly provide it. As for the matter that you mention, we leave it to your discretion. Farewell.

To Archbishop Ralph of Tours   (*1073–85*)

Gregory, bishop, servant of the servants of God, to Archbishop Ralph of Tours, greeting and apostolic blessing.

This knight, the bearer of this letter, has complained to the apostolic see that, having put away by judgement of his bishop a kinswoman whom he had wrongfully joined to him, he has lost without lawful judgement the wife whom he had lawfully married. We therefore request you with apostolic charity regarding this matter that you confer with the bishop of Poitiers[1] and charge him by our apostolic authority to see to it that he justly puts right what he has done unjustly, knowing that if this matter is dealt with otherwise than is proper it will by no means be left unavenged by the apostolic see.

Ramackers, *Q.F.I.A.B.* xxiii (1931–2), no. 8, p. 41. Morin, *R.B.* xlviii (1936), no. 3, p. 121. Ramackers, *P.U.F.* v, no. 18, pp. 80–1.

----

[1] Isembert (1047–86).

64

To Archbishop Ralph of Tours and Bishop Eusebius (or Geoffrey) of Angers: Gregory attempts to bring about a settlement in a long-standing dispute between the monasteries of Marmoutier and Redon   (*1073–85*)*

G. episcopus seruus seruorum Dei dilectis in Christo fratribus et coepiscopis Turonensi et Andecauensi salutem et apostolicam benedictionem.

Discordia Maioris monasterii¹ et Rotonensis² diu protracta nec adhuc ad finem perducta multotiens aures nostras fatigauit.³ Vnde uolumus ut fraternitas uestra rationes utriusque partis diligenter inquirat, et si potest certum ac legitimum finem imponat. Quod si apud uos fieri non potest, procurate nobis rescribere ueritatem et iusticiam ipsius negotii, et utrumque abbatem uel eorum idoneos nuntios nobis transmittere.

65

To King Sancho Ramirez of Aragon: Gregory encourages him to continue the exemplary character of his kingship, and commends to him Bishop Raymond of Roda   (*1076–85*)†

Gregorius episcopus seruus seruorum Dei Sancio glorioso regi salutem et apostolicam benedictionem.

Gratias omnipotenti Deo referimus quod in administratione desuper tibi data iuste et racionabiliter incedis, adeo ut spiritales et religiosi uiri famam bonitatis tuae ad noticiam nostram reportent, gaudium nobis et maximam de bonis et bene inceptis studiis tuis fiduciam ministrantes. Illud enim est quod desideranter esurimus atque sitimus, ut Christiana gens eos habeat reges qui Deum ueraciter timeant et magis diuinum honorem quam suum

---

* Not in J.L. MSS.: Budapest, Bibl. nat. Széch. lat. med. aeui 5, fo. 8ᵛ, *c.* 1100. Paris, Bibl. nat. Duchesne 4, fo. 109ᵛ, seventeenth cent. Printed: Ramackers, *Q.F.I.A.B.* xxiii (1931–2), no. 9, p. 41. Morin, *R.B.* xlviii (1936), no. 5, p. 123. Ramackers, *P.U.F.* v, no. 19, p. 81.

† King Sancho Ramirez (1063–94) had made his kingdom a papal fief in 1068. Bishop Raymond of Roda was elected in 1076 or 1078; the date of his journey to Rome is not known.

To Archbishop Ralph of Tours and Bishop Eusebius (o Geoffrey) of Angers   (1073–85)

Gregory, bishop, servant of the servants of God, to his brothers in Christ and fellow bishops of Tours and Angers, greeting and apostolic blessing.

The dispute between Marmoutier[1] and Redon,[2] long drawn out and not yet brought to an end, has many times wearied our ears.[3] We therefore desire you to make thorough inquiry into the cases of both sides and if possible to make a final and just settlement. If it is not possible to do so before yourselves, see to it that you prepare us a written account of the truth and justice of this affair, and send to us both abbots or their competent envoys.

To King Sancho Ramirez of Aragon   (1076–85)

Gregory, bishop, servant of the servants of God, to the renowned King Sancho, greeting and apostolic blessing.

We offer thanks to Almighty God because you walk justly and rightly in the stewardship which you have been given from above, so that spiritual and religious men bring to our knowledge a good report of you, affording us joy and all confidence in the good endeavours which you have so well begun. For it is just what we eagerly hunger and thirst for, that Christendom should have kings who in truth fear God, and who choose his honour rather than

Not in J.L. MS.: Lérida, Archivo de la Catedral, Archiuum Rotense, Roda Cartulary, no. 16, p. 32, twelfth cent. Printed: Kehr, 'Papsturkunden in Katalanien, ii', *Abh. Gött.* xviii, pt. 2 (1926), no. 13, pp. 271–2.
The text which follows is Kehr's.

---

[1] Dioc. Tours.
[2] Saint-Sauveur, Redon (dioc. Vannes).
[3] Cf. Ramackers, *P.U.F.* v, no. 7, pp. 69–70; *R.H.F.* xiv. 152–3. The dispute was not finally resolved until 1111–12.

et iusticiae quam rerum temporalium amorem diligant. Sed quia diuino testimonio perseuerantia commendatur,[1] studeat deuotio tua non solum in his que de te dicuntur bonis perseuerare sed de uirtute in uirtutem bene incedendo mentem ad altiora semper erigere. Quantis enim calamitatibus mundus iste pulsetur, quot et quantis regibus, quot principibus, postremo quot millibus hominum mentiatur, uides. Cuius gloriam uanam utique et fragilem[2] si contempseris et officium tibi commissum laudabiliter perages, et Deum tibi propiciatorem et clementissimum facies. Et quia humana uita momentanea est et fugitiua,[3] necessarium tibi est ut diem mortis cotidie ante oculos ponas et tanto in amore et seruitio Dei crescas quanto ipsius districti iudicis sine intermissione iudicio appropinquas, quatenus cum ante presentiam eius ueneris, non districtum sed misericordem eum sentire merearis. Hunc autem karissimum confratrem nostrum Raimundum reuera tibi fidelissimum dilectionis tuae intuitu honorifice recepimus. Quem nobilitati tuae commendantes rogamus, ut ipse deinceps pro caritate nostra augmentum dilectionis et auxilii tui et qui ad nos uenit apud te semper sibi proficiat.

---

[1] Cf. Matt. 10: 22; 24: 13.   [2] Cf. Sallust, *Catilina*, 1. 4.
[3] Possibly a reference to Pseudo-Augustine, *Sermo* lvi. 3, *P.L.* xxxix. 1852.

their own and the love of his righteousness rather than that of
worldly goods. But because perseverance is urged upon us by
divine testimony,[1] you ought not only to continue in the good
works for which men praise you but also to go on from virtue to
virtue and ever to lift up your mind to higher things. For you see
by how many disasters this world is shaken, and by how many great
kings, princes, and men in their thousands it is deceived. If you
despise its vain and passing glory[2] and laudably fulfil the office
committed to you, you will make God the more favourable and
merciful towards you. And because the life of man is short and
passing,[3] it is needful that you should regularly set the day of your
death before your eyes, and ever increase in the love and service
of God as you continually draw nearer to the judgement of so
strict a judge; then, when you come before his presence, you will
deserve to find him not severe but merciful.

Because of your love we have honourably received our most dear
brother Raymond, who is indeed a most faithful servant of yours.
We commend him to you and ask that as a return for our love he,
having come to us, may henceforth always enjoy the increase of
your favour and help towards him.

APPENDIX A

This Appendix contains a small number of texts from canonical collections and of other papal decisions which probably emanated from Rome during the pontificate of Gregory VII. Where references to the manuscript sources are not stated the documents are taken from the printed sources as indicated. References to canonical collections are made according to the titles in W. Holtzmann, 'Kanonistische Ergänzungen zur *Italia Pontificia*', *Q.F.I.A.B.* xxxvii (1957), 55–102.

66

A ruling concerning simony in respect of prebends

(*1073–85*)*

Si quis dator uel acceptor Dei ecclesias uel ecclesiastica beneficia, que quidem prebendas uocant, sub pecuniae interuentu susceperit, siue dando emerit siue accipiendo uendiderit, a Symonis non excluditur perditione.[1] Sed si perseuerans fuerit perpetua mulctetur dampnatione. Nam qui sub religionis obtentu Deo famulari uoluerit, si quid acceperit et meritum perdit et beneficio accepto frustratur. Rationis ergo uigore cogitur quod iniuste recepit restituere et quicquid turpis lucri gratia receperat non tenere.

---

* Gratian's inscription is: 'Idem [i.e. Gregory VII] Rotomagensi episcopo et Gallicis omnibus.'

J.L. 5276. Printed: Gratian, *Decretum*, C. I, q. iii, c. 2, *Corpus iuris canonici*, ed. Friedberg, i. 412. *Ep. coll.* no. 49, pp. 575–6.

---

[1] Cf. Acts 8: 9–24.

67

An insistence that truth is superior to custom (*1073–85*)*

Si consuetudinem fortassis opponas, aduertendum fuerit quod
Dominus dicit: 'Ego sum ueritas et uita.'[1] Non ait: 'Ego sum
consuetudo', sed 'ueritas'. Et certe, ut beati Cypriani utamur
sententia,[2] quaelibet consuetudo, quantumuis uetusta, quantumuis uulgata, ueritati est omnino postponenda et usus qui ueritati
est contrarius abolendus.

68

*Rules for the penance of clerks who carry arms and commit
homicide* (*1073–80*)†

Gregorii papae VII et . . .ᵃ

Si quis clericus contra patrum regulas . . .ᵇ ordines arma arripit
et homicidium perpetrat,ᶜ huiusmodi penitentiam sibi iniungentes

---

ᵃ *MS. illegible for 36 mm.*   ᵇ *MS. illegible for 11 mm.*   ᶜ *et*
homicidium perpetrat *interlined in the same hand*

---

* In his *Decretum* Ivo of Chartres gives this fragment the following inscription:
'Vsum qui ueritati contrarius est abolendum esse.
Gregorius VII Wimundo Auersano episcopo.'
In all probability Guitmund did not become bishop of Aversa until the time of
Pope Urban II (1088–99), who thus might be the source of this fragment. But
Ivo may refer to Guitmund anachronistically by his familiar title. See Ladner,
'Two Gregorian Letters on the Sources and Nature of Gregory VII's Reform
Ideology', *S.G.* v (1956), 225–42.
    J.L. 5277. *I.P.* viii, pp. 281–2, no. 2. Printed: Ivo of Chartres, *Decretum*, iv.
213, *P.L.* clxi. 311; *Panormia*, ii. 166, *P.L.* clxi. 1121. Gratian, *Decretum*, *D.*
VIII, *c.* 5, *Corpus iuris canonici*, ed. Friedberg, i. 14. *Ep. coll.* no. 50, p. 576.
Ladner, *S.G.* v. 225.
    The fragment also occurs in the *Tripartita*, e.g. Oxford, Bodleian Library,
d'Orville 46, fo. 181ʳ, twelfth cent.
    † J.L. 5289. MS.: Paris, Bibl. nat. lat. 8922, fo. 173ʳ, *c.* 1100. Printed:
(partly) Loewenfeld, *N.A.* vii (1882), no. 8, pp. 163–4. Loewenfeld, *Epist.
pont. Rom. ined.* no. 120, pp. 58–9.

---

[1] Cf. John 14: 6.
[2] The immediate source of the reference to Cyprian, bishop of Carthage
(249–57) seems to be Augustine, *De baptismo*, iii. 6. 9, *C.S.E.L.* li. 203, where
Augustine quotes Bishop Libosus of Vaga who was at the council of Carthage
(256): cf. *Sententiae episcoporum numero LXXXVII de hereticis baptizandis*,
C.S.E.L. iii, pt. 1, p. 433.

carceri XL diebus mancipandum decreuimus; deinde aecclesiae
gremio inter laicos miserationis intuitu sociamus; deinde penitentiam XIIII annorum imponimus, sed II accipimus ita ut proximo
quadrigenio a dominici corporis et sanguinis et omnium carnium
abstineat perceptione. Quartam et sextam feriam in pane et aqua
et crudis herbis ieiunet; quadragesimali tempore secundam et
quartam et sextam feriam eodem tenore obseruet; unam quadra-
gesimam ante natalem Domini annuatim persoluat. Ceterum si
in regulari monasterio monachus effici uoluerit siue in regulari
canonica esse maluerit, haec omnia in abbatis sui uel decani
potestate consistit; ita tamen ut quicquid horum fuerit, ipse
ulterius ad gradum aecclesiastici ordinis non promoueatur nisi
per gratiam.

69

To Peter, a subdeacon: a form of oath is prescribed for a
bishop   (*1073–85*)*

Gregorius Petro subdiacono.

Ego Petrus episcopus ab hac hora inantea fidelis ero sancto
Petro sancteque Romane apostolice ecclesie, domino meo
pape illiusque successoribus canonice intrantibus. Non ero in
consilio nec in synodo ut uitam perdat uel membrum aut capiatur
mala captione. Consilium quod mihi per se aut per litteras aut
per nuntium manifestabit ad eorum damnum nulli pandam.
Papatum Romane ecclesie et sancti Petri adiutor ero ad retinen-
dum et defendendum, saluo meo ordine, contra omnes homines.

---

* In his notes W. Holtzmann suggests that Gregory VII may have addressed
this item to his legate Peter, to whom he refers in *Reg.* v. 12, 9 Jan. 1078, p. 365;
if so it may embody a form of oath prepared for Bishop Peter of Antivari (*c.*
1060– ?), whom Gregory summoned to Rome. Holtzmann also records its
appearance with the inscription 'Gregorius Petro subdiacono' in *Florianensis,
Cusana*, and *Bambergensis*. In the *Decretales* the inscription is 'Idem [i.e.
Gregory VII] Petro subdiacono'. This form of oath is very similar to that
prescribed for Patriarch Henry of Aquileia at the Lent council of 1079: *Reg.*
vi. 17*a*, pp. 428–9.

Not in J.L. MSS.: *1 Berolinensis*: Berlin, Deutsche Staatsbibl. Phillipps 1742,
fo. 290ᵛ, thirteenth cent. *Duacensis*: Douai, Bibl. municip. 590, fo. 248ᵛ, thirteenth cent. (part only). Printed: Gregory IX, *Decretales*, I. 24. 4, *Corpus iuris
canonici*, ed. Friedberg, ii. 360. This text also occurs in *I Compilatio*, I. 4. 20:
cf. *Quinque compilationes antiquae*, ed. Friedberg, p. 3.

Vocatus ad synodum ueniam nisi prepeditus fuero canonica prepeditione. Legatum apostolice sedis quem certum legatum esse cognouero in eundo et reddendo honorifice tractabo et in suis necessitatibus adiuuabo. Apostolorum limina singulis annis aut per me aut per certum nuntium meum uisitabo, nisi eorum absoluar licentia. Sic me Deus adiuuet et hec sancta euangelia.

APPENDIX B

This Appendix contains a selection of letters and canonical material which circulated under the name of Gregory VII. In all cases the ascription is probably or certainly false, but the documents are all referred to with some frequency in connection with Gregory, and most of them have some significance for the study of his pontificate.

†70

To Bishop Hugh of Die: Gregory instructs him to settle the dispute between Bishop Landeric of Mâcon and Abbot Hugh of Cluny (*1079, summer*)*

Gregorius episcopus seruus seruorum Dei confratri et coepiscopo H. salutem et apostolicam benedictionem.

Causam Matisconensis episcopi quae est inter illum et fidelem nostrum abbatem Cluniacensem fraternitati tuae determinandam*a* mandauimus, episcopo multum condolentes, uidentes in illo columbae simplicitatem in abbate autem serpentis astutiam; neque ad dextram neque ad sinistram amplius declinare uolumus, sed ex utroque unum temperamentum facere et secundum canones quod iustum est iudicare. Nos autem secundum apostolum absentes corpore presentes autem spiritu[1] tam iudicauimus ut

---

a om. determinandam *and add* de sibi M, *which also leaves a space of 27 mm.*

---

* The two MSS. which contain this letter preserve material derived from a MS. Cartulary of the church of Mâcon, which was destroyed *c.* 1567. The letter was written, on behalf of the canons of the cathedral of Saint-Vincent, at an early stage of their quarrel with Cluny which issued in Gregory's vindication of the monks: see nos. 38–9 above. The quarrel began when the canons caused their bishop, Landeric, to complain at Rome about Cluny's alleged infringement of their temporal rights: cf. *Reg.* vi. 33, 14 Apr. 1079, pp. 446–7. The present letter seems to have been drafted soon afterwards in an attempt to involve Gregory's standing legate against the monks.

J.L. †5183. MSS.: Paris, Bibl. nat. lat. 17086, no. 20, pp. 11–12, seventeenth cent. (*P*). Mâcon, Archives de Saône-et-Loire, G. 198, no. 20, fo. 15ʳ, eighteenth cent. (*M*). Printed: Ragut, *Cartulaire de Saint-Vincent de Mâcon*, no. 20, p. 17.

---

[1] Cf. Col. 2: 5.

presentes iudicio canonum, domnum abbatem Cluniacensem
contra praefatum episcopum nihil sinistrum facere debere,
mutationes non amare, nouitates non curare, sed sicut antiquitus
fuerit ecclesiae ita eas desiderare, ne lux sua lucens coram hominibus aliquo naeuo deturpetur.[b] Sanctiorem episcopo suo uelle
uideri quodammodo iniuriam in episcopum . . .[c] contra canones
agere est, contra canones autem agere a fide est exorbitare,
exorbitare autem a fide in Christum peccare est, quod quanta pena
plectendum sit tu ipse cognoscis. Cui ergo iustitiam fauere per
discussionem tuam declaratum fuerit, fraternitatem tuam monemus
et praecipimus ut ei firmiter adhaereas et ad obtinendum ius
suum ministerium debitae fraternitatis impendas.

†71

*To Bishop Amatus of Oléron: Gregory instructs him to hold
a council and settle a dispute between the abbots of Saint-
Sever and Sainte-Croix, Bordeaux, regarding the church
of Soulac*   *Benevento, (1079)* 25 Apr.*

Gregorius episcopus seruus seruorum Dei fratri Amato sancte
Romane aecclesie uicario salutem et apostolicam benedictionem.

De querela filii nostri Arnaldi abbatis sancti Seueri Guasconiae
super aecclesia beatae Marie de Solaco quae tamdiu est uentilata

---

   [b] nouo detraxetur *M*   [c] *Space of 27 mm. in P; add* autem realiter *M*

---

   * The abbots were Arnald I of Saint-Sever, dioc. Aire (1072–92) and Arnald
Trencardus of Sainte-Croix, Bordeaux (*c.* 1066–*c.* 1087). For the course of the
dispute cf. *Reg.* i. 51, 14 Mar. 1074, pp. 77–8; vi. 24–5, 8 Mar. 1079, pp. 436–8;
Amatus of Oléron's charter of 12 Oct. 1079 recording the decision of the council
of Bordeaux in favour of Abbot Arnald of Sainte-Croix: *G.C.* ii, instrumenta
no. 10, cols. 273–4; Paschal II, Ep. xvi, *c.* 1105, *P.L.* clxiii. 461. Gregory VII is
not known to have been at Benevento on 25 Apr. in any year of his pontificate.
In the MS. this letter is preceded by one in the name of Pope Alexander II which
was clearly written with it. It is addressed 'fratri Ranbaldo sanctae Romanae
aecclesiae uicario', and directs that 'congregato concilio si abbas beati Seueri septima manu abbatum tricennalem possessionem legali querimonia inconcussam
se tenuisse probauerit a tua caritate auctoritate sanctae Romanae aecclesiae
sanctorumque canonum et nostra confirmatione reuestiatur ei dominaturus
in ea in perpetuum.' Both letters are clearly spurious and were probably written
before the council of Bordeaux (1079).
   Not in J.L. MS.: Paris, Bibl. nat. lat. 8878, fo. 289ᵛ, twelfth cent. (*P*).
Printed: Wiederhold, *P.U.F.* vii, no. 4, p. 37.

et nondum difinita, litteris praesentibus fraternitati tuae mandamus
quatenus ex auctoritate beati Petri apostolorum principis sanctae-
que Romane aecclesiae ac nostra*a* quoadunato coetu*b* tam episcoporum quam abbatum sicut mos est legatorum nostrorum,
praesente fratre nostro A. abbate sancte Crucis, si filius noster
abbas sancti Seueri probare poterit septima manu sui ordinis se
obtinuisse tricennalem possessionem in aecclesia beatae Mariae
de Solac, per tuam manum reuestiatur auctoritate beati Petri et
nostra possessurus eam in perpetuum. Valete.

Data vii kal. Madii, Beneuentani.

†72

*To Archbishop Ralph of Tours and Bishop Eusebius of
Angers: Gregory charges them to protect Berengar of Tours
from his enemies, and especially Count Fulk of Anjou*
(*1079, Feb.*)*

G. episcopus seruus seruorum Dei R. Turonorum archiepiscopo
et E. Andecauorum pontifici salutem et apostolicam benedictionem.

Audiuimus F. comitem Andecauensem quorumdam instinctu
qui filio nostro karissimo B. sacerdoti inimicantur in eius odium
exarsisse. Quapropter fraternitati uestrae mandamus quatinus
ipsi comiti nostra uice praecipiatis ut non ulterius supradictum
uirum inquietare praesumat. Nec solum . . .*a* sed et contra
omnes inimicos et perturbatores rerum ipsius uicem nostram
ad ferenda illi auxilia suscipiatis, praecipiendo praecipimus ex
auctoritate beatorum apostolorum Petri et Pauli. Valete, et nulla
ratione quae praecipio contempnite.

---

a nostri P   *b* coeto *corrected to* coetu P   †72   *a* *P has a full stop
but no break in the text*

---

* Gregory condemned the eucharistic errors of Berengar, archdeacon of
Tours (died 1088) at his Lent council in 1079: *Reg.* vi. 17*a*, 11 Feb. 1079,
pp. 425–7. Berengar himself drafted this letter and the oath which follows
in anticipation of a more satisfactory outcome. Cf. Erdmann, 'Gregor VII. und
Berengar von Tours', *Q.F.I.A.B.* xxviii (1937–8), 54–5.

J.L. 5197. MS.: Paris, Bibl. nat. lat. 152, fo. 39ʳ, *c.* 1100, (*P*). Printed: Roye,
Vita Berengarii, pp. 75–6. *Ep. coll.* no. 36, p. 564.

†73

To all the faithful of St. Peter: Gregory forbids anyone to harm the person and possessions of Berengar of Tours
(*1079, Feb.*)*

G. episcopus seruus seruorum Dei omnibus beato Petro fidelibus salutem et apostolicam benedictionem.

Notum uobis omnibus facimus nos anathema fecisse ex auctoritate Dei omnipotentis Patris et Filii et Spiritus sancti et beatorum apostolorum Petri et Pauli omnibus qui iniuriam aliquam facere praesumpserint Beringerio, Romanae ecclesiae filio, uel in persona uel in omni possessione sua, uel qui eum uocabunt*ᵃ* hereticum. Quem post multas quas apud nos quantas uoluimus fecit moras domum suam remittimus, et cum eo fidelem nostrum, Fulconem nomine.¹

†74

To Abbot William of Brioude: Gregory calls upon him to do justice to the monastery of Lérins with respect to a church which he has seized   Lateran, (*1073–83*), *14 Dec.*†

G. episcopus seruus seruorum Dei G. abbati Briuatensi² salutem et apostolicam benedictionem.

Clamorem fratrum Lyrinensium³ accepimus, quod eis aecclesiam sancti Iusti, quae est sita in pago Briuatensi, quam episcopus

ᵃ uocabit *A*

---

* J.L. 5103. MS.: Angers, Archives de Maine-et-Loire, 67, on fo. 1 of a MS. of Haimo, *Explanatio in Pauli apostoli epistolas*, inserted inside back cover, eleventh cent. (*A*). Printed: Roye, *Vita, haeresis, et poenitentia Berengarii*, pp. 76–7. Labbe and Cossart, *Sacrosancta concilia*, x. 410. D'Achéry, *Spicilegium*, iii. 413. *Ep. coll.* no. 24, p. 550.

† J.L. 5244. MS.: Nice, Archives des Alpes-Maritimes, H. 10, fo. 130ᵛ, thirteenth cent. (*L*). Printed: Pflugk-Harttung, *Acta pont. Rom. ined.* i, no. 54, pp. 52–3. *Cartulaire de l'abbaye de Lérins*, no. 271, p. 278.

---

¹ Berengar himself spoke of a Fulk amongst Gregory's spokesmen: *Iuramentum Berengarii Turonici clerici*, in Martène and Durand, *Thesaurus nouus anecdotorum*, iv. 103.
² William, abbot of Saint-Martin and Saint-Julien, Brioude (dioc. Clermont).
³ Saint-Honorat, Lérins (dioc. Antibes).

Clarimontis[1] et praepositus Briuatensis[2] dederunt eisdem monachis, iniuste abstuleris nec etiam eorum auctoritates audire uolueris. Vnde fraternitatem tuam karitatiue ammonentes et eciam praecipientes, ut praedictam ecclesiam cum omnibus ad eam pertinentibus usque ad proximam Christi ressurreccionem eidem monasterio restituas uel ante praesentiam Arelatensis archiepiscopi[3] eius iudicio statuto die ne deinceps querimoniam audiamus cum praefatis monachis definias. Quod si facere contempseris apostolica auctoritate introitum omnium ecclesiarum tibi interdicimus et ecclesiam illam ab omni diuino officio praeter babtismum et penitenciam in finem cessare praecepimus.

Datum Laterani, xviiii kal. Ianuarii.

†75

A ruling about how to determine the age of adulthood *

Manifestum est eum puberem esse qui gesticulatione sui corporis talis est ut iam procreare possit, licet ad metas legibus diffinitas non peruenerit.

* J.L. 5291. This text appears, with minor variant readings, in several canonical collections. In some it occurs without inscription, e.g. *Cheltenhamensis*: London, Brit. Mus. Egerton 2819, fo. 58ᵛ, twelfth cent.; and *Cottoniana*: London, Brit. Mus. Cotton Vitellius E XIII, fo. 271ᵛ, twelfth cent. W. Holtzmann notes it thus in these collections, also in one MS. of *Appendix concilii Lateranensis*. It has the inscription 'Gregorius' in *Francofurtana*, e.g. London, Brit. Mus. Egerton 2901, fo. 2ʳ⁻ᵛ, twelfth cent.; Holtzmann also notes it in the other *Appendix* MSS., in *Petrihusensis*, and in *I Compilatio*, iv. 2. 3, *Quinque compilationes antiquae*, ed. Friedberg, p. 45. With the inscription 'Gregorius VI' Holtzmann notes it in *Brugensis*. It is sometimes inscribed 'Gregorius VII', e.g. in *Coll. Tanneri*, Oxford, Bodleian Library, Tanner 8, *c.* 1200, p. 700; Holtzmann also notes it thus in *Bambergensis*, *Casselana*, and *Lipsiensis*.

It is improbable that the ascription to Gregory VII is correct. Holtzmann in his notes points for a possible model to Isidore of Seville, *Etymologiarum*, xi. ii. 13, ed. W. M. Lindsay, ii (Oxford, 1911), ad loc.

---

[1] William (1073–6) or Durand (1088–95).
[2] Stephen.　　　[3] Aicard (*c.* 1067–90).

†76

*A ruling concerning Embertides**

Licet noua consuetudo[1] aecclesiae, nulla fulta auctoritate,[a] numeret inter ieiunia et ordinationes quattuor temporum primam hebdomadam primi mensis Martii et secundum quarti, id est Iunii, uetus tamen auctoritas sanctorum patrum est[b] ut in initio quadragesimali et in hebdomada Pentecostes debeant obseruari.[2]

   [a] *add* semper *V*   [b] *corr. to* statuit *B*

---

  * J.L. 5290. MSS.: London, Brit. Mus. Addit. 8873, fo. 73ʳ, twelfth cent. (*B*). Rome, Bibl. Vallicelliana, tomo XXI. xlvii, fo. 245ᵛ, twelfth cent. (*V*).[3]

---

  [1] *B* has the rubric 'Gregorii papae VII de ieiunio Pentecostes et de ordinatione in prima hebdomada quadragesimae et Pentecostes'.
  [2] In both MSS. a lengthy catena of ancient authorities follows.
  [3] This text also appears in the late-eleventh-century *Liber Tarraconensis*, where it is also ascribed to Gregory VII: cf. P. Fournier, 'Le *Liber Tarraconensis*. Étude sur une collection canonique du xiᵉ siècle', *Mélanges Julien Havet* (Paris, 1895), p. 274.

ADDITIONAL NOTE

THE DATE OF NOS. 6–11

It is debated whether nos. 6–11, which were evidently written during the same year, followed the Lent council of 1074 or that of 1075, at both of which decrees against simony and clerical marriage were enacted. In *Ep. coll.* Jaffé assigned nos. 6–8 to Mar. 1074 and nos. 9–11 to Dec. 1074: pp. 523–6, 528–31. But criticisms by Giesebrecht, *Geschichte der deutschen Kaiserzeit*, iii. 1121, and Meltzer, *Papst Gregors VII. Gesetzgebung und Bestrebungen in Betreff der Bischofswahlen*, p. 60 n. (pp. 203–4 in later edns.), led the revisers of Jaffé's *Regesta pontificum Romanorum* to place nos. 6–8 at the end of Feb. 1075: J.L. 4931–3; and nos. 9 and 10 in Dec. 1075: J.L. 4970–1. More recently the date 1074 has been defended by Fliche, *La Réforme grégorienne*, ii. 136, n. 5, and Borino, 'I decreti di Gregorio VII contro i simoniaci e i nicolaiti sono del sinodo quaresimale del 1074', *S.G.* vi (1959–61), 277–95, with a full review of the literature. Erdmann, on the other hand, like almost all recent German historians, argued for 1075 as the date of all six letters, placing no. 11 with nos. 9 and 10 because of its exclusive concern with celibacy, Gregory's principal reforming aim in late 1075: *Studien zur Briefliteratur Deutschlands im elften Jahrhundert*, pp. 227 n. 3, 247 n. 3, 275.

The arguments in favour of 1074 are not decisive. The chief of them are as follows: (i) The chronicler Lampert of Hersfeld says that in 1074 Gregory VII 'crebras litteras ad episcopos Galliarum [i.e. to the provinces of Cologne, Mainz, and Trier] transmittebat' against clerical marriage and concubinage (*Ann. a.* 1074, pp. 256–8). But Lampert, who was writing after 1077, dissociated these letters from the legatine work of Cardinals Gerald of Ostia and Hubert of Palestrina whom Gregory sent to Germany after his Lent council of 1074; Lampert may well have antedated letters sent in 1075.

(ii) If no. 7 is dated 1075 it duplicates Gregory's letter of 29 Mar. 1075 to Archbishop Werner of Magdeburg: *Reg.* ii. 68, pp. 225–6. But this letter is of a very different character. It does not communicate the text of the decree and refers only to the promoting of clerical chastity; it could well have followed no. 7 after a month's interval.

(iii) Gregory's letter to Patriarch Sigehard of Aquileia of 23 Mar. 1075 (*Reg.* ii. 62, p. 217), which was written during Lent 1075, refers to statutes and decrees against simony and nicolaitism which Gregory enacted 'in peracto consilio preteritae quadragesimae', i.e. Lent 1074. Thus Gregory's key legislation was that of 1074. But the manifest purpose of *Reg.* ii. 62 is to procure the adherence of Sigehard's province to very recent papal legislation, and it in any case throws no light on the forms in which Gregory's decrees were communicated to Germany.

(iv) On 4 Dec. 1074 Gregory expressly summoned Siegfried of Mainz and through him Otto of Constance to attend the Lent council of 1075: *Reg.* ii. 29, pp. 161–2. They failed to attend; Gregory could hardly have omitted to allude to their failure in nos. 6 and 8 if these letters were of Feb. 1075. But Gregory does not seem to have proceeded severely against them at the council, in view of the silence of *Reg.* ii. 52*a*, pp. 196–7; and soon afterwards Siegfried played an active part in Germany and at Rome in Gregory's proceedings against Bishop Hermann of Bamberg: *Weitere Briefe Meinhards von Bamberg*, ed. Erdmann, no. 41, *M.G.H. B.D.K.* v. 242–4. Gregory's attitude to Siegfried and Otto in Feb. 1075 thus seems to have been conciliatory and to have been directed towards seeking their collaboration; hence the absence of rebuke in nos. 6 and 8.

(v) Various of Gregory's letters to Germany refer to the promulgation of his decrees against simony and nicolaitism at the Lent council of 1074: Fliche cites *Reg.* ii. 11, 26 Oct. 1074, pp. 142–3; ii. 45, 11 Jan. 1075, pp. 182–5; and ii. 66, 29 Mar. 1075, pp. 221–2. In 1075 he confirmed this legislation. But there is no evidence to suggest that in Feb. 1074 as well as condemning clerical vices Gregory already proposed one of the most important measures in the letters under discussion: a lay boycott of the sacraments of married clergy.

The main reasons for preferring 1075 are these: (i) In 1074 Gregory sent two legates to Germany as the principal means of implementing his decrees of that year; in 1075 he sent no legates but publicized his decrees principally by sending such letters as nos. 6–8: cf. *Reg.* ii. 66, 29 Mar. 1075, pp. 221–2. (ii) Legates of the bishop of Constance, referred to in no. 8, are known to have been at the council of 1075: *Reg.* ii. 60, 13 Mar. 1075, pp. 214–15. (iii) The references in nos. 6–8 and 10–11 to Gregory's stipulation that laymen should refuse to receive the ministrations of disobedient clergy allude to a demand which Gregory is not known from his letters to have addressed to Germany before the winter of 1074–5: cf. *Reg.* ii. 45, 11 Jan. 1075, pp. 182–5, for the earliest clear allusion. (iv) A number of German chronicles refer to Gregory's legislation of Lent 1075 as including the prohibition of laymen from having recourse to sinful clergy: e.g. Berthold, *Ann. a.* 1075, *M.G.H. Scr.* v. 277; Bernold, *Chron. a.* 1075, *M.G.H. Scr. v. 430–1*; *Annales Augustani, a.* 1075, *M.G.H. Scr.* iii. 128. No contemporary chronicle speaks of such a prohibition in Feb. 1074; the letters under discussion thus appear to be based upon the legislation of 1075. (v) Otto of Constance is known to have held a council in the second half of 1075 at which Gregory's decrees about celibacy were rejected: Bernard of Constance, *De damnatione scismaticorum, M.G.H. L. de L.* ii. 45; cf. Erdmann, *Studien zur Briefliteratur Deutschlands im elften Jahrhundert*, p. 274, n. 3. This council is manifestly the background of nos. 9–11.

LIST OF MANUSCRIPTS USED

References are to the numbers of the letters in this edition. The indications of date which accompany the letters show when they were copied, and are not necessarily a guide to the dates of the manuscripts themselves.

Admont
 Stiftsbibliothek
  24: 8–11, 14, 17, 18, 25
Angers
 Archives de Maine-et-Loire, Bibliothèque municipale
  67 (59): †73
  368 (355): 48, 52, 55, 61
Berlin
 Deutsche Staatsbibliothek
  Phillipps 1742: 69
  — 1870: 9–12, 14, 15, 18, 19, 25, 30, 31, 54
Boulogne
 Bibliothèque municipale
  72: 24, 41
Budapest
 Bibliotheca nationalis Széchenyiana
  lat. med. aeui 5: 3, 22, 23, 33, 35, 37, 63, 64
Cambridge
 Corpus Christi College
  135: 34
  299: 34
 University Library
  Dd. i. 11: 1
Douai
 Bibliothèque municipale
  590: 69
Dublin
 Trinity College
  578 (E. 3. 10): 57
Einsiedeln
 Stiftsbibliothek
  169 (468): 8
Florence
 Archivio di Stato
  A.S.F., Corporazione religiosi soppresse, arch. 260, 223: 2
 Biblioteca Medicea Laurenziana
  Plut. 16. 15: 32

Hanover
 Niedersächsische Landesbibliothek
  XI. 671, codex I: 9, 10, 14, 17, 18
  — — III: 5
Heiligenkreuz
 Stiftsbibliothek
  12: 8–11, 14, 17, 18, 25
  13: 58, 59
Karlsruhe
 Badische Landesbibliothek
  Rastatt 27: 8, 14
Kremsmünster
 Stiftsbibliothek
  27: 32, 51
Leipzig
 Universitätsbibliothek
  201: 17, 18
  1323: 14, 25–7
London
 British Museum
  Addit. 4791: 57
  — 8873: †76
  Cotton Claudius A I: 57
  — — E V: 1
  — Vitellius E XIII: †75
  Egerton 2802: 56
  — 2819: †75
  — 2901: †75
  Sloane 1449: 57
 Lambeth Palace
  59: 34
  224: 34
Mâcon
 Archives de Saône-et-Loire
  G. 198: †70
Melk
 Stiftsbibliothek
  492: 8–11, 14, 17, 18, 25
Monte Cassino
 Archivio abbaziale
  Petri Diaconi Registrum: 28, 29

Munich
  Bayerische Staatsbibliothek
    lat. 4594 (*olim* Benedictoburanus
      94): 14
    — 6236 (*olim* Freising 36): 6
    — 16054 (*olim* St. Nicholas,
      Passau, 54): 7
    — 18526*b* (*olim* Tegernsee 526*b*):
      58, 59
    — 18541*a* (*olim* Tegernsee 541*a*): 7
Nice
  Archives des Alpes-Maritimes
    H. 10: †74
Oxford
  Bodleian Library
    D'Orville 46 (16924): 67
    Laud Misc. 611 (1133): 57
    Tanner 8 (9828): †75
Paris
  Bibliothèque nationale
    Baluze 41: 56
    — 74: 56
    — 77: 36
    Duchesne 4: 3, 22, 23, 33, 35,
      37, 63, 64
    franç. 22322: 16
    lat. 152: †72
    — 275: 62
    — 933: 42
    — 1458: 53
    — 2478: 34
    — 3839*A*: 21
    — 8625: 50
    — 8878: †71
    — 8922: 68
    — 11851: 14, 25–7
    — 14762: 34
    — 17086: †70
    Moreau 31: 49
    — 283: 39
Reichersberg
  Stiftsbibliothek
    1: 32

Rome
  Biblioteca Vallicelliana
    tomo XXI. xlvii: †76
  Vatican Library
    Barberinus lat. 538: 43
    lat. 1208 (*olim* 186), 39
    — 1363: 8
    — 1974: 51
    Palatino-Vaticanus 830: 32
    Reginensis lat. 285: 1
Saint-Omer
  Bibliothèque municipale
    188: 24, 41
Sarnen
  Kollegsbibliothek
    Muri-Sarnen 10: 32
Sélestat (Schlettstadt)
  Bibliothèque et Archives munici-
    pales
    13 (*olim* 99): 9, 10, 14
Stuttgart
  Württembergische Landesbiblio-
    thek HB. VI. 107: 8
Trier
  Bistumsarchiv
    Abt. 95, 93 (*olim* 102): 25, 27
Vienna
  Österreichische Nationalbibliothek
    336 (*olim* hist. eccles. 5): 8–11,
      14, 17, 18, 25
    398 (*olim* ius can. 45), 9, 10, 13,
      14, 17, 18, 26, 51
    611 (*olim* ius can. 130): 14
    2198 (*olim* ius can. 99): 60
Wolfenbüttel
  Herzog-August Bibliothek
    Helmstedt 1024: 9, 10, 13, 14, 17,
      18, 26
Zwettl
  Stiftsarchiv
    283: 9, 10, 13, 14, 17, 18, 26, 51

INDEX OF LETTERS

	J.L.	*Ep. coll.*	No.
Admonemus atque praecipimus	5285	..	61
Ad notitiam tuam	5253	44	53
Apostolicae sedis benedictionem	..	..	3
Apostolicam benedictionem libenter	5192	35	40
Aquensis archidiaconus A.	5241	43	44
Archiepiscopi uestri diligenter	..	..	22
Audiuimus F[ulconem] comitem	5197	36	†72
Audiuimus quod Cenomanensi	5226	..	48
Audiuimus quod quidam	4902	10	11
Audiuimus, quod sine	5129	29	28
Audiuimus quosdam inter uos			
(Audiuimus inter uos quosdam)	4999	14	14
Causam Matisconensis episcopi	†5183	..	†70
Clamorem fratrum Lyrinensium	5244	..	†74
Clamor et querimonia	5188	..	41
Compertum esse celsitudini	5005	16	16
Cum apostolica auctoritate	4931	3	6
Cum apostolica auctoritate	4932	4	7
Cum Veritas ipsa	5108	27	26
De controuersia que	5223	..	42
De querela filii	..	..	†71
Deuotionem uestram circa	5286	..	62
Dilectissimi fratres et	5042	21	21
Dilectissimus confrater noster	..	..	35
Disoordia Maioris monasterii	..	..	64
Ego Petrus episcopus	..	..	69
Ego qualiscumque sacerdos	5014	18	18
Fraternitatem uestram, dilectissimi	4849	6	12
Gratias omnipotenti Deo	..	..	65
Iam saepius excellentiae	5247	42	47
Instantia nuntiorum tuorum	4933	5	8
Interrogauit nos religio	5275	47	58
Licet noua consuetudo	5290	..	†76
Licet uenerandae memoriae	4814	2	2
Manifestum est eum	5291	..	†75
Miles iste, harum	..	..	63
Miramur fraternitatis tue	4997	13	13
Mirari ualde compellimur	5182	37	38
Misimus fratri nostro			
(Misimus ad uos; Misimus episcopo uestro)	4971	9	10
Non eget, o fili	5043	22	20
Nos indigni et			
(Nos et indigni et)	5013	17	17
Notum tibi esse	5242	40	45
Notum uobis fieri	5273	..	55
Notum uobis omnibus	5103	24	†73

INDEX OF REFERENCES TO GREGORY VII'S
REGISTER AND PRIVILEGES

A. THE *REGISTER*

References are to the numbers of the letters in Caspar's edition

	page		page
i. 29a	34, 36	iv. 28	35, 56
i. 35–6	9		
i. 42	xxix	v. 12	152
i. 46	11	v. 14a	65, 68, 100, 105
i. 49	11, 12	v. 17	58
i. 51	9, 155	v. 20	59
i. 57	8		
i. 76	9	vi. 1	61
i. 81	xxix	vi. 5b	65, 68, 73, 78
i. 82	83	vi. 7	62, 63
i. 85a	9	vi. 13	35
		vi. 17a	100, 152, 156
ii. 3	11	vi. 18	69
ii. 9	3	vi. 24–5	155
ii. 11	161	vi. 33	77, 154
ii. 19	60	vi. 37	73
ii. 29	161	vi. 38	80
ii. 31	11, 12		
ii. 37	11, 12	vii. 1	63
ii. 45	19, 27, 161	vii. 3	81
ii. 52a	161	vii. 14a	30, 101, 130
ii. 56	28	vii. 16	102
ii. 60	160		
ii. 62	160	viii. 16	100, 101
ii. 64	28	viii. 20a	103
ii. 66	161	viii. 23	129
ii. 68	160		
		ix. 10	142
		ix. 13	114
iii. 10	38, 52	ix. 24	126
iii. 10a	28, 30, 41, 100	ix. 29	122
iii. 15	31	ix. 31	114
iii. 18	xxix	ix. 32	xxix
		ix. 33–4	114, 115
iv. 1	32, 42–3	ix. 35	114, 115
iv. 3	42	ix. 35a	123, 137
iv. 4–5	47	ix. 36	114
iv. 12	50	ix. 37	128

B. PRIVILEGES

References are to the numbers of the privileges, etc., in Santifaller, *Q.F.*

106	xxvi
107	98
110	xxvi
198	103
216	xxvi

INDEX OF QUOTATIONS AND ALLUSIONS

A. BIBLICAL

References are in the first instance to the Vulgate; where the English Versions differ, references to them are given in parentheses

Num. 21: 22	124–5	24: 12	122–3
1 Reg. (1 Sam.) 15: 22–3	24–7	24: 13	128–9, 148–6
15: 23	86–7	Luke 10: 16	10–11, 58–9, 100–1
2 Reg. (2 Sam.) 19: 38	88–9	John 10: 1	10–11, 100–1, 108–9
3 Reg. (1 Kgs.) 12: 25–33	98–9	10: 1–2	44–5, 70–1, 80–1
19: 18	98–9	10: 10	100–1
Ps. 2: 1–2	128–9	Acts 5: 29	30–1
2: 2	2–3	8: 9–24	150
10 (11): 8	90–1	8: 21	38–9
18: 6–7 (19: 4–6)	138–9	14: 21	50–1
58: 13–14 (59: 12–13)	40–1	17: 28	132–3
83: 8 (84: 7)	12–13	Rom. 1: 32	26–7
Isa. 3: 7	38–9	8: 27	70–1
57: 7	130–1	13: 7	28–9
58: 1	130–1	1 Cor. 5: 11	20–1
60: 14	138–9	10: 24	28–9
61: 8	54–5	16: 13	6–7, 40–1
Ezek. 13: 5	68–9	2 Cor. 1: 3–4	124–5
Mal. 2: 2	86–7	Gal. 4: 26	12–13
Tobit 4: 16 (15)	28–9	Eph. 3: 16	40–1
Ecclus. 8: 3 (2)	40–1	6: 10	6–7
34: 24 (20)	54–5	Phil. 2: 21	2–3
Matt. 5: 10	66–7	4: 1	50–1
5: 16	6–7	Col. 3: 1–2	20–1
7: 7	88–9	2 Tim. 2: 5	67–8
7: 12	28–9	4: 1	40–1
10: 16	42–3	4: 2	34–5
10: 22	148–9	Jas. 5: 16	88–9
13: 24–30	6–7	1 Pet. 5: 5	38–9
		Rev. 2: 23	40–1

B. CLASSICAL, PATRISTIC, AND MEDIEVAL

Augustine:		Hegesippus:	
De baptismo		*Historiae*	
iii. 6. 9	151	1. 11. 2	12–13
Doctrina Apostolorum	28–9	5. 43. 2	12–13
Gregory the Great:		Horace:	
Homiliarum in Ezechielem		*Carmina*	
i, Homil. xi. 5	130–1	3. 2. 13	12–13
Moralium		Isidore of Seville:	
vii. 26	48–9	*Etymologiarum*	
xxv. 28	24–7, 86–7	xi. ii. 13	158

Leo I:
  Epistolae
  xiv. 4   20–1
  clvii   108–9
Pseudo-Augustine:
  Sermones
  lvi. 3   148–9
Sallust:
  Catilina
  i. 4   34–5, 148–9

  20: 4   56–7
  58: 21   12–13
Seneca:
  Epistolae
  122. 4   12–13
Virgil:
  Aeneid
  4. 336   6–7

GENERAL INDEX

Adalbert, bishop of Worms (1070–1107), 84–5

Adelpreth, messenger of Gregory VII, 38–9

Agnes, empress (died 1077), widow of Emperor Henry III, 10–13

Aicard, archbishop of Arles (*c.* 1067–90), 158

Alan Cagnart, count of Cornouailles (died 1058), 136

Alanus III, count of Brittany (1008–39/40), 44–5

Albert, abbot, 62–3

Alexander II, pope (1061–73), 58–9, 104, 155

Altmann, bishop of Passau (1065–91), xix, xxvi, xxvii, 68–9, 140–3

Altzelle bei Nossen, monastery of (dioc. Meissen), xxii

Amatus, bishop of Oléron (1073–89), papal standing legate in France, xix, xxvii, 56–9, 101, 108–9, 114, 118–19, 126–7, 155–6

Anno, archbishop of Cologne (1056–75), 54–7

Anselm, abbot of Bec (1078–93), archbishop of Canterbury (1093–1109), xxv, xxviii, 88–91

Anselm II, bishop of Lucca (1073–86), papal standing legate in Lombardy, xix, 105

Arnald I, abbot of Saint-Sever (1072–92), 155–6

Arnald, archdeacon of Dax, 106–9

Arnald, bishop of le Mans (1066–81), 116

Arnald Trencardus, abbot of Sainte-Croix, Bordeaux (*c.* 1066–*c.* 87), 155–6

Arnold, abbot of Berge, xxii

Arnulf, archdeacon of Thérouanne, provost of Saint-Omer, 114–15

Augsburg, proposed *Reichstag* at, 46

Aymeric, vicomte of Narbonne (*c.* 1080–1105/6), 100–1

Azzo II, marquis of Este (1029–97), 8–9

Bartholomew, abbot of Marmoutier (1064–83), 91–3

Beatrice, countess of Tuscany (died 1076), 12–13

Benevento, letter dated at, 155–6

Berengar, archdeacon of Tours (died 1088), condemned by Gregory for his eucharistic teaching, xxviii, 156–7

Bernard, abbot of Saint-Victor, Marseilles (1064–79), legate of Gregory VII in Germany, 70–1

Bernard, monk of Constance, xxv

Berthold I of Zähringen, duke of Carinthia (1061–77), 72–3

Boniface VIII, pope (1294–1303), xvii

Bordeaux, council of (1079), 155

Borgo San Donnino, near Parma, 82

Brauweiler, St. Nicholas, monastery of (dioc. Cologne), 54–7

Brixen, council of (1080), 129

Bruno, author of *Saxonicum bellum*, xxi–xxii

Byzantium, Gregory VII's proposal for an expedition to help, 10–13

Camaldoli, San Salvatore, monastery of (dioc. Arezzo), xxvii, 104–7

Canossa, meeting of Gregory VII and Henry IV in Jan. 1077, xxvii, 51–3, 55, 64

Carthage, council of (256), 151

celibacy, clerical, xvii, xxvi–xxvii, 14–28, 44–7, 84–6, 102–3, 160–1

Châlon-sur-Saône, diocese of, 79–80

Clement III, anti-pope (1080–1100), 129

Cluny, monastery of (dioc. Mâcon), xxviii, 76–9, 94–9, 154–5

Codex Udalrici, xxiii–xxv

Cologne, St. Mary *ad Gradus*, church of, 54–7

Conques, monastery of (dioc. Rodez), xxvi

Constance, see of, 19–26, 161

Constantine the Great, emperor (306–37), 132–3

Cyprian, bishop of Carthage (249–57), 151

Dalmatius, archbishop of Narbonne (1081–96), formerly abbot of la Grasse, 100–1, 103–5
David, abbot of la Trinité, Vendôme (1083–5), 142–3
Dax, dispute concerning churches at, 106–9
Desiderius, abbot of Monte Cassino (1058–86), later Pope Victor III (1086–7), 74–5
Dodo, bishop of Grosseto (c. 1060–c. 79), 72
Dol, city in Brittany, 44–7
Durand, bishop of Clermont (1077–95), 157–8

Egilbert, archbishop of Trier (1079–1101), 82–3
Ekkehard, abbot of Reichenau (1077–88), 68–9, 80–5
Election Decree (1059), xvii
Eusebius, bishop of Angers (1047–81), 142–3, 146–7, 156
Ezzo, palsgrave of Lorraine (died 1034), 54

Figeac, monastery of (dioc. Cahors), xxvi
Forchheim, assembly of German princes at (Mar. 1077), xxvii, 64
Frotger, bishop of Châlon-sur-Saône, 78–9
Fucecchio, San Salvatore, monastery of (dioc. Lucca), xxvii, 104–7
Fulk IV, le Réchin, count of Anjou (1060–1109), 8–9, 92–5, 116–17, 126–7, 156
Fulk, spokesman in the Berengarian controversy, 157

Gebhard, bishop of Constance (1084–1110), 72–3
Gebhard, bishop of Würzburg (1122–5), xxiii
Gebuin, archbishop of Lyons (1077–82), 76–9, 80–1, 94–7
Geoffrey, bishop of Angers (1081–93), 142–3, 146–7
Gerald, cardinal-bishop of Ostia (1067–77), 36–7, 160

Gerhoh, provost of Reichersberg (1132–69), xxv
Gisulf II, prince of Salerno (1042–deposed 1076; died after 1088), 129
Godfrey, duke of Lower Lorraine (1069–76), 12
Goslar, an unidentified decanus of, 72–3
Gotteschalk, messenger of Gregory VII, 38–9
Guitmund, bishop of Aversa, 151
Gunther, clerk of Magdeburg, 67

Hanover letter collection, xxiii–xxv
Hartwig, archbishop of Magdeburg (1079–1102), 72–3
Henor, Breton priory of, 91
Henry, bishop of Liège (1075–91), xxvi
Henry, bishop of Trent (1062–82), 30–3
Henry III, emperor (1039–56), xvii, 12
Henry IV, emperor (1056–1106), xvii, xviii–xix, xxii, xxiii, xxvi–xxvii, 12, 30–43, 46–53, 64, 68–71, 80–3, 123–5, 129, 137
Henry V, emperor (1106–25), xxiii
Henry, patriarch of Aquileia (1077–84), 152
Hermann, bishop of Bamberg (1065–75), 161
Hermann, bishop of Metz (1073–90), 68–9
Hildolf, archbishop of Cologne (1076–8), 54–7
Hirsau, monastery of St. Aurelian (dioc. Speyer), 19
Hoel, bishop of le Mans (1082–96), 116–17, 126
Hoel II, count of Brittany (1066–84), 136–7
Homburg-on-the-Unstrut, battle of (9 June 1075), 36–7
Hubert, bishop of Thérouanne (1078/9–82), 102–3, 108
Hubert, cardinal-bishop of Palestrina (1073–82), 36–7, 160
Hubert, subdeacon of the Roman church, 60–3, 90–1
Hugh, abbot of Cluny (1049–1109), 60–1, 76–9, 92–7, 120–1, 154–5

Hugh, bishop of Die (1074–82), archbishop of Lyons (1082–1106), papal standing legate in France, xix, xxi, xxvii, 28–9, 58–63, 76–81, 101, 106–9, 112–14, 118–19, 126–9, 154–5

Hugh, bishop of Langres (c. 1065–85), 62–5

Hugh, clerk of Sainte-Radegonde, Poitiers, 118–19

Hugh of Flavigny, chronicler, xxi, xxiv

Humbert, archbishop of Lyons (1065–76), 9

Hunald, abbot of Moissac (1072–95), 120

Ingelrannus, canon of Saint-Omer, 114–15

Ireland, Gregory VII and, 1–5, 138–41

Isarnus, bishop of Toulouse (1071–1105), 120

Isembert, bishop of Poitiers (1047–86), 144–5

Ivo (Evenus), bishop of Dol (1076–81) formerly abbot of Saint-Melaine, Rennes, 44–7

Jarento, abbot of Saint-Bénigne, Dijon (1078–c. 1112), xxi, 129

John Gualbertus, abbot of Vallombrosa (1036–73), 4–7

Jordan, prince of Capua (1078–90), 72–6

Judith, countess of Cornouailles, 136

Juhel, bishop of Dol (c. 1039–76), 44–7

Klotten, vill of, on the Moselle, 54–7

La Grasse, Sainte-Marie, monastery of (dioc. Narbonne), 102–5

Lambert, intruded bishop of Thérouanne, 108–15

Lampert of Hersfeld, Chronicle of, 160

Landeric of Berzé, bishop of Mâcon (1074–96), formerly archdeacon of Autun, 8–11, 94–7, 154–5

Lanfranc, archbishop of Canterbury (1070–89), 1–5

Langres, diocese of, 80–1

lay investiture, 78–9

Leo IX, pope (1048–54), xvii

Lérins, Saint-Honorat, monastery of (dioc. Antibes), 157–8

Letter collections, xxii–xxv

Liber censuum of the Roman church, 28

Liber Tarraconensis, 124, 159

Libosus, bishop of Vaga (third cent.), 151

Liutprand, priest of Milan, xxvi

Lucca, diocese of, 104–7

Mâcon, diocese of, xxviii, 8–11, 76–9, 94–7, 154–5

Magdeburg, see of, 66–73

Magnum Legendarium Austriacum, xxi

Maldolus, count, founder of Camaldoli, 105

Manasses I, archbishop of Rheims (1069–80), 78–9

Manegold of Lautenbach, Gregorian publicist, xxv

Mantua, as rendezvous for Gregory VII and his escort to Germany (1076), 46–9

Marino, letter perhaps dated at, 138–41

Marmoutier, monastery of (dioc. Tours), 90–1, 146–7

Matilda, countess of Tuscany (1052–1115), xxvii, 10–13, 32–3, 50–1

Mazé (Maine-et-Loire), 142–3

Meaux, council of (1082), 114

Melfi, treaty of (1059), xvii

Mellrichstadt, battle of (7 Aug. 1078), 67, 85

Milan, Patarenes of, 6; dukes of, 144

Moissac, Cluniac monastery of (dioc. Cahors), 120–1

Monte Cassino, abbey of, xxvii, 72–7

Montmajour, monastery of (dioc. Arles), 103

Nürnberg, meeting of Henry IV with papal legates at (1074), 37

Odericus, abbot of la Trinité, Vendôme (1046–82), 142–3

Odo I, bishop of Bayeux (1049–97), 128–9

Odo I, cardinal-bishop of Ostia, see Urban II, pope

Otto, bishop of Constance (1071–86), 16–25, 161

Padua, Henry IV's diploma of 1079 for the church of, 81

Paschal II, pope (1099–1118), 155

Patarenes of Milan, 6

Paul of Bernried, author of *Gregorii VII uita*, xx–xxi

Peace of God, 124–5

Peter, abbot of San Salvatore, Fucecchio, 104–7

Peter, bishop of Antivari (*c.* 1060– ?), 152

Peter, bishop of Rodez (1046–79), 100–1, 103

Peter, cardinal-bishop of Albano (1072–89), *also* Peter Igneus, 4, 65, 70–1, 80–5, 94–7, 129

Peter Mezzabarba, bishop of Florence (1062–8), 4

Peter, a subdeacon, 152

Philip I, king of France (1060–1108), 9, 44–5, 108–11, 126

Piacenza, assembly of (1076), 38–9

Poitiers, council of (1078), 58, 86

Poitiers, Sainte-Croix, monastery of, 118–19; Sainte-Radegonde, church of, 118–19

Quimperlé, Sainte-Croix, monastery of (dioc. Quimper), 136–7

Quiriacus, bishop of Nantes (1060–79), 90–3

Radbod, messenger of Gregory VII, 38, 52–3

Ralph, archbishop of Tours (1073–86), xxv, xxviii, 8–9, 58–64, 86–9, 90–1, 92–5, 116–17, 126–7, 142–7, 156

Ralph, earl of Norfolk, 44

Raymond, bishop of Bazas (1057–84), 108–9

Raymond, bishop of Roda (1076–94), 146–9

Redon, Saint-Sauveur, monastery of (dioc. Vannes), 146–7

Regensburg, Henry IV's meeting with papal legates at (1079), 80

Register, Gregory VII's, xix–xx

Richard, abbot of Saint-Victor, Marseilles (1079–1108) and papal legate, 103–5, 106–9, 120–1

Richeza, queen of Poland, 54

Rivière (Indre-et-Loire), 142–3

Robert I, count of Flanders (1071–93), 62–3, 108–15

Roger, subdeacon of the Roman church, 58–9

Rome, St. Paul's-without-the-Walls, 137; St. Peter's, 51, 74–5, 137

Romuald, St., founder of Camaldoli, 104

Rouen, an unnamed archbishop of, 150

Rudolf, abbot of Saint-Vanne, Verdun (1076–99), xxi

Rudolf, anti-king, (1077–80), formerly duke of Swabia, xxvii, 64–71, 80, 82–3

Rudolf, prior of Camaldoli (1074–*c.* 87), 104–7

Saintes, council of (1081), 118–19

Saint-Gilles, abbey of (dioc. Nîmes), xxvi

Salerno, Gregory VII's withdrawal to (1084), 129

Sancho Ramirez (1063–94), king of Aragon, 146–9

Sichelgaita, wife of Robert Guiscard, duke of Apulia and Calabria, xxx

Siegfried, archbishop of Mainz (1060–84), 14–16, 18–21, 33, 161

Siegfried II, bishop of Augsburg (1077–96), 82–3

Siegfried, count of Spanheim, 72–3

Sigehard, patriarch of Aquileia (1068–77), 160

Sigewin, archbishop of Cologne (1079–89), 82–3

Silvester, bishop of Rennes (1076–96), 86–7, 90–1

simony, xvii, xxvi–xxvii, 4, 9–11, 14–25, 34–9, 100–3, 112–13, 150, 160–1

Speyer, Henry IV withdraws to after Tribur-Oppenheim, 50

Stephen, *praepositus* of Brioude, 158

Sutri, letter dated at, 138–41

Thérouanne, see of, 102–3, 108–15

Tivoli, letter dated at, 42–3

Toirdhealbhach Ó Briain, king of Ireland (died 1086), 5, 138–41

Toulouse, council of (1079), 101–3; Saint-Sernin, church of, 120–1

Tours, Saint-Martin, canons of, 126–7; Saint-Maurice, canons of, 126–7
Tribur-Oppenheim, negotiations of Henry IV with the German princes at (1076), 46, 50
Troyes, proposed council of (1079), 78–9

Ughiccio, son of Count William Bulgarelli, 104–7
Ulrich, bishop of Padua (1064–80), 65, 68–71, 80–5, 142
Ulrich, canon and *scholasticus* of Bamberg, xxiii
Ulrich, patriarch of Aquileia (1086–1121), formerly abbot of Saint-Gall and Reichenau, 82–5
Urban II, pope (1088–99), formerly Odo I, cardinal-bishop of Ostia (1080–8), 28, 129, 151

Vallombrosa, monastery of, xxvii, 4–7
Verdun, monastery of Saint-Vanne, xxi

Warmund, archbishop of Vienne (1077–81), 94–7
Werner, archbishop of Magdeburg (1063–78), xxi, 16–17, 66–7, 71
Werner, bishop of Merseburg (1059–93), xxi, 160

Wifred, archbishop of Narbonne (1019–79), 31, 100–1
Wifred, Patarene leader at Milan, 31
Wighard, *decanus* of Notre-Dame and Saint-Paul, Besançon, 60–1
William, abbot of Brioude, 157–8
William, abbot of Saint-Florent-lès-Saumur (1070–1118), 90–1
William, archbishop of Auch (1068–96), 108–9
William, archbishop of Rouen (1079–1110), 116
William, bishop of Clermont (1073–6), 157–8
William Bulgarelli, count, 104–5
William VIII, duke of Aquitaine (1058–87), 11
William, count of Burgundy (died 1087), 10–11
William I, king of England (1066–87), duke of Normandy (1035–87), 44–7, 116, 128–9
Wolfenbüttel letter collection, xxiii-xxv
Wolfhelm, abbot of Brauweiler (1065–91), 54
Worms, assembly of (24 Jan. 1076), 32, 38–9
Würzburg, plans for German assembly at (1079), 80, 81